BILLY GRAHAM
The Making of a Crusader

The Making
of a
BILLY GRAHAM *Crusader*

By CURTIS MITCHELL

Foreword by

GEORGE M. WILSON

CHILTON BOOKS
A DIVISION OF CHILTON COMPANY
Publishers
Philadelphia and New York

"What shall I find if I accept your gospel and become Christ's man?" asked the King.

Brindon replied, "If you become Christ's man, you will stumble upon wonder after wonder, and every wonder will be true."

Acknowledgment is made to the following sources for permission to quote from previously published material:

Henry S. Coffin, *Meaning of the Cross*, 1959, Charles Scribner's Sons, New York.

Glenn Daniels, *Billy Graham*, 1965, Paperback Library, New York.

Billy Graham, "The Autobiography of Billy Graham," *McCall's*, April, May, June, 1964.

Billy Graham, "Background of Segregation," *Life*, October 1, 1956.

Stanley High, *Billy Graham*, 1956, McGraw-Hill, New York.

Ernest M. Ligon, *Psychology of the Christian Personality*, 1962, Macmillan, New York.

Harold Martin, "Revivalist Billy Graham," *Saturday Evening Post*, April 13, 1963.

William C. McLoughlin, Jr., *Billy Graham, Revivalist in a Secular Age*, 1960, The Ronald Press Company, New York.

John Pollock, *Billy Graham, the Authorized Biography*, 1966, McGraw-Hill, New York.

Time, "Sickles for the Harvest," November 14, 1949; "Civil Rights—The Central Point," March 19, 1965.

Foreword

If one were to pick out the two primary qualities that characterize Billy Graham, I am positive they would be sincerity and singleness of purpose.

We met first in the summer of 1944 during the fledgling days of Youth for Christ International. He became the first Vice President of YFC and I was International Secretary.

When Mr. Graham first came to Minneapolis in February, 1945, he faced the first large audience of his life. The city auditorium was packed with over ten thousand lively teenagers. That night scores of these young people made decisions for Christ. Some of them are on the mission field as a result of that message.

This was the youthful Billy Graham, just out of college. From the outset he has presented the claims of Christ with power and authority, and it was evident from that first meeting that the hand of God was upon him. Every generation has had its evangel. In our day it is readily apparent that Mr. Graham has been raised up of the Lord.

I think the wonderful influence of a godly mother and father who never shirked their responsibility had a great deal to do with the making and molding of this spokesman for our age. In the presence of his mother during the recent London Crusade, he told some thirty thousand listeners, "She reared me to know God! I kicked off the traces in my youth, but I couldn't get away from her early training." Therein lies a lesson for all parents: "Train up a child in the way he should go; and when he is old, he will not depart from it." (Proverbs 22:6)

The shaping process of that early training is the subject of this study of his life from the time of his birth to the 1949 crusade in Los Angeles when the world first learned of this evangelist.

Since then he has preached many times—and millions have gladly heard.

You will read with pleasure THE MAKING OF A CRUSADER.

GEORGE M. WILSON

Preface

This book is an attempt to describe some of the steps up which a man of great fame and public esteem climbed in order to reach the unique position he occupies.

It is unarguable, I think, that Dr. Billy Graham has outdistanced all his evangelistic contemporaries and outdone all his predecessors.

But no man travels alone. The source of his power is widely dispersed, originating in chromosomes, in traditions, in failures and triumphs and in inspiration.

So I have asked, "How did it happen?"

Dr. Graham has his own answer, as this work reveals. I would add a factor mentioned, in connection with the 'prophets Moses, Samuel, Jeremiah, and Isaiah, by Henry Sloane Coffin, Jr., of Yale. He says they were successful "because they didn't fall down on their knees. They reared up on their hind legs."

Speaking theologically, Dr. Graham long ago "reared up" against the contemporary tendency of many churchmen to dilute the veracity of Scripture. Socially, he "reared up" against a host of human failures, including racial prejudice.

Some day other biographers will tell the complete story of the evolution of this phenomenal evangelist. I feel that a more immediate examination will be valuable now, because the problems with which he concerns himself are desperately pressing.

My judgments are entirely personal and probably prejudiced. Nevertheless, they are as accurate as conscience and contemplation can make them. They represent conclusions and revisions of conclusions reached over the years, plus insights not available to others who have not, as I have, closely "covered" Billy Graham and his team for the last ten years.

In 1956, I wrote *God in the Garden,* a book which described the revival campaign he waged in New York. We have since collaborated on many magazine pieces. This present work describes the forces which gradually assumed command of his heart and will, evolving through years of play and study and experience, until finally their mobilization equipped him for the explosion of faith and works that took place in Los Angeles in 1949.

So here is the human story of the making of a crusader, containing perhaps more than a hint of the superhuman.

I am indebted to so many persons for their assistance that I cannot name them all. Indeed, with due apology to all those omitted, I shall name only two:

Ruth Bell Graham, the evangelist's remarkable wife.

William Franklin Graham, Jr., known as Billy.

I thank them for many things, but most of all I thank them for the privilege of witnessing their life together and viewing their joint testimony of a home in which Christ dwells.

CURTIS MITCHELL

Westport, Conn.

BILLY GRAHAM
The Making of a Crusader

Chapter One

Billy Graham, the growing boy, was filled with self-doubt.

Dr. Billy Graham, the mature man, is the most effective evangelist in world history.

Between boyhood and manhood, he discovered a power which changed the course of his life. Utilizing its force, he set and achieved one apparently impossible goal after another.

This account will tell about that discovery and how he used it.

We begin on a Sunday evening in suburban Charlotte, North Carolina. Billy Frank Graham, a teenager with a firm jaw and wavy hair, folded his long frame into the back seat of his father's car. The gaunt lines of a rustic church rose through the twilight. The soft country air moved gently as young voices were raised in hymn singing.

The girl beside him asked, "Why do you always come to these youth meetings and never go inside?"

This gathering of young people was both social and religious. Ardent teenagers recited their personal experiences 'in the troublesome art of living a Christian life. One after another, they rose and reported in slurring southern accents, imitating the testimonies of their parents in other convocations.

Outside, Billy Graham squirmed with guilt. How does a boy with a great yearning tell a girl that he is too goose-pimply scared to go into that church meeting because he knows he might be asked to testify? His close friend Grady

Wilson was running the service, and he had threatened to get Billy onto his feet for a public declaration. Billy wanted to respond, but something held him back. Mute witness to his fear were ten fingernails bitten to the quick and an occasional fierce stutter which tied up his tongue.

"I just caint say things in front of people," he explained. "I wish I could. Gee, I really want to do it, but I caint."

His school teachers knew that Billy Frank was a shy one whose grades were scandalously low and that he had an indifferent attitude and a painful awareness of being a foot taller than his classmates. But some of them sensed another quality, a slumbering potential that could not be named but which burst forth occasionally with improbable excellence.

One school year he laid aside his baseball mitt long enough to play the role of George Washington in a school play. His performance stunned his audience. "I felt I was really seeing the father of our country up on that stage," a classmate remembers. And his mother, brushing away tears of pride, allowed herself the luxury of dreaming that her firstborn might yet play a role in God's kingdom.

Some Scotch and Irish clans have a custom of dedicating the first male heir to God's service, and the tradition has reached across the Atlantic to lodge in the gracious soil of the Carolina Piedmont. So Morrow Graham's first act after the birth of William Franklin Graham, Jr., was to say a fervent Presbyterian prayer and lay her bairn at the feet of her Lord.

"In the beginning . . . was God!"

Today that child has become a man whose outreach embraces the world.

The growth of an aimless youth into such a dynamic leader happens so rarely that its elements challenge assessment. One wants to learn all about it.

What wellsprings of nature were tapped?

2

What resources of mind and soul?

What is owed to environment?

How much to heredity?

A biographer can describe what happened and why he thinks it happened, but personality remains a jungle thicker than the Mato Grosso and trickier than the Sargasso Sea. If his insights are valid, he may discover and write the truth. If his insights are faulty, he may perpetuate a fraud.

So the voyage of discovery begins, with no known destination, but with the feeling that it may hold as many surprises as a journey to a new planet. And we open with the plain question:

What manner of man is Dr. Billy Graham?

Gigi, his eldest daughter, whose marriage took place in 1963, when she was only eighteen, might say, "He's the most understanding father in the world."

Nelson Edman, youngest of the five Graham children and now age seven, might say, "He's the man who comes home every two or three months and tells me wonderful stories."

Ruth, his wife, might say, "He's a man appointed by the Lord to the work of evangelism, and I'd rather have him the few weeks each year that we are together than anyone else full time."

Dwight D. Eisenhower might say, "He was one of those who persuaded me to run for the Presidency of the United States. Later he was helpful to me in religious matters."

Lyndon Baines Johnson might say, "He is one of my spiritual advisors."

What of those others, those multitudes who have listened from the bleachers of ball parks and the balconies of football stadiums or heard the electronic projection of his voice on radio and television? Their response is reflected by at least three public opinion polls.

A poll taken to choose the world's best known personalities named Billy Graham along with Winston Churchill and Charles De Gaulle.

Another poll asked thousands, "What other person would you most like to be?" His name was among those most frequently mentioned.

A poll asked, "What personality do you most admire?" He was among the top three.

His itinerary takes him around the world in jet-propelled steps. Since 1964, he has crusaded in Hawaii, Denmark, Alabama, Colorado, England, and Germany in addition to making innumerable side trips.

Each December he delivers a Christmas message, by official invitation of the U.S. Goverment, to our cadets or midshipmen at either West Point or Annapolis.

Each New Year he stands before the nation's top brass in a chapel at the heart of the Pentagon and tells them of the Prince of Peace.

Annually he "brings the message" to a lofty gathering of government officials, military leaders, businessmen, and intellectuals attending the President's Prayer Breakfast in the Capital.

Between speaking engagements, he conducts Christian missions to such skeptical institutions as Yale, Harvard, California, and MIT, as well as to the campuses of emerging nations.

Statistically, the world has never seen his like.

This much can be summarized:

He has preached more widely than any evangelist in history, having conducted crusades in fifty countries and states. He has preached on every continent and in a plane flying fifteen thousand feet above America's Middle West.

He has preached to more people (now more than eighty million) face-to-face than any other evangelist.

He has seen more than one million people decide to give their lives to God through Christ.

His organization, the Billy Graham Evangelistic Association, has received contributions and earnings amounting to many millions of dollars, the biggest program of free-will offerings in the annals of the Protestant church. It currently amounts to more than ten million dollars annually.

His radio program, "The Hour of Decision," is the most far-reaching religious program of all time, serving listeners through the facilities of over eight hundred stations in a dozen countries.

His telecasts, which reproduce actual crusade services, draw letters by the millions from admirers and inquirers.

His newspaper column, "My Answer," appears several times each week in three hundred publications.

His books, *World Aflame, Peace With God* and *The Secret of Happiness,* are best sellers at home and abroad.

He holds honorary degrees from many colleges and universities.

He has been urged by responsible citizens of North Carolina to run for the United States Senate, an invitation several times rejected.

He has been urged by men who have pledged huge financial support to run for the Presidency of the United States, a possibility he also rejected.

He has refused a salary of a million dollars per year for five years to make one weekly broadcast for a national television and radio network.

He draws an annual wage from his Evangelistic Association of about $20,000.

Who is Billy Graham?

A Catholic woman once asked her priest if she could attend one of his crusade meetings. He replied, "You know very well it's forbidden. The bishop himself said you can't go."

She said, "I think I'll go just the same."

The priest said, "I think I'll go, too."

A Protestant minister says, "I don't agree with his whole theology, but I cannot get over the fact that God is with him."

A teenager says, "I don't know what he's got, but whatever it is, he's got more of it than anybody else."

A Christian editor and statesman says, "He's a man filled with the passion and purpose of his evangelical faith—an open channel for the Holy Spirit."

His own words supply this answer, as reported in *The Saturday Evening Post:* "I myself am nothing," he says. "I am what every evangelist has been: the herald, the trumpeter, telling the good news of the Gospel. I can't convert anybody. God converts them. I am only the channel through which he works."

At a press conference upon his arrival in England for his Greater London Crusade of 1966, a newsman asked, "What have you to say to your total world following?"

"My world following?" Graham said. "I hope I have none. I want people to follow Christ. I'm simply a messenger, calling people to Christ. The word evangelist, by the way, is a New Testament word. It's used three times. It means herald or proclaimer. My job is to be a proclaimer, to say to a man, 'God loves you, God is willing to forgive you, God can change you, God can make you a new person in Jesus Christ. . . .' "

I have interviewed hundreds of famous persons in the course of my career as a writer. A reporter usually follows the procedure of asking questions which elicit anecdotes of difficulties encountered, obstacles overcome, and successes enjoyed. I had probed the Graham personality for years before I finally hit upon the query that most nearly explains him, at least to my satisfaction.

"Tell me about your failures," I asked.

He gave me a patient smile. "A true Christian has *no*

6

failures in the worldly sense," he said. "His friends may judge him to be either a misfit or an achiever, but the real question is—how does God judge him? Within his heart, does he know that he has tried to follow God's will?"

That sentence told me more about Billy Graham's way of looking at things (and about my own way of looking at things) than I had learned from countless interviews, thousands of clippings, and whole libraries of science and philosophy.

With those words I came to an understanding of his unprecedented—what else can you call it?—success.

I recall the first time he faced newspapermen in New York City. Early in his career he admitted, "I pray more about press conferences than I do about my sermons. It's so easy to put one word in the wrong place, to say a sentence that someone can misunderstand. It's so easy to be misquoted and misinterpreted."

But a press conference is the launching pad of most of today's ideas, hopes, and dreams. Men and women from every news medium—press, radio, television, and magazines—are summoned to some smoke-filled room where they crowd each other savagely when they anticipate a sensational story or hobnob in fraternal rivalry when the stakes are low.

Graham's New York conference was unique in that it offered no alcoholic refreshment; instead, there were coffee and doughnuts. The questions began. Why are you coming to New York for a crusade? Is this the wickedest city in the world? Do you think you can clean it up? Don't your converts backslide as soon as you leave town? How many do you expect to convert? How many do you expect to join the churches? How much do you think the crime rate will drop?

Those newsmen used every trick to put him on the spot. That was their job. Finally, they ticked off his preparations for the New York crusade: posters and ads, radio and TV spots, committees and choirs, all devices that Madison Avenue experts would use in like circumstances.

"How do you account for your success?" a newsman asked.

Billy replied, "The only answer I know is God."

"But Dr. Graham, why did God choose *you?*"

The blue eyes twinkled. "When I die and go to heaven," he said, "that's the first question I'm going to ask him."

"When I get to heaven. . . ." he had said.

No ifs, no ands, no buts. . . .

In an age given to skepticism and to eye-witness reports from Russian astronauts that certainly there is no heaven "up there," he spoke with absolute conviction.

This attitude is the core of a faith that glows in him day and night. Its conviction is catching.

"What I can do," he says, "you can do, too."

But how?

The best clue is to be found in the transformation of Billy Graham from a Carolina country boy to a global ambassador for the Kingdom of Heaven. I have followed this process for more than a decade. Its twists and turns have intrigued and, at times, frustrated me so greatly that I have had to become a sort of psychological James Bond. Indeed, I, too, have asked myself why God chose Billy Graham.

My trade of journalism has forced me to become an amateur character analyst; it is a skill which comes from studying humanity and placing your conclusions on paper for others to read. My pilgrimage in search of the truth about Billy Graham began in 1954 when magazine editor Ernest V. Heyn sensed that something of importance was happening in the British Isles. Already, British newspapers were reciting the details of an unprecedented religious meeting that had all of London talking. Thousands of staid Englishmen had, on a rainy day, left their cozy homes to overflow two of London's largest stadiums.

Sixty thousand persons had filled the White City stadium to hear his afternoon sermon.

Later in the day, 120,000 others stood or sat in the rain at Wembley to hear his second sermon.

This, mind you, took place after ninety days of revival meetings at a converted dog track called Harringay Arena.

The editor said, "This may be the most important story you'll ever write."

I should confess that I am a preacher's son, also a preacher's grandson, also a moderately backslid Baptist from Missouri's Bible belt, and I am convinced that I can smell the aroma of religious rascality a little sooner than most. And back in 1954 I thought I smelled it all the way from jolly old England.

I must confess further that I knew something about the promotion of public personalities. I learned this art during a period in which I succumbed to Hollywood's golden lure to participate in the business of star-making. In brief, I knew from personal experience the right buttons to press to assure the kind of hot air that would balloon a modest talent into a box office attraction.

Nor did I take this assignment lacking a standard of performance by which to measure public figures. My pursuit of copy had involved General Eisenhower at the "little red school house" in France, Eleanor Roosevelt in the White House as she realized her husband was failing, and John Foster Dulles when he spoke memorably at New York's Brick Church. My bosses had included Cecil B. DeMille and General George C. Marshall.

No, I was not to be taken in by glowing reports from England. Mass evangelism was a thing of the past, as every informed person knew, having succumbed to more modern techniques, along with behaviorism, the Black Bottom dance, and two-dollar wheat.

Before admitting that the star of a new evangelist was rising, I wanted to inspect his credentials, check his sleeve cuffs for extra jokers, and examine his bank account.

Chapter Two

Most adult Americans go to church regularly on Easter Sunday and on Christmas, and most are members of some Christian congregation, but relatively few have even an inkling of the church's evangelistic role as expressed in Scripture.

Billy Graham's practice of evangelism, though requiring unprecedented financial support, is not money-centered but, rather, dedicated to obtaining from his hearers a personal response. "Go ye and tell" is the motto on his crusading banner, and the organism by which he communicates God's Word to the public is called a crusade.

Each crusade is an entity built upon and around the churches and the Christians of a community. "I am not come to destroy but to fulfill" is an applicable text. If you understand this fact, then you can begin to understand and know the crusader himself.

Here are examples of several different types of crusades:

First, his 1965 "instant crusade" in the state of Alabama, which took him unexpectedly into the heart of the Southland at the height of its racial tension.

Second, two crucial crusades in Nashville, Tennessee, and New Orleans, Louisiana, which were the first to be held in the United States following his "impossible" success in early 1954 in London, England.

Third, his "break-through" crusade of 1949 in Los Angeles, California, which shattered the stubborn and widely held view that "evangelism is dead."

The 1965 crusade in Alabama, which visited several cities and ended in Montgomery, was not a production-line model developed after two years of meticulous preparation, enlisting thousands of prayer partners, and penetrating the spiritual life of hundreds of churches, but it does represent an unprecedented application of Christian influence to social conditions. Possibly, future generations will judge it to be the ultimate development of the evangelist's potential, more effective than even the mammoth productions of New York, London, and Los Angeles. Certainly, it had a soothing effect on the bosom of the South.

Like all Billy Graham crusades, it sprang from his burdened heart and received its strength from his will.

Early spring saw him in a sickbed in Honolulu, where he had worn himself to a frazzle in an all-island campaign. Newspaper headlines were shouting of violence in his beloved Southland. Despite fatigue and fever he made an urgent phone call to his Atlanta headquarters.

"Go to Selma, Alabama," he told two assistants. "Tell me what we can do."

A few days later he ignored caution and discarded precedent to announce his Alabama crusade. As matters stood, it was bound to be the most poorly prepared, the least likely to succeed, and yet the most desperately needed crusade of his fabulously fruitful career.

He went first to the cities of Dothan, Tuscaloosa, Auburn and Tuskegee, where he held the first nonsegregated religious mass meetings in these locales' history.

Then, after a jump via seven-league boots to Copenhagen, Denmark, for a fortnight of campaigning, he brought his team back to Montgomery, Alabama's capital and the focal point on the most virulent racial tension America had experienced since the days of Reconstruction.

The story began when the big transport plane lifted off the glistening runway on Kauai, most Asiatic and most distant of the islands of Hawaii, carrying a weary cargo.

The Hawaiian crusade had begun with months of choir rehearsals and counselor training sessions. More than 175,000 homes had been visited by workers inviting people to attend meetings. Over twelve hundred homes had held morning and evening prayer groups. From Honolulu the campaign had spread to the islands of Maui, Kauai, and Hawaii, where hundreds of inquirers came forward each night to signify their desire to accept Jesus Christ as their Lord.

In colorful Lihue town Billy Graham had preached his final sermon, given his final invitation, waved his last farewell, smiled his last smile, and spent his last ounce of strength. Now he could rest.

The pilot swung his gleaming craft off the westbound beam that led to distant Wake and Midway and set his course east by southeast toward the Honolulu International Airport. The evangelist and his team settled down briefly for the run home. Cliff Barrows, song leader, buried his head in his hands, thinking of all the watery miles he had covered since his decision, back in 1945, to become Graham's teammate. Dr. Akbar Haqq, who had preached every sermon at Kauai until Graham relieved him on the final night, closed his eyes and thought of all the memorable revivals he had seen since his resignation as president of the School of Islamic Studies in New Delhi and his acceptance of the evangelist's invitation to be his interpreter in India and subsequently a member of his team. Ethel Waters, celebrated Negro actress and singer, who had made a guest appearance every night to sing "Oh, How I Love Jesus," smoothed her whitening hair, recalling how her life had changed in the decade since she had gone unannounced and near poverty to Madison Square Garden to sing with the crusade choir.

The others were silent, like runners after a hard race, their spent minds seeking comfort in thoughts of home: Grady Wilson would rejoin his family in Charlotte, North Carolina, Beverly Shea would return to Western Springs, Illinois, and T. W. Wilson to Montreat, a half-mile down the mountain from Billy Graham's house.

The evangelist felt his temples. They were hot. His body throbbed, and his throat was raw. He had preached day after day and delivered countless addresses to special groups. He felt utterly weary. It had been a glorious experience, singing hymns to a ukulele accompaniment, addressing eight hundred leaders of the fiftieth state at the Governor's Prayer Breakfast, preaching in sunshine in Honolulu stadium before 15,500 persons. Now his bones ached. After a hard crusade, he often felt that way. The plane, holding a microcosm of the world's races droned south and east.

Billy Graham thought of the countless faces he had seen, faces that showed all the colors and lineaments of most of the earth's population but with all their eyes gloriously reflecting the fire of a single faith. Their origin did not matter, only their character. One of his sermons had been entitled "God and the Color of a Man's Skin." Its impact had been deep and hard.

And now he could return to his wife Ruth and to Anne Morrow, sixteen, who would graduate from high school in June, and Ruth Bell, fourteen, and William Franklin, Jr., twelve, and Nelson Edman, seven, and his three big dogs.

The transport crossed the Oahu coastline and began to descend, slanting toward the green earth beyond gleaming, glistening Pearl Harbor. With Waikiki Beach and Diamond Head to starboard, the pilot circled into the west-

14

erly wind and touched down. Unfastening seat belts, the team had a single thought: one more lap and they would be home.

Instead, friends took Billy Graham to a hospital. Physicians read his elevated temperature and hurried him to bed, demanding complete rest. His body was exhausted, incapable of fighting off the viruses that threatened him. They called it a bronchial infection. Now he needed treatment and rest.

"How long?"

"About two weeks," the doctors said.

That was the fortnight during which Selma, Alabama, exploded.

Lying abed, he listened to the radio reports of Martin Luther King's activities. King was in Selma organizing a protest march to call attention to the fact that Negroes in that Alabama town, who made up about 50 per cent of the population, were permitted to cast only 1 per cent or so of the vote. Pinpointing this target, this inequality, disclosed the greater iniquities and injustices that afflicted the colored people.

Further south in Dothan, Graham's brother-in-law, Rev. Clayton Bell, was pastor of the First Presbyterian Church. They had already discussed the hazards of change in Alabama. Since the Supreme Court decision of 1954, in fact, many Alabama pastors and laymen had begun to work together to encourage obedience to both the moral and statutory law.

Quietly, Graham prayed that God would guide both white and Negro leadership into honorable channels.

Gathering strength, he was struck by the coincidence that this fortnight was the only time during the next half-year in which he could afford to be abed. As he improved further, he began to answer his mail and plan the addresses

15

he had promised. In Minneapolis and New York he would deliver addresses at prayer breakfasts. Immediately after, looking toward his London crusade beginning June 1, 1966, he would leave for speaking engagements in England and on the Continent. A crusade in Copenhagen would claim him in early May. Then he would return home for a short rest, deliver a commencement address at daughter Anne's high-school graduation, and hold successive crusades in Denver and Houston, this last in the famous Astrodome.

For every speaking engagement Billy Graham accepts, he must turn down scores, so he puts most invitations to a unique test. I heard him use it once when a famous clergyman sought him to address ten thousand Baptist preachers. I considered it a flattering invitation, but he refused. "You don't need me. You'll have ten thousand Christians," he explained. "Now you get me ten thousand sinners, and I'll come."

On Sunday, March 7, Doctor King led his marchers down Selma's Sylvan Street, turned them right at Water Street and followed the road to the Edmund Pettus Bridge over the Alabama River. A quarter of a mile beyond, Highway 80 was blocked by state troopers wearing sky-blue helmets and carrying billy clubs, sidearms, and gas masks. They were reinforced by Selma possemen and sheriff's deputies.

Major John McCloud of the state police shouted into a bullhorn, "Turn around and go back to your church. You'll not be allowed to go any further. You've got two minutes."

The Negroes stopped, their songs silenced. The two seconds ticked by. McCloud ordered, "Troopers—forward!" The solid rank of officers moved ahead until white body met black body. Several Negroes sprawled on the road. Officers slipped, falling heavily amid a tangle of feet and legs. Suddenly a police club rose and fell, and its impact sounded like a firecracker.

Instantly other clubs flashed, beating, thrusting, jabbing, and the waiting sheriff's deputies and possemen rushed into the one-sided fray. The unresisting Negroes retreated until a space lay between them and the slowly advancing officers. A new sound suddenly crackled—the detonation of tear gas cannisters. White and green and yellow smoke billowed across the road. The marchers choked and began to run.

A *Time* newsman reported, "Choking and bleeding, the Negroes fled in all directions while the whites pursued them."

The news flashed across the world, given authenticity by news pictures as unforgiving as the moment Jack Ruby, in television view of the nation, shot and killed Lee Harvey Oswald. Born of the South, loving the South, Billy Graham's Christian conscience demanded that he take some action to heal the rupture.

But he was weak and bedridden, with more days of recuperation ahead.

Two nights later, the Rev. James Reeb and two other ministers were assaulted and beaten in front of Selma's Silver Moon Cafe. On Thursday, four days after King's aborted march, the Rev. Reeb died. And indignation flared across the land, bringing a torrent of angry demonstrations, proclamations, and letters to editors and congressmen.

During those days, those tense and terrible days when despair gripped so many people of good will, Graham picked up his bedside phone and talked to his new team headquarters at the Atlanta airport in Georgia. He directed trusted associates Walter Smythe and Stanley Mooneyham to visit Selma and other Alabama cities, to talk to every person they could find who was concerned about human dignity and God's love for all his children. A dozen Alabama speaking invitations were pending. "Ask all those people how we can be of help now," he said.

"But you've got appointments in Europe."

"We can cancel them."

He had no plan, but he had some experience. On Easter Sunday, 1963, when tension was high in Birmingham, he had flown to that city for a mass meeting at which black and white Christians worshipped together in a vast stadium. Threatening letters and phone calls came, but the meeting went ahead, with biracial ushers, a biracial choir, biracial platform guests, and an audience of thirty-five thousand, almost equally divided between whites and Negroes. Not one incident marred the service.

"The race question will not be solved by demonstrations in the streets, but in the hearts of both Negro and white," Dr. Graham had said. "There must be genuine love to replace prejudice and hate. This love can be supplied by Christ—and only by Christ."

Afterwards, Claude Keathley, religious editor of the powerful Birmingham *News,* reported, "Birmingham will never be the same."

Earlier, Graham had gone to Clinton, Tennessee, challenged by newspaperman Drew Pearson to hold a nonsegregated meeting following a pre-dawn bombing that had destroyed an entire high school. Writing about it, Graham said, "One of the segregationist leaders who had vowed to break up our meeting was among the first persons to step forward to receive Christ."

Lying in bed in Honolulu, he searched the Bible for clues to the future. "I don't think there's a single problem man faces that cannot be solved by Scripture," he says.

Billy Graham has a unique habit that is wholly personal, wholly intellectual. Repeatedly, he demands of himself, "Did I do enough?" He wrestles with the question after each crusade, after each address to a state legislature or body of business leaders. On his conscience are occasions when he closed a crusade or permitted it to be terminated by weary committees, when one more week might have ignited the true fire of revival. At these times his realization had come too late.

That March he asked, "Have I done all that I can to diminish this agony in Alabama?" With respect to civil rights, he had no reason for self-reproach.

Harold H. Martin has reported to *Saturday Evening Post* readers, "Mr. Graham has spoken out so strongly for love and justice toward the Negro that many of his warmest supporters in the Deep South have fallen away. . . . No Graham crusade has been segregated since 1954 . . . and (he) has made a point of going to Clinton, Tennessee, Little Rock, and New Orleans to hold unsegregated meetings following outbursts of racial troubles. . . ."

Holiday magazine said, "Graham's record on intolerance, injustice, and discrimination is unassailable. This is astonishing considering that he was brought up in a Bible belt where segregation was God's law, and some of his early teachers still quote the Bible to prove that it is. Long before the Supreme Court decision, Graham had the 'White' and 'Colored' signs removed from Southern auditoriums where he was invited to preach."

Time recently said, "Billy has often been accused of ignoring segregation, but it is a charge that does not bear scrutiny. Since 1950 he has refused to speak before segregated audiences and has quietly integrated his own staff. Speaking in the South, Billy has denounced racial discrimination as a product of man's sinfulness; and he has refused to preach in South Africa because his audiences would be segregated.

"Civil rights advocates, among the clergy who prefer

19

picket lines to preaching, are skeptical about the worth of Billy's Southern crusade. 'I think my ministry is a little bit different from marching,' answers Billy, who believes that the church must cleanse itself before attacking secular ills. 'I've often said that the most segregated hour of the week is 11 o'clock Sunday morning.' "

He remembered with that clarity of detail possible only to a person born in the context of white supremacy a personal confrontation with discrimination. In 1952 he was leading a crusade in Dallas, Texas. To relax, he invited a Negro masseur from the local YMCA to come to his hotel room and give him a treatment. He was standing in the lobby when the man arrived. In previous meetings they had developed a warm friendship.

Graham said, "I'm going right up. Come along with me."

The Negro said, "Sorry, sir, but I'm not allowed on the elevator."

"Nonsense. How else can you get to my room?"

"Oh, I go round back and walk up," the masseur said.

Graham said, "You just come along." He conducted the Negro to the elevator.

A bell captain stopped the Negro, saying, "I'm sorry, but he isn't allowed on the front elevator. It's a regulation, sir."

"But I've invited him. He's my friend."

"Sorry, sir."

"Either he rides with me, or I go out back and walk up with him."

An assistant manager arrived, breathing peace. "It's a misunderstanding," he said. "If he's your guest, he can use the front elevator."

But it had not been a misunderstanding. Graham told me, "This was only one more incident in a series that made me realize the insults that occurred to other human beings. The Scripture says there's a place for righteous

20

indignation. That day I felt the heat of righteous indignation."

Signs of acute race hatred had begun to appear after the Supreme Court decision of 1954. Earlier, crusades in Southern cities had been guided by local custom. But even in 1952, Graham had challenged his organizing committees.

"I quietly urged them to seat people wherever they wanted to sit," he says. "I had become convinced in my own heart that segregation in religious meetings was wrong. Not only was it against the dignity of the Negro, but I felt it was a sin against God. Most committees complied, nothing was said, the people were just seated where they wanted to be."

He told me of a crusade in Jackson, Mississippi, a city later to become a trouble spot. The local committee made the customary arrangements for segregated sections. The nightly attendance of Negroes was between two and three thousand, but when they responded to the evangelist's invitation, as hundreds did, they mingled with white persons in the group at the altar. In the counseling room they were not segregated.

One day a local minister took Graham aside, saying, "Do you realize we're on the verge of a tragic racial explosion?" In a few minutes he spelled it out. Graham had never heard such a reasoned and frightening prediction. None of the Negro clergymen he knew had spoken so plainly.

The minister had used a new word, "integration"; this was the first time Graham had heard it. "I resolved then to hold integrated meetings in the future," he says, "even though I was barely aware of what the word meant."

But a strange and confusing thing happened. When special sections for seating Negroes were abolished, they avoided his meetings. Before, two or three thousand had attended. Now they numbered only two or three hundred.

He consulted Negro ministers and other leaders. Their reply dug into the heart of the matter.

"Negroes really don't want to intermingle with whites," they said, "but they rebel at the laws and ropes that bar them. Take the *dare* out of it and 90 per cent of the civil rights problem is solved."

Intolerance is not the sole property of America, as Graham discovered on his trip to India in 1956. He was exploring a village with a Jain—Jains are one of the high-caste groups—when he saw a snake charmer at work. He suggested, "Let's watch this man charm that cobra." The Jain looked at the man and spat on the ground, his face contorted with loathing. The snake charmer was from a very low caste, and the Jain could not look at him without spitting.

Prime Minister Nehru understood prejudice and the need for men to change. Billy Graham went to see him at his office one day in New Delhi. In Washington he had been briefed by John Foster Dulles on how to talk to the Indian Prime Minister. In India, when he delivered Dulles' message, it elicited a mere nod. He told of the respect Americans felt for the Indian nation. Mr. Nehru played with his letter opener. Mr. Graham expressed Secretary Dulles' hope for continuing friendship. The Indian sifted through his papers.

Finally, the young American abandoned his "official" role and turned evangelist. He leaned forward, saying, "Mr. Nehru, when I decided to live for Christ, he changed me. He gave me peace and joy. Before this decision, I didn't care about God, the Bible, or other human beings. I was filled with intolerance. But the simple act of accepting him changed my nature. I began to worship God, and I loved people, no matter what color their skins might be. Mr. Nehru, Christ can do that for everyone."

He expected to be thrown out. Instead, the Prime Minister's eyes brightened. For the first time, his manner showed concern. "And how does he do this?" he asked. They talked on and on, far beyond the time set for the visit.

On his return to the United States, President Eisenhower called him to the White House. Graham reread his notes on the conditions he had observed in India, the Malay States, and the Philippines, preparing to report his observations. The President never mentioned foreign affairs. He wanted to talk about the worsening drift of American race relations and of how they could be improved. He believed the church could help more than any other institution. Graham went back to his hotel room and knelt in prayer, asking God's guidance. Nine years later, another President with a similar burden would call for similar aid.

Since 1956, when his crusades became totally nonsegregated, they have been witness to no incident of racial conflict. In Richmond, Virginia, a white crusade usher once resigned when he learned that he would have to escort Negroes to their seats. But the man attended the initial meeting, listened to Graham's sermon, and went forward at his invitation. Next day he sought out the chief usher. "Since last night, I'm changed," he said. "I'd like my job back."

Graham says, "His prejudice had melted in the wake of a spiritual experience. You cannot argue and debate away prejudice, but it can melt in the fervor of supernatural love that God gives you. This is why I'm convinced that conversion, on the part of the individual Negro and white person alike, can solve most of the race problem."

Virginia City supplied another example. Two of the town's social leaders decided to give a party for crusade workers. Invitations were rushed out. Presently, the host and hostess learned they had unwittingly invited several Negroes. They had never entertained colored guests, but they went ahead with the party. The evening went off without a hitch. Graham says, "I think it was the first time some of those white people had met Negroes on an equal social basis. I know they were amazed at their intelligence, wit, perfect manners, and culture. We had one of the most delightful social events of our experience."

For years a pressure group of sincere colored Christians have urged Graham to use his television time to dramatize the need of love between the races. One of them told a crusade associate, "I pray that some day Brother Graham will call a white man from his audience and a black man from his audience and have them stand beside him in the pulpit. And then how glorious it would be if he would take a black hand and place it in a white hand and put them together on the Bible so everyone in America could see that this is what Jesus Christ teaches."

On the other hand, the prejudice is not all on one side. An important Negro leader told the evangelist, "I have prejudice in my heart simply because a man's skin is white. I can't conquer this feeling. I know it's sinful, and I'm working on it, but it's still there."

Billy Graham refuses to use his pulpit for anything but the message of the Bible. Elsewhere, he is far from silent. In 1956, *Life* published his article entitled "Plea for An End to Intolerance," a powerful call for racial friendship. In 1960, the same periodical published his policy, the result of four years of study, under the title, "Men Must Be Changed Before a Nation Can Be Changed." At luncheons, at conventions, in private conversation, he speaks forcefully about civic freedom and white responsibilities.

"We must enter into the Negroes' difficulties and problems, and their burdens must become our burdens if we are to fulfill the law of Christ," he says.

Meanwhile tensions were mounting in Alabama.

Governor Wallace had visited President Johnson. Martin

Luther King had been given permission to lead a group from Selma to Montgomery on Sunday, March 21, to arrive in the state capital on Thursday, March 25. Civil rights sympathizers of all shades, political and physical, were funneling into the steaming South.

Chapter Three

About the middle of the month, Billy Graham left the hospital in Honolulu and flew to Montreat, North Carolina. Smythe and Mooneyham reported that Alabama friends were eager for him to tour the state. They said that thousands of decent white citizens were ready to disavow the tyranny of noisy minorities. Given a chance and firm leadership, they were ready to demonstrate their brotherly love. They could be mobilized to help arrange nonsegregated mass meetings.

Laymen and ministers had said, "God bless you, we're glad you're here. We're glad somebody cares."

Furthermore, many local pastors were hopeful that a religious revival might initiate a period of understanding and mutual tolerance. At that time Northern opinion was berating Southern clergymen for not taking a public stand, for not throwing their church doors wide to all comers.

"We've tried that," one explained. "The result was a shambles. We are willing to worship with our colored brethren, but instead, we're invaded by bearded hooligans and women wearing stretch pants and bikinis. They don't come to worship. They come to agitate."

Another said, "My best friend took a courageous stand. He preached immediate integration, and his congregation split right down the middle. He had to resign. Now he's left the community, and his Christian influence is lost forever. I wish our brothers up North would understand

26

there's more than one way to skin a cat. I'm working with my church officers and deacons. Most of them have changed their thinking and are ready right now to support biracial activities. Our next step is to have them try to change *their* friends and relatives. When we've done that, we can take a strong, united position. And we're already a lot further along than anybody imagines."

On March 25, Doctor King's big march from Selma reached Montgomery. The marchers included a cripple, a blind man, a nun, preachers galore, and plain citizens of both colors. Troops had guarded them every foot of the way.

That night civil rights worker Mrs. Viola Liuzzo was murdered by members of the Ku Klux Klan.

Sixteen hours later President Lyndon Johnson was on television, announcing their arrest.

And Billy Graham made up his mind to take his crusade to Alabama.

"You may be in some personal danger," friends told him.

"I don't think so."

"The Klan won't want you to come. They may try to stop you."

"It's a chance I'll take."

"Right now half the crackpots and religious fanatics in America have gathered in Alabama. They've threatened you before."

"I'm coming."

He stopped off in Washington to tell his friend Lyndon Johnson. First, he would tour several trouble spots and hold a nonsegregated stadium meeting in each. Then, in June, he would return to Montgomery for an all-out, old-fashioned Billy Graham crusade that would involve as many churches and church people throughout Alabama as could be enlisted.

Cables postponed English and Continental appearances.

His team had scattered to their homes. Many, after Hawaii, were on vacation, but his Atlanta headquarters traced them, ordering them to a command post in Montgomery.

They would ordinarily spend two years preparing for a major crusade. Here they would have only two weeks to prepare for his one-night stands and two months for the big Montgomery crusade. Their helpers would be some of the individuals and organizations that had invited Billy Graham to address them, plus pastors and churches representing both races, ministerial alliances, and laymen's groups. A crash program was needed.

The news broke first in Washington, D.C. Newsmen called Montreat, N.C., and spoke to Graham. The Associated Press reported, "Evangelist Billy Graham says 'It is wrong for people in other parts of the country to point an accusing self-righteous finger at Alabama.'

"Graham made his statement Monday as he canceled engagements in Great Britain to go to Alabama for four speeches this month.

"The evangelist added he believes the only permanent solution to the racial problem is the 'Message of God's love in Jesus Christ and our obligations to love our neighbors as ourselves.'

"The evangelist said he will 'preach the same Gospel I have preached all over the world, which is the same message the early apostles preached in the first century.' "

Segregationists were quick to react and criticize. Recalling the evangelist's recent visit to the White House, members of White Citizens Committees sent rumors buzzing along their grapevines. "Lyndon Johnson is sending his buddy Billy Graham down here to tell us how to run our state."

Reporters next found Billy Graham at his Minneapolis headquarters where he was scheduled to address the Minnesota Governor's Prayer Breakfast and the Kiwanis Club. "Did Johnson ask you to go to Alabama?" they asked.

The Religious News Service reported, "Mr. Graham said he had been encouraged by President Johnson to conduct a series of religious meetings in racially tense Alabama late in April.

"The evangelist laughed off a report that he had become 'chaplain' of the White House.

"He said he is a great admirer of President Johnson and expressed the opinion that 'in many ways he carries the heaviest load of any man since Lincoln. I think we need unity and should pray for the President that God will help him. I have a sense he is depending on God and looking for His guidance in many directions. No one can imagine the loneliness in which the President must make his decisions.' "

The report continued, "Mr. Graham told how he and Mrs. Graham had visited President Johnson's room at one A.M. during their recent overnight stay in the White House. Lying on his bed were envelopes filled with documents that the President had to read before he went to bed. In the lonely hours in that room, the President had to make decisions that affect the lives of millions around the world."

The New York *Times* news service reported from Atlanta, "Everywhere he goes these days, the Rev. Billy Graham carries with him a little black-covered memorandum book inscribed with the names of those he prays for. There are presidents and professional golfers, members of his evangelistic team and people he has met only once. One of the most recent entries was the name of Governor George C. Wallace, of Alabama.

"In the modest royal-blue-gold office he occupies at the International Park, he talked of his mission. . . . 'I am a Southerner,' he said. 'I don't feel I have the whole answer, but at least for the time being I have a voice in the South and I will try to provide the leadership I can.

" 'Some things down here are changing very slowly, and there will be more Selmas. But the friendships are closer, too, and we haven't reached the stage yet where we have the ghettos.

" 'What we are doing, I think, all over America, is laying the foundation for a multiracial society for the next generation. We are the generation of revolution. The next will be the generation of peace.' "

The race against time began.

Invitations from ministerial groups and other organizations were accepted from four Alabama cities: Dothan, Tuscaloosa, Auburn, and Tuskegee. The ministers and churches of Montgomery asked for a full-length crusade.

On Saturday, April 24, Billy Graham drove into Dothan, a city of thirty thousand in the deepest part of the deep South, just a few miles from the Florida line. It is a thriving trading and farming center surrounded by miles of rich earth nicknamed the Black Belt. Dothan calls itself the peanut capital of the world, and it was crowded that Saturday with visitors. Extra police and state troopers were on duty. Because several threats had been intercepted, two state investigators were assigned to guarantee Graham's personal safety, and they were never more than a few feet from him, except when he preached; even then they guarded the steps to his platform. At night, they slept in rooms on either side of the evangelist's suite.

Earlier the Dothan *Eagle* had carried a full-page advertisement paid for by segregationists which said, in effect, "Billy Graham, go home!"

On another page the *Eagle*'s editorial column was polite but restrained. "Billy Graham, the noted evangelist will make two appearances in Dothan this weekend. There exists something less than unanimity of opinion regarding the timing of his visit in relation to recent events in Alabama. . . . Dothan is playing host, thus regardless of the views that people may have on the subject, it is incumbent on individuals and the community alike that there be no incident capable of causing unpleasantness, embarrassment, or regret. If this means restraint on the part of anyone inside or outside, then so be it."

By Saturday the downtown crowds were buzzing with rumors. One report said that Billy Graham was bringing the detested Martin Luther King with him. Another said he was bussing two hundred Negro women from Harlem to sing in his choir. Handbills appeared mysteriously on the street, presenting side-by-side portraits of Graham and King, along with scurrilous comment. Rabid segregationists, it was clear, would do all they could to disrupt the meetings. No one knew how far they would go.

Chairman of the Dothan Crusade Committee was the Rev. Harper Shannon, pastor of the First Baptist Church. He and his fellow clergymen had worked hard to make this crusade a success. At Dothan's Rip Hewes football stadium that Saturday, the seats filled slowly as forty policemen and troopers watched. The audience was about half white, half Negro. So was the 450-voice choir. So were the guests on the platform. This had never happened before.

Finally, when about six thousand persons were present, the meeting began. Cliff Barrows directed the hymn singing. Beverly Shea sang his beloved songs. Grady Wilson read the Scripture. And Billy Graham preached. In Hawaii he had spoken on the color of God's skin. In Dothan his message was "The End of the World."

On the street before the stadium, a procession of cars passed back and forth, back and forth, filled with faces peering at the biracial assembly. These were the timid ones, the cautious citizens who wondered if it would be safe for them to attend tomorrow's service, unwilling as yet to "mix," and wondering if they would lose face with their neighbors if they sat publicly with Negroes.

At the end, when Graham asked for persons to come forward who would pledge their lives to Christ, 239 made their way to the speaker's pulpit.

No incident of any kind occurred. The Reverend Shannon declared, "This meeting has set a new level of personal relationships. Lives will be challenged by what has happened here. Some persons expected—some even wanted—a calamity to happen. But the Spirit was present."

On Sunday Alabama's sunny springtime turned to rain. Now the segregationists must have rejoiced. What they had not achieved with all their rumor-mongering, nature would do for them. The Sunday afternoon meeting would be washed out. At their motel the Graham team wondered if anyone would be foolhardy enough to come to the stadium. Already, he had made arrangements to deliver his address via a local television station.

"Nobody will come in this storm. Why not issue a formal cancellation?" an assistant suggested.

"But if people do come, I can't disappoint them," Graham said.

A scout hurried to the stadium and phoned in a startling report. Every water-logged seat was empty, but three thousand persons were already huddled beneath the stands. The evangelist threw on a raincoat and hurried to join them.

Claude Keathley of the Birmingham *News* reported, "Dr. Graham told the rain-drenched congregation he was going to speak for only five minutes and then let them go home to listen to a hurriedly arranged telecast. The five minutes lengthened to ten, fifteen, and then twenty minutes.

"The interracial audience standing shoulder to shoulder could not move as Billy Graham made his invitation to follow Christ. He asked them to just lift their hands in decision. Many did."

Keathley's story also mentioned Wallace Malone, financial power and vice-president of the segregationist Houston County Citizens Council. On his own request, he was received by Graham. Malone later said, "I was at the Saturday night service, and it was a great service. Dr. Graham and I agreed on one thing, that the South has made great progress. I'm sure Dr. Graham did not come here to stir up trouble, and he did preach the Gospel. Dr. Graham is a great preacher and our kind of man."

So Dothan's twin meetings, abbreviated by rain, became history. Their success seemed to be a good sign, but the route ahead might be booby-trapped; certainly it was shadowed by bloody memories.

Monday night Graham would preach in Tuscaloosa at the University of Alabama.

Tuesday morning at Auburn University.

Tuesday night at Tuskegee.

Then unbreakable commitments would call him to Copenhagen, Denmark.

In June he would return to Alabama's capital for a major crusade.

Tuscaloosa, Alabama, was named for a famous Chocktaw Indian chief. It means "black warrior," and it is the seat of the beautiful sixty-acre campus of the state university. Dr. Frank A. Rose, a no-nonsense president, believes in desegregation and accepts the registration of qualified Negroes. The policy works.

But Alabama is also the university where Governor George C. Wallace stood "at the schoolhouse door" to maintain racial segregation until he was overwhelmed by national pressure and the power of his federalized National Guard. When he stepped aside, two Negro students, Vivian Malone and James Hood, were promptly enrolled.

The university's Student Government Association was sponsoring Graham's appearance. Claude Keathley invited

33

me to accompany him. Rolling along Highway 11, we discussed the situation.

"Do you expect any trouble here?" I asked.

He said, "Well, we've got the Imperial Wizard of the Ku Klux Klan living in Tuscaloosa." He glanced at thunder-heads piling up in the south and west. "We often have showers this time of year. That'll keep the crowd down."

"How about the ministers?"

"Two hundred churches are supporting this service. They're sending delegations. Of course, we've got some renegade preachers who say segregation is supported by the Bible."

The use of Scripture to justify segregation is a phenomenon that seems to be limited largely to the South, and many segregationists sincerely believe that it authorizes their stand for white superiority.

It is worth examining.

They refer you to Genesis, ninth chapter, and its story of Noah and his sons and grandsons. After the flood, Noah planted a vineyard, drank the wine, and got drunk. In his stupor, he lay naked in his tent. His son Ham, seeing his father exposed, told his brothers Shem and Japheth. The latter two took a garment, and, averting their faces so they would not witness their parent's shame, covered him.

When Noah awoke, he learned that his youngest son Ham had "tattled." In fury he cursed all of Ham's offspring starting with Canaan, Ham's firstborn. "Cursed be Canaan," he cried. "A slave of slaves shall he be to his brothers." He named his son Shem, saying that Canaan would always be his servant, and he named Japheth, saying Canaan would also be his servant.

The Genesis story runs from the eighteenth to the twenty-eighth verse. For years English, Dutch, and Yankee slave traders used it to ease their consciences, claiming that the Negro race had been cursed by God and placed forever in an inferior position.

Graham has written, "Let's look at the facts. First, Shem, Ham, and Japheth were blood brothers, and the Bible says that from these all earth was peopled. They had the same mother and father, and there was no discrimination between them. Second, *God* never did curse Canaan; it was Noah, and Noah had been drunk. Third, most scholars agree that the Canaanites, the descendants of Canaan, were all white tribes, and that the Negro peoples are descended from Canaan's brothers whom Canaan was to serve.

"Jesus put no color bar on the Golden Rule. There is no evidence of racial discrimination in the early church. James wrote, 'If you show partiality, you commit sin.' Let's not make the mistake of pleading the Bible to defend it."

We drove to the columned ante-bellum mansion that is President Frank Rose's home. The entire Billy Graham team was there, plus white and Negro guests, student leaders of both races, Paul Bear Bryant, idol of Alabama football fans and an ardent worker for his faith, and young Zach Higgs, president of the Student Government Association, who had a prepared statement:

"On behalf of the Student Government Association, I want to welcome Dr. Billy Graham and his staff to the campus. It is our hope that this program will continue the goal set by the Student Government, that of having enlightening speakers come to our campus to speak on various topics."

Dr. Rose said, "We are delighted to have this great man of God with us, and we are confident that great good will come from this occasion. We hope that Dr. Graham and the members of his party thoroughly enjoy the hospitality of this university."

Outside, the sky was turning black, and the warm air stirred uneasily. As we walked to Denny Stadium, joining thousands of other pilgrims, spears of lightning shot down to the horizon. "Maybe it will pass around us," we thought.

In the stadium, floodlights illuminated the darkness,

35

turning grass to shining green, whitening the raw wood of the platform where Graham and many university dignitaries sat. Microphones made an electronic hedge before the lectern. A grand piano stood at its right, an organ at its left. Billy Graham, bareheaded, wore a light tan raincoat.

As the service began, the first drops fell, and ten thousand umbrellas opened, painting the stadium with an incredible patchwork of colors.

Student President Zach Higgs welcomed Graham and the crowd. Huge drops fell slowly, like feathers, widely spaced and harmless. Cliff Barrows, leading a song, suggested that a more appropriate number might be "Let There Be Showers of Blessing." Football quarterback Steve Sloan, star athlete and student leader, read the Scripture. Beverly Shea's solo was cut to a single verse, as were hymns, and introductions were curtailed. The storm was gathering directly above Tuscaloosa. Amazingly, nobody left the stadium.

Billy Graham rose to preach, and the rain stopped. The people folded their damp umbrellas and relaxed.

"I don't know of any place in the world where we've had a warmer welcome," he began. "President Johnson has said we are living in a world of crisis. . . . We are living in a world of tremendous social revolution. . . . Young people are on the march everywhere. . . . President Kennedy said, 'Each day the crisis moves on. Each day the crisis grows more difficult. . . .'"

Then the thunder began, not in the distance but overhead, rolling across the top of the stadium and muffling the evangelist's words.

"Many people are asking, 'What can we do?'" Graham continued, and large raindrops began to multiply in the floodlights. "Is there an answer? I say tonight there is an answer. There is one that came two thousand years ago and said, 'I am the way, the truth, and the life.' He said, 'I'm your way out!' And I say tonight you people are facing a war. You are a people facing racial tension and crisis. There is a way out. For your problems and your difficulties and your sins, Jesus Christ is the way. He is the truth. He is the life. . . ."

Suddenly, the heavens seemed to open and the rain came with the force and density of a thousand high pressure hoses. Water beaded Graham's forehead and made rivulets down his cheeks. He wanted to continue, but his voice was lost in the drumming of rain and thunder. Men on the platform unfolded sheets of plastic and held them over their heads. Others covered the piano and organ. People in the stadium got to their feet reluctantly, and some began to leave. Others merely stood looking at the bizarre beauty of ten billion diamonds swirling in the floodlight and teeming onto the green gridiron and onto the face and shoulders of the evangelist, who, through it all, did not move from his microphones.

Almost immediately it became clear that the storm had won. As lightning flashed, the electrical equipment blinked and sparked. Wet connections began to sputter. Graham finally closed his watersoaked Bible. "Thank you so much," he said. "If it quits raining, I'll continue."

Grady Wilson, associate evangelist, lifted his umbrella overhead with one hand while using the other to tug a plastic canopy over the heads of the platform guests. A thunderbolt split the lowering clouds straight overhead, lacing the blackness with white fire, and Grady found himself flat on his back, his arms numbed by a vagrant electrical shock. Picking himself up, he saw that no one was hurt and that ten thousand men and women, students with dates, faculty members, reporters—all were making their way out of the stadium. Many simply folded their useless umbrellas and carried their shoes and stockings in their hands. Most were smiling. They had heard a brief address, but it had meaning. To me it seemed that their wet faces, both white and colored, were suffused with a fraternal radiance.

The Billy Graham team got into cars, turned on their heaters, and drove, soaking wet and sneezing, the hundred miles back to their motel in Montgomery. Tomorrow they would hold two more services, one at Auburn, one at Tuskegee.

Auburn, Alabama, is a small college town far from the rumblings of commerce. Its streets are tree-lined, its homes are gracious, its atmosphere restful. Its principal industry is the education of young minds. Almost a hundred years ago, the State Agricultural and Mechanical College was founded there. Later it was renamed the Alabama Polytechnic Institute, and today it is known to every football fan as Auburn University.

Most of its students know what they want and where they are going. They get first-rate professional training in addition to a fine cultural background from Auburn's several colleges. Because they will be the generation to run much of Alabama's industrial and agricultural machinery, Billy Graham accepted an invitation from their Student Government Association to bring his crusade to their campus.

The day was brilliant, and Cliff Hare Stadium at the edge of town was filled that morning with sixteen thousand persons . . . students, faculty, and townspeople. Eighty-five ushers of both races seated them on the south side of the bowl. Again the message concerned God's work in men's hearts; again its embodiment was visible in the audience, in the choir, and on the platform. The Auburn community was predominately white, so Negro spectators were far less numerous than they would be that same evening in the Tuskegee stadium.

Graham does not ask for decisions in his campus crusades. Instead, he appeals to conscience and shows that man is un-
38

able to go it alone. Then he underscores the unimaginable power for good man has once he surrenders to the guidance of God through Christ. When Auburn's first interracial mass service was over, its students and faculty and homesteaders walked out to their cars in a sober and thoughtful mood.

Again I heard the words, "This town will never be the same."

As Graham and his team drove toward Tuskegee, convoyed by state troopers and guarded by a detail of state investigators in an unmarked car, they talked quietly of what might happen on this last night of their crusade.

Thus far no untoward incident had marred the pilgrimage. But Keathley had said, "If there's going to be trouble, it'll come at Tuskegee."

Tuskegee Institute is in Macon County, a political entity in which a white minority, until recently, held iron-clad power over a Negro majority.

Before accepting the invitation from the Institute's famous John A. Andrew Clinical Society, the Graham team had asked questions:

"What's the climate among your whites and Negroes? Are tempers high?"

"We think not, but all the highways are open. White racists can easily come to Tuskegee to make trouble." They were thinking of Ku Klux Klan bombings and Black Muslim murders.

"Is the stadium properly lighted for a night meeting?"

"We could never afford to light our stadium," Negro leaders said. "We've never had the money."

"Won't it be dangerous for thousands of persons to mill around in the darkness? Can you install temporary lights?"

"We'll light the stadium somehow."

Trouble could come in Tuskegee, but then so could a great blessing. These thousands of colored students, guided by idealism and wills of iron, were getting the training

39

they would need to lead their communities toward the Great Society. Already, local white and Negro leaders had met together, stated their cases plainly and with honesty, and made concessions to each other. Here, it seemed that reconciliation already had a foothold.

I drove into town at dusk and saw a huge banner saying, "Tuskegee Welcomes Billy Graham." Small stores fringed the empty central square, enough to serve its population of seven thousand. Tuskegee is not a pretty town. Only when one leaves the business section and heads into the tree-lined streets that run through the Institute campus does it become attractive.

Macon County, with its rolling hills and green trees, is a lovely county, but I have never seen so many miles of dreary roadsides. On the outskirts of Tuskegee, in contrast to most American urban border areas, you cannot find a motel or a highway restaurant. This part of the city looks as though it is still back in the time of the Great Depression.

"Where do travelers sleep? Where do they eat?" I asked a local citizen.

"They don't stop here," he said. "Except for merchants, a couple of ministers and their families, and a few others . . . this is a Negro town, six to one."

"Can I get a meal here?"

He said, "Well, there's a club. You drive back to the corner and. . . ."

I followed his directions to a low building carrying a huge "Cafe" sign. Across the street a line of Negro and white teenagers took turns at buying malted milks and ice cream from a roadside shop. I parked and walked to the cafe door. It was closed and locked. A small card said, in smudged ink, "Private Club. Ring the bell."

I rang, and a waitress came to study me through the curtain. After a moment she opened the door and said, "Come in."

40

While eating, I saw other men come to that door, insert a key, and enter. A few came and went, as I did, with no apparent credentials except the color of their skin.

An Alabama reporter told me, "It's being done all over. The club is a dodge to keep out Negroes. Everybody is supposed to buy a key." He showed me his crowded key ring. "Mine cost me thirty-five cents."

I drove toward Billy Graham's meeting at Alumni Stadium, wondering where in Tuskegee such dark-complexioned persons as Mahatma Gandhi or Booker T. Washington or Prime Minister Nehru could have found a place to eat. I wondered, too, if that pretty waitress, who judged me through her locked door, would have admitted the bearded Jew, Jesus Christ.

Negro soldiers and airmen, booted and scarved, all members of the Tuskegee Reserve Officers Training Corps, guided a line of cars down dirt roads to a field. Negro policemen directed me to a parking place. I had been told that Negro policemen and Negro councilmen were a recent concession by the formerly all-white government.

Alumni Stadium is in a valley, with seats along two sides, a structure so modest—one stand is covered by a tin roof supported by bare iron columns—that most city high schools would disown it. In this unprepossessing structure I met more ROTC soldiers, the smartest I've ever seen, lighting the way with flashlights. Fathers held their children's hands and mothers carried cushions and blankets for protection from the cool night air. I saw not one other white face.

Chairs covered the football field, eleven hundred of them borrowed from classrooms. Bare bulbs mounted on tall poles spread a dim light over the crowd. But at one open end of the stadium, the speaker's platform was brilliantly illuminated and its steps were guarded by a white plainclothesman and a Negro noncommissioned officer.

When the service began, ten thousand were present, most

of them colored. The platform guests were prominent doctors and dentists from all over the South, all the city's councilmen, and school officials. The medical men were there because of the Andrew Clinical Society. Months earlier, it had asked Graham to be the banquet speaker that year. When his presence was assured, they opened the meeting to the public to assure him a large audience. We newsmen were handed the Society's printed program of medical and cultural discussions and saw that his address fell between talks on "Complications of Diabetes Mellitus" and "Hiatus Hernia."

The evening, aided by the famed Tuskegee Choir, quickly moved from prayer to hymn to Scripture. When Graham stepped to the lectern, everyone was not relaxed. This was the handful of educators who had been present at an afternoon confrontation between the evangelist and a dissident group of students. They did not want oil poured on troubled waters. He had offered the hand of fellowship. They had rejected it with disrespect and discourtesy, using language unworthy of either their race or their university. Despite an apology from the officials, some wondered how Graham would handle the inflammatory incident. Would the North Carolinian, stung by the slurs he had heard, strike back? He began to preach, and a whippoorwill in a nearby tree started to sing. Microphones picked up the birdsong, mixing its notes with the Graham exhortation. Otherwise, the audience heard about the same message others had heard, emphasizing the need of people to fill their empty lives.

The evangelist said, "Before Ernest Hemingway killed himself, he told friends, 'I live in a vacuum. It's as lonely as a radio tube when the batteries are dead and there's no current to plug into.'

"And people are asking, 'Which way can we turn?' I say to you . . . for your problems and your difficulties and your sins, Jesus Christ is the way. He is the truth. He is the life!"

He said our race problems should be seen in perspective: "The difference in many countries is between religion and race. That's the problem in Cyprus, in India, in Malaysia, in the Middle East, and even in Russia. But greater improvement has been made in America recently than in any other country."

He said science offers unprecedented benefits for the future, but we must not forget that "God is the creator of it all. And you cannot put God in a test tube."

A police escort picked up Graham and his associates and started them on the long drive to Atlanta, where they would catch planes for their homes for a day or two with their families before crossing the Atlantic to carry their crusade to the people of Denmark.

The crowd waited until the Graham party had climbed the hill, and then they, too, left the stadium. Within minutes every seat was empty. Two electricians began to dismantle the sound system and the electric lights. To a newcomer it would look as if nothing much had happened there.

But a biracial group had heard a Negro college president and a Negro physician conduct a service in which a white banker read the Scripture, a white evangelist preached the Gospel, and Negro and white musicians together produced sacred music. And to round out the amazing picture, a Jew who had recruited dozens of extra singers for this unprecedented event sat in the choir's back row among his colored friends, mouthing the words of Christian hymns despite being tone deaf and unable to sing a note.

And brotherhood reigned in Tuskegee that night.

What is the core of Billy Graham's zeal? What logic persuades him that men can love one another?

"Christ said, 'You must be born anew,' " he explains. "He taught that human nature must be transformed, changed,

43

and redirected. He taught that before we can have a better society we must have better men."

He says, "But man is not able to bring about this transformation by his own efforts. It is a superhuman act of the soul *which takes place when men repent and exercise faith in Christ.*

"This is why we call on men to be converted to Christ first. Only *after* Christ transforms their lives, will they have the power to love their fellowmen properly. Christ gives men this capacity."

What is his mission? What does he hope to achieve in his seven-league boots, crossing oceans and mountains, a few weeks here, a few days there?

An evangelist, he says, is simply a proclaimer of the good news, which, in capsule form, is that "Christ died for our sins according to the Scriptures . . . was buried . . . and rose again on the third day, according to the Scriptures. The Bible declares that man is a sinner, that Christ is the only Savior, that Christ lives evermore, and that the Scriptures are trustworthy."

What would he have people do?

He would have them experience conversion, live their Christianity in every daily contact through courtesy, patience, and humility, teach love for other races in the home, accept responsibility as their brother's keeper, take a stand in their church for neighbor-love, be honest with themselves and realize that they can never do enough, and act always on principle, never condoning a wrong.

"Christian laymen must speak out against the social ills of our times," he says. "I am convinced that faith without works is dead."

In his plea for tolerance, published several years ago in *Life,* he tells the following illuminating story:

"After the close of the Civil War, a Negro entered a fashionable church in Richmond, Virginia, one Sunday morning

44

while communion was being served. He walked down the aisle and knelt at the altar. A rustle of shock and anger swept through the congregation. Sensing the situation, a distinguished layman immediately stood up, stepped forward to the altar, and knelt beside his Negro brother. Captured by his spirit, the congregation followed his magnanimous example. The layman who set the example was Robert E. Lee."

In May, Billy Graham completed his ten-day campaign in Copenhagen, Denmark. For the first time in modern history, hoodlums repeatedly invaded Christian services and tried to break them up by shouting, singing, and troublemaking. One night they threw acid in the eyes of a guard and blinded him. It was an unsettling, disturbing experience for Graham.

Back in Montgomery he immediately plunged into another exhausting crusade, speaking several times each day, whipping up interest throughout Alabama's Protestant community, encouraging the weary, and inspiring the young.

"How long can you keep this up?" a worried friend asked.

"Until God gives the signal," he replied.

"What about the next ten years? What do you think will happen?" Several months earlier, he had anticipated the question.

"They could be the most critical in human history. And I'm glad to be alive at a time like this. What a moment to be an ambassador for Christ. What an hour for the proclamation of his Gospel. Christianity is the religion of crisis. For a world in ferment, it fits the heart and the needs of man. This is the time to make Christ known, whether it be by pastor, teacher, evangelist, or layman.

"And I intend to continue," he concluded, "until He says, 'It is enough.' "

Like the Apostle Paul, he is Christ's happy prisoner. And his eyes forever see a vision and a promise that, in the words of Harold A. Martin, "the people in the pews, frail, weak, and frightened mortals though they may be, have within themselves the power to shake and change the world."

Chapter Four

"I'm going to Nashville to get a story on Billy Graham," I told another newsman in 1954. The evangelist was en route to Tennessee after his resounding success in England. "You'll never see him."

"Why not?"

"I tried it in London," he said. "I heard him preach and I wanted to talk to him. But he's busier than any head of government or movie celebrity I've ever interviewed. That day he had over two hundred long-distance calls, visits from a score of old friends, consultations with a half-dozen new Christians who were in trouble, and two committee meetings.

"He also made a talk to a luncheon club, visited a factory, and appeared on the radio. At three o'clock he began his quiet time, which he reserves for studying and praying and writing his sermons. I'd say he needs it."

So I flew to Nashville to get my first glimpse of the world's busiest young evangelist. By arrangement with George Wilson, an official of the young Billy Graham Evangelistic Association, I was welcomed by the evangelist's press secretary, Mrs. Betty Lowry. Modest hotels housed the Graham team. Modest offices, contributed by a local benefactor, contained a small secretarial staff and provided a base of operations. The team's work, I was soon to learn, involved a tremendous amount of preliminary correspondence aimed at organizing large committees among participating churches. Hundreds of persons had been recruited to sing, to usher, to counsel (after special training) with inquirers, and to pray.

That first night I heard a singular sound as I walked through the September dusk, one I learned later to associate with all Billy Graham crusades: it was the liquid sound of thousands of feet beating against sidewalks and overflowing into gutters, creating a sibilant monotone like that of waves breaking on the shore. Occasionally voices rose above it or broke through in spurts of talk and laughter. They had a special quality, almost like those of children. Time and again, I turned toward them, expecting to see a Sunday School class and found only normally dressed men and women.

Many of the pedestrians carried books colored white, black, or red, and I was startled to see that these were Bibles. "Bring your Bibles," Graham always exhorted. And the people did.

Within the giant dish of the stadium a million candlepower's worth of light bathed the slanting tier of seats to form an oval alive with visitors. One could hear them settling into seats, along with the braking of busses and the door slamming of cars in the adjacent parking lot as other thousands arrived. A moon hung overhead like a reminder of the mystery of God's universe.

A high platform the size of a badminton court stood on the fifty-yard line across the running track. Rising behind it, a solid mass of white-clad singers held hymnbooks. A powerful, tall figure stood on the platform, both arms upraised, outlined by the powerful beam of a floodlight. Suddenly his hands reached out and a paean of thanksgiving filled the air. It was a hymn I had sung many times in my father's church.

The press section—I was a little surprised that a church service would have a press section—was a grass-carpeted space at the base of the platform. Several tables and chairs held bored reporters. By the time I found a place, Billy Graham was speaking.

I watched his lean, lance-like figure and his spotlighted arm holding aloft his Bible. A reporter looks first at externals. The young evangelist from North Carolina was obviously attractive. A reporter looks secondly for word tags to help him remember. The first word in my mind was "dramatic!" Watching his gestures, I wondered if Graham had visited Greece and learned how their ancient actors managed to communicate effectively with audiences sitting a half-block away.

The Greeks had used larger-than-life masks that showed joy or rage or sorrow. Graham used larger-than-life gestures which flowed from his entire body. Many preachers lounge at their work or stand immobile in the pulpit like horses at their hitching posts. This evangelist darted about like a pugilist, sure-footed as a cat, purposeful as a tiger.

I began to count his steps.

In one minute he took twenty-two steps, in another forty-four steps, in another forty steps. Weaving and side-stepping, right, left, and right again, then backward to a kind of home base directly behind the lectern. Certainly, he was the most active minister I had ever seen, his every phrase strengthened by an accompanying physical attitude.

"Jesus is love!"—stride—"Jesus is mercy!"—stride—"Jesus is forgiveness!"—stride. . . .

His hands became many things, banners or rapiers or sledgehammers, as his message required, moving even more rapidly than his feet. "Now hear this!" Clap. "You cannot kill your soul." Clap. "The part of you that thinks and remembers and imagines will live on always." Clap! No single gesture was low or mean or meager. When he wanted to thrust an idea home, the wrist stiffened with authority.

He changed pace often, leaning on the pulpit, left foot

49

forward, right hand punching. Then he sprang back, his body taut as a bow, arms outspread, simulating the cross. His words hit the ears like bullets. Booming from mighty loudspeakers, they bounced off scoreboards, and rolled over the tiers of listeners, seeming, finally, almost to overflow the stadium itself.

Their source was a tiny microphone pinned to the evangelist's four-in-hand tie. A thin wire ran from it, went through a belt clip, and then emerged almost invisibly from beneath Graham's coattails. Snaking across fifteen feet of space, it vanished into the practiced hand of Cliff Barrows, now no song leader but a Nimrod tending his line with the dedication of a fly fisherman, flicking it this way and that, keeping it clear.

His voice described a confrontation between God and sinner, with Graham acting both roles. His hands stretched forward, imploringly. "God, I'm a church member." The long arms folded, the neck stiffened. "Depart from me. I never knew you." His back bent in supplication. "God, I tithed and was good to my wife." His fists doubled menacingly. "Depart from me. I never knew you!"

He told a story about preachers, and, mind you, soberfaced ministers from Nashville churches were sitting in rows on the platform behind him. "Two preachers were supposed to talk for twenty minutes each. The night was hot. The first preacher got on his feet and poured himself a glass of ice water. As he spoke, he alternately fanned and drank. He was full of his message, and he went over his time, but finally, when he had emptied the water pitcher, he concluded his talk and sat down. The second minister rose and said, 'New things happen in all our lives, and this has been a great evening for me in this respect. For the last thirty-five minutes, I've seen a new thing. For the first time in my life, I've seen a windmill that runs on ice water.'"

The audience roared, the ministerial council chuckled,

and the young evangelist held them all in the palm of his hand. "People think a believer in Jesus has to be sad," he said. "On the contrary, a Christian is the only person in the world who has something to be happy about. A violinist who came to help me in a meeting once got off the train wearing a black suit, black hat, black tie, black socks, and a black look. I asked him what was the matter, and he told me he'd just been converted. So I took him down town and bought him a red tie and a red handkerchief and a pair of argyle socks, and I told him to wear them or to get out of town. That night he came up on the platform, resplendent in his bright new clothes, and he wore a smile on his face that was like a thousand sunbeams. He looked at me and said, 'Reverend, how'm I doing?' And I said, 'Brother, you're cookin' with gas.'"

Again laughter exploded. He damped it quickly to clarify the structure of his message. His sermon also listed the woes of the world in which we live, the dilemmas of which we despair, and the failure of science and philosophy and education to solve them.

"But there is a way out," Graham said, and his words bounced against the opposite side of the stadium.

Suddenly I began to feel uneasy. In that improbable setting under a yellow moon, with my feet solidly planted on the turf of an athletic field, I began to think seriously of my own relationship with God. For years I had been too busy, even while attending some of the largest and richest churches in America and Europe.

Graham held up his leather-bound Bible. Folded now, it became a spearpoint to prick the tardy conscience. Open, it was a beacon. I recalled that someone had said he wore out two Bibles every year.

Without warning, he became silent, his arms folded across his chest. Then he said, quietly and soberly, "With every head bowed, every eye closed, with no one leaving or moving about, let us pray that those who are so minded will come to the front of the platform to signify that they want to live for Jesus Christ."

Muted music flowed into the stillness. "Just as I am, without one plea. . . ."

Billy Graham stood four feet behind his lectern, his head bent forward prayerfully. Abruptly withdrawn, he looked like a man who has given his all and now, utterly spent, must regather his strength. The moment was electric, all motion suspended, and then, like a distant rustle of leaves, the sound of moving feet began to blend with the choir's soft entreaty.

Grady Wilson, one of Graham's principal assistants, moved quietly into the open space before the platform to become the focus almost immediately for a half-dozen converging human rivulets. Singly, in couples, in family groups, those inquirers streamed forward with faces composed yet strangely alight. A few eyes gleamed with tears, but there were no sobs, no emotional excesses.

Graham lifted his head and spoke gently but with power and authority to the thousands before him. "You come," he bade them.

And the people came.

Next day I went to his hotel suite and waited in a spiritless sitting room. Faint splashes on carpet and wallpaper suggested earlier, more frolicsome tenants. Graham's briefcases and books were spread over a corner desk. A dictating machine stood ready, its plastic belt half-used.

A Bible lay on the mantel, a King James version with added maps, concordance and charts. I was examining it when Billy Graham came through the door, smiling and brisk, hand extended.

"I'm glad you're here. Betty told me about you and the story you're writing. I'm honored to be its subject."

52

A good reporter usually begins his interview with a needle. I was, I hope, a good reporter.

"I'm not so certain I like going to church in a football stadium," I said. "I have a feeling you're missing a lot of people who ought to be listening."

He leaned forward, resting his forearms on his knees. "It started in Shreveport. We were preaching to about four thousand people a night in the largest auditorium in town. When I suggested that we go outdoors, they were shocked. They said, 'We'll never get an audience.' But we did. We called it 'Revival under the Stars.' And we had an audience of eighteen thousand people. On the last Sunday night we had twenty-eight thousand."

"Are numbers all that important to you?"

"Not numbers," he said earnestly, "but the kind of people who come. It's easy to get together an audience of churchmen. I must reach the un-churched. I've learned this since Shreveport. Every time we go outdoors we get about four times as many non-churchgoers as when we preach indoors."

He talked easily, dodging no question, smiling when my needling was most apparent. In those days most Americans who had heard of Billy Graham were asking, "Is he sincere?" The query came from men on the street and housewives, from cabdrivers and ministers. Only much later would the litany change.

Phil Santora, reporting for the New York *News,* was another visitor in Nashville, another needler. Returning to New York, he wrote, "Millions of persons want to know if Billy Graham is sincere, if he's as dedicated to the cause as he seems. They wonder if he isn't taking advantage of a situation to make himself a million dollars on the side while he preaches humility and abject surrender to Christ. . . .

"To understand Billy Graham, you should spend a great deal of time with him, examine him under a magnifying glass, then step away from him for a few days so that he can be reexamined coldly and logically. . . .

"After all this you reach the conclusion that this young man who has so much influence on the more than thirteen million persons who have gone to hear him is exactly as he purports to be: a dedicated person who believes in what he is teaching, whose aim in life is to harvest as many souls as possible. . . ."

But sincerity alone cannot transform a Carolina farm boy into an internationally recognized evangelist whose fame is comparable to that of a prime minister or the brightest Hollywood star. How had this change come about?

Whenever I approached this mystery, Billy Graham answered by saying, "It is God's doing."

"But Billy. . . ."

"We have simply followed his leading."

"But how do you know his will? In all the crises you have faced and with all the directions in which you could go, how do you know where God leads?"

He said, "I can give you some rules, but the thing is so personal that it is hard to find words to express it. The rules tell only part of the story. For example, I believe that God never leads anyone contrary to the Bible. So if you have a feeling that is contrary, it isn't God, but it might be the Devil. Pay no heed!"

He sank deeper in his chair, concentrating. "Secondly, God doesn't lead contrary to circumstances. I had a ninety-year-old man come to me and say he was called to the missionary field. I told him he was wrong. God wouldn't put a man that old, all alone and without medicine, in a foreign country.

"Third, God doesn't go against common sense. I was preaching in a poor area once, a very poor part of town, and I was wearing a wristwatch with a gold band. As I preached, I noticed how it flashed, and, without even think-
54

ing, I knew that flashy gold was standing between God's message and the people I was addressing. I took it off, and immediately I was free with my sermon."

I picked up the Bible, preparing another query. He said, "That's a Kirkbride. Somebody just gave it to me."

I said ,"I was thinking of ordering one like it."

He said, "I've got a duplicate. You take this one. I want you to have it." He took the Bible from me, opened it to the flyleaf, and wrote, "To my friend Curtis Mitchell. God bless you." He thought for a moment and added "Psalm 16:11."

Later I looked it up.

"Thou wilt show me the path of life; in thy presence is fulness of joy; at thy right hand there are pleasures for evermore."

I thought, "What a nice beginning."

Chapter Five

Billy Graham's New Orleans crusade was held in Pelican Stadium. I flew down from New York one day and met Graham for lunch. I expected to put the final touches on our story of his life. Around us, other diners were staring curiously.

The waiter set plates before us, and I picked up my knife and fork like the average man in a hurry. Graham folded his hands on the table's edge, his head bowed and his eyes closed. The gesture was not obtrusive or attention-grabbing, but there it was, a man at prayer in the center of a brightly lighted restaurant. I sat in amazement and embarrassment. Never in many years of business luncheons had any companions paused to thank God.

Later I learned that public prayer was common to all members of the Graham evangelistic team, and to their wives and children, as well. Be it fashionable restaurant or dingy cafeteria, they never omitted giving thanks with either a moment of silence or a few sentences.

Have I explained that I was formerly a promoter of Hollywood films as well as of a stable of cinema stars? Now I was co-authoring an article on Graham's life to be published in *The American Weekly* magazine, a newspaper Sunday supplement for twenty-five of the largest newspapers in the United States. For the first time it would disclose in his own words the course by which Graham emerged from obscurity.

His story seemed to follow the venerable Horatio Alger formula of rags to riches. Our arrangement was that he would dictate the details and that I would record them, polish them, and submit to him the result for final revision. The method is practiced by almost all busy celebrities, scientists, and government officials. The story would be entitled "I Was Born Again," with the byline reading, "by Billy Graham as told to Curtis Mitchell."

Here, in New Orleans, my part of the work was finished, and the days passed while I waited to see him again. Each night I went to the stadium. Mrs. Lowry, his press secretary, promised, "You'll get an appointment as soon as he's free. He's terribly busy." The afternoon paper carried a picture of the evangelist playing golf.

My editor called from New York, complaining that he needed the story immediately. Next night I followed Graham to a trailer he used for a dressing room out behind the football field. He changed from his perspiration-soaked clothing and came into his tiny "sitting room." For five minutes I tried in vain to reach him with my problem. He was polite, but his mind was on other matters.

Later I was to learn never to talk to him immediately following his delivery of a sermon. That night, as always after preaching, his mind was spent and his nerves were strung tight. Since we got nowhere, I assumed he was fobbing me off with no regard for our joint labors. He did it with charm, with a smile, with a hearty goodnight handshake.

"Go back to New York and wait," Mrs. Lowry advised.

"I'll go back to my room," I said. "You tell him for me. . . ."

She interrupted. "Let me try once again."

In my motel I polished and tightened every sentence of the story Graham had given me. It was an exciting yarn, full of surprises and almost unbelievable "lucky breaks."

57

I talked to other reporters at Pelican Stadium. When they learned I was doing a "national" story, they all asked the same question:

"Do you think he's sincere?"

A religious editor said, "I think God's with him. Moving so many people, God must be with him."

A newsman from a small paper chimed in. "I'm not used to preachers wearing matching cuff links, tie clasps, and belt buckles. And did you notice those suits the team wears? They're *tailored*. How do they afford it?"

"Gifts," I said. "It's an old Southern custom. Preachers never have much money, so a well-heeled layman will often buy his pastor a suit of clothes." I was on solid ground. During my own childhood such largess had often covered the nakedness of our family.

He said, "What about that publicity picture of him kneeling on the White House lawn? That was phony."

"Graham was young. He made a mistake."

John McCormack, present Speaker of the House, had invited Graham to meet President Truman. Wanting to share the honor, Billy had brought along associates Cliff Barrows, Grady Wilson, and Jerry Beavan. They wore white suits and white buck shoes.

Graham says, "I'd never dreamed of meeting the President. I wondered what we would talk about. However, I was determined to present the Gospel to him if an opportunity arose. I knew he had a Baptist background. He greeted us warmly and cordially. We chatted about our crusades, and after about twenty minutes he stood up. I said, 'Mr. President, could we have a prayer?' Without hesitation, he said, 'Certainly.' I prayed, and I could hear Cliff muttering 'amens.' When I prayed for the President, I heard him say, 'Do it, Lord!' Then we left."

Leaving the White House, they walked through the anteroom in which newsmen traditionally question presidential visitors. Reporters and photographers pounced on them.

"I made one of the great mistakes of my ministry," Graham confesses. "No one had briefed me, so I told them everything we talked about. I quoted the President. I told them that I had led a prayer. Photographers insisted that we go out on the lawn and kneel again. Next day that picture was printed all over America. The caption said, 'Evangelist prays with President.' "

Truman never invited him again.

"I've learned my lesson," Graham says. "Now I never quote from any private conversation I have with an outstanding person."

While waiting in New Orleans to see Graham, I attended several more services at Pelican Stadium. Each night I studied his message in the light of what he had told me about his life. Each night hundreds of people in the audience walked down those long aisles and across the gridiron to stand before his pulpit. Why did they respond? Why so many? He was handsome and dramatic, but this was also true of many less successful ministers. He spoke clearly and urgently, but so did others. I moved from the press rows to the bleachers, from the midfield to the choir, trying to fathom his appeal.

The audience seemed to be composed of unusually happy folk carrying Bibles and religious literature. They came from all over. One night the evangelist singled out a group of thirty visitors from Chattanooga, Tennessee, asking them to rise and be recognized. They had met first when they joined Cliff Barrow's choir in an earlier crusade. Since then they had attended every subsequent Southern campaign.

Graham announced another group. "A special train will bring one thousand Nashvillians and Governor Clement of Tennessee," he said. "They'll sit up all night in coaches to attend our service here."

At the conclusion of one service, with several hundred inquirers clustered about the platform, he held up his hands, stopping the music. The huge bowl became silent, and I felt an air of urgency. He said, "We ordinarily close at this point, but I feel the spirit of the living God moving here tonight. I feel there is someone in this audience right now who is struggling, someone who wants to come forward. We're going to sing 'Just As I Am' one more time, just for you."

His glance swept the distant benches for a long moment, and then his eyes closed and his head bowed. About a score of persons rose and came forward.

Neither I nor the public suspected it, but the entire team was near exhaustion. They had come straight from months of labor in Great Britain and plunged into a crusade in Nashville. Now, with no rest, they were fighting in New Orleans. The city was no pushover.

At least one of its powerful political hierarchies was deeply involved in operating gambling and "sporting houses."

Its famous Bourbon Street is where American jazz was born and nourished, and it offers a full menu of earthy pleasures. One night a police official put Graham in an unmarked car, and they toured the area. Subsequently, when he preached against what he had seen, the one Bourbon Street club he happened to mention advertised, "This is the club that Billy Graham recommends."

The rainy season did not help. The crusade began in the rain and continued in the rain. Graham stood under an umbrella one night and said, "In Korea I met three soldiers, one from Minnesota, one from Texas, and one from Louisiana. They said to the boy from Minnesota, 'Doesn't it get cold up there?' He said, 'Yes, but it's a dry cold, and you don't feel it.' They asked the boy from Texas, 'Doesn't

60

it get hot in Texas?' He said, 'Yes, but it's a dry heat, and you don't feel it.' They turned to the boy from New Orleans and said, 'Don't you have a lot of rain in New Orleans?' And he said, 'Yes, but it's a dry rain, and you don't feel it.' "

At long last my phone rang. "Can you meet Dr. Graham at the hotel for lunch?"

I was led to a table for two. Graham arrived five minutes late. I was astonished at the change in him. He had lost much weight. "I lose from ten to twenty pounds in each crusade," he said. Dark patches lay beneath his eyes. But his manner was courteous and considerate. "I'm sorry we couldn't get together sooner," he said, and I had to believe him. "A very important Englishman has been here in New Orleans, and I've had to spend many hours with him."

Those hours were devoted to personal consultation and advice, I learned later, and to the spiritual process which evangelists call "leading a person to Christ." Compared to the winning of a soul, I was to learn, nothing else matters.

While we ate, he read and revised the story about his life, inserting a few new facts, correcting errors. Finally, it was finished. Its first paragraphs were:

"Yes, Christ changed my life.

"What he did for me, He can do for you, exactly as He is doing it daily for thousands of other people.

"I want to tell you some glorious news. Jesus said you can be born anew. You can step forth a new person. No matter how soiled your past may be, no matter how snarled your present, there is a way out."

(Once Graham told me, "I write things in magazines and I go on television programs for only one reason: to bear witness to Jesus Christ. I'm not interested unless the editor or the producer will let me preach a little.")

After several thousand words, our story concluded: "I

wouldn't change with the wealthiest and most influential man in the world. I would rather be a child of the King, co-heir with Christ, and a member of the Royal Family of Heaven. For twenty years, since I accepted Christ as my savior, my life has been complete. After my conversion I had no fear, because 'perfect love casteth out fear.' I had no loneliness, for Jesus said, 'Lo, I am with you always.' And I had no insecurity because of the promise, 'He that overcometh shall inherit all things.' What the future holds, I know not; but I know Who holds the future."

I asked, "From the evangelical point of view, are you satisfied with the story?" He nodded and said, "From the journalistic point of view, are you satisfied?"

"You don't talk much about your grade-school years," I said. "Weren't they important? Didn't anything happen?"

He thought a while. "I kind of slept through grade school," he said. "I'd grown faster and was much taller than anyone else. I was busy with chores at home. In school I kept busy having fun. Nothing much important happened."

He was only partly right.

Chapter Six

"How do you get a man out of a boy?"

A philosopher asked that question many years ago, calling it the most important query of all time.

In this space-and-rockets twentieth century most adults seek an answer in the field of science. Out of habit they turn to the laboratory and test tube to ascertain the chemical mix that does the job. And they learn little or nothing.

Or they call in psychologists with their questionnaires which measure one's narcissism, Oedipus complex, intelligence, social adjustment, and emotional stability. And they learn little or nothing.

Or they ask physiologists to establish norms for blood count, alkalinity, the speed of a nerve current, and the production rate of adenosine triphosphate. And they learn almost nothing.

All these methods fail for the same simple reason. Dietrich Bonhoeffer, the German theologian, expressed it when he wrote, "God is being edged out of life."

Ancient man faced the dilemma of choosing one God from among many. Modern man has gone to the other extreme. As Trevor Huddleston says, "He (man) is not tormented in having to choose between so many. He thinks God is dead."

This creates a new dilemma.

Without God, who sets the rules?

Without authority, what force arises during those split

seconds of indecision when the critical mass of a man's character is under stress? What internal weight overcomes expediency to tilt the balance in favor of generosity instead of selfishness, compassion rather than persecution?

The Christian view holds that God must enter man through the Holy Spirit. Billy Graham says, "If you would change the world, you must first change man."

How does this happen? Or, in one case, how *did* it happen? How did Billy Frank the boy become Billy Graham the man?

The world has witnessed an enormous development in the character of the country youth who sat tongue-tied outside that rustic church in North Carolina. Today he is a religious statesman and a fluent, powerful orator. We are aware that he is driven by a humble yet intense dedication to principles of justice and freedom and to his evangelistic role.

Is he right? Is he wrong? Is he to be followed or disregarded? The church is split on many things, and it is split on Billy Graham, too, with one wing insisting on increasing social action, the other claiming that a cursory inspection of the New Testament reveals that Christ sought to change men's lives far more often than he resorted to civil disobedience.

But that was agricultural Judea, and this is freeway-laced, LSD-testing, pleasure-bent America. That was a bucolic land of placid peasants, and this is a pressurized continent of swingers facing the possibility of instant doom. Yet is there a real difference in what God commanded then and what he commands now? Billy Graham's electronic voice, magnified by unprecedented power and hurled to the four corners of the ear, says there is no difference. And because he says so, millions of people listen and truly believe.

64

Regardless of one's personal opinion, all must agree that we find, in the person of Billy Graham, a remarkable character delivering with extraordinary effect an ageless message. What if the next few generations were to produce ten thousand religious leaders of the same caliber?

To explore this dizzying idea and to delineate some of the influences that molded Graham is the purpose of the remainder of this work. Ultimately, the creation of a man's character is God's doing through the operation of the spiritual laws that vivify the countless caresses and buffetings required to shape every developing human being.

Our question becomes, then, "How can those laws be grasped and directed so that their manifestations can be cultivated and harvested?" Indeed, how did Franklin and Morrow Graham do it?

Our search begins in the religious climate of the Carolina Piedmont, that plateau between the mountains to the west and the littoral to the east where armies of the American Revolution once fought. Forty years ago North Carolina was a have-not state suspicious of all visitors. A Yankee who strayed beyond the limits of its cities became an object of suspicion.

Most farm and small-town families were church members with a profound respect for the learning and leadership of their pastors. One's denomination was important, too, and a man was a "born Methodist" or a "born Baptist" or, more rarely, "a born Presbyterian." Other sects were little understood, and Billy still recalls the day when he and his father encountered several darkly strange newcomers on a Mecklenburg County back road. "Who are they?" he asked. And the father replied, his voice low, "They're Lutherans, son. They hold strange beliefs."

Faith in God was as natural as faith in planting and harvest. Older church members remembered tales of revival meetings that had swept their Appalachian highlands in the 1800's. In those days the supreme Christian experience was thought to be a personal conversion manifested in irresistible physical contortions, twistings, writhings, faintings, and prostrations. Cynics, as well as true believers, had been struck down.

One scoffer, a famous legend insisted, had gone to church to laugh, but, hearing the Lord's call, had plunged from the back of his horse to lie on the ground in a trance for thirty hours.

Cane Ridge, Tennessee, became the scene of a conversion Olympics when fifty preachers assembled for a colossal revival that attracted twenty-five thousand squirrel hunters and farmers and their families. They preached from stumps, wagon beds and the backs of horses, many of them simultaneously, and the carnage was memorable. An observer wrote, "The nights were filled with people lying all over the ground, some praying, some crying, some begging God for mercy, some lying as if dead. Many fled into the woods, and their groans came from the groves like those of dying men."

Whatever else frontier revivalism achieved, it opened up salvation to all, as opposed to the theology of Calvin, which held that God, regardless of man's trust or deed, chose his own. Here was the heady doctrine that human rebirth was the essential ingredient; and it rested its case on Saint John's testimony in the third verse of his third chapter:

"Except a man be born again, he cannot see the kingdom of heaven."

As frontier families grew wealthy or weary and returned to the cities, they brought with them this new Christian doctrine. Seminary-trained city pastors suddenly found themselves challenged by an influx of self-elected evangelists who were also solid-citizen farmers or small merchants with established families. These newcomers were
66

ignorant of theology, but every last man among them had been reborn, and they had taught themselves the art of exhortation.

Strong leaders contended with one another during these years of ferment. Denominational structures cracked around the edges or split wide open as congregations refused to follow this or that new doctrine. In Carolina religion was a topic to be argued with the same vehemence as politics. But talk was not enough; a man's religion was to be *lived*.

Sundays and weekdays were all holy days, for the Bible guided one's total life. Thousands of families, believing that they had inherited their share of original sin, lived every day of every year in a state of painful righteousness.

This was the climate into which Billy Graham was born in November of 1918.

For days after that event, the road before the modest Graham farmhouse was choked with rigs from town and neighboring farms, with an occasional high-wheeled Overland or Reo snorting up to scare horses and mules. Relatives brought jams and jellies, did the cooking and cleaning, and then returned to their own farms, filled with the joy of a successful birthing.

After a while farm life at the Graham place resumed its normal tenor. The mild Carolina winter passed swiftly, and a first springtime warmed the kitchen yard where Morrow laid her child in a clothes basket.

She thought he might become a minister.

His father thought he might become a farmer.

And the slow process of maturation began, moving the child toward an unsuspected destiny. How would Billy Frank, as his mother called him, learn to face the twentieth century?

A Charlotte newspaper printed stories about new theories of child-rearing that stemmed from the teachings of an Austrian doctor named Freud, who claimed that a child's development depends on its sexual urge. Another physician named Adler claimed that a feeling of inferiority, not sex, is the true basis. (Dr. Benjamin Spock, at this time, was still an unheralded medical student.)

Morrow Graham did not need their assistance. She opened the family Bible and turned to the Book of Proverbs. Admonitory verses were as thick as the springtime dandelions in her yard.

"The fear of the Lord is the beginning of wisdom. . . ."

"Train up a child in the way he should go, and when he is old, he will not depart from it. . . ."

"He that spareth the rod hateth his son, but he that loveth him chasteneth him betimes. . . ."

Those were the mother's precepts, and she applied them. But a boy changes, and Frank Graham knew that the time would come when his firstborn would need the application of a heavier hand to enforce the discipline of chores and the muscling-up required for plowing and milking. Recalling his own youth, he anticipated that the task of herding young Billy through puberty would demand a more stinging reprimand than could be extracted from Scripture. His practicality was the leavening in this particular blending of parental supervision.

Actually, Billy Graham's heritage included a generous share of turpitude. His paternal grandfather was said to be considerably less than a saint. Graham once told a friend, "He was a Confederate veteran who was anything but religious. Grandfather drank and swore and had little time for God or the church." However, the formidable piety of his wife made up for him. She was a remarkable woman of Scotch descent who bore eight daughters and three sons and fed them oatmeal and Bible verses at every breakfast. All eleven children became dedicated Christians, and several of their children became ministers.

Morrow Coffee Graham was a Confederate soldier's

child, too, with a full measure of her father's pride and spunk. Expecting a son, wanting a son, her father had picked the name Morrow, and when his wife gave him a daughter, he refused to change it. Morrow says that during the Civil War her father served under General Pickett, right through the famous charge at Gettysburg. There, a burst of shrapnel cut him down, mangling a leg. Lying amid the carnage, he was hit again by a bullet that gouged out an eye. Litter-bearers rushed him to a hospital in Richmond, Virginia.

"He woke up from the operation and looked around the operating room," she recounts. "Doctors had completed the shrapnel's job. They had cut off his leg. He saw it lying there beside him, with the shoe still on it."

Chapter Seven

The odds against the marriage of Frank Graham and Morrow Coffee were astronomical. She was deeply devout, whereas young farmer Graham was more concerned with his fancy rig and high-stepping horse. She was a graduate of Elizabeth College in Charlotte, a cradle of learning for the cream of Dixie's belles; he had quit school after the third grade to help farm his father's acres.

They met in a picnic area west of Charlotte called Lakewood Park. She was one of a group of young ladies on a house-party outing. When a mutual friend introduced them, she thought he was the tallest, handsomest man she had ever seen. He must have felt parallel emotions, for he asked to drive her home.

His horse was the sleekest and fastest and his buggy the sportiest of all those in the hitching lot, and he took her away from her friends in a memorable cloud of dust.

"I'd like to see you again Saturday night," he said.

It was the beginning of a honeymoon that lasted four decades.

Their marriage brought together a pious Presbyterian and a reckless "born Methodist." Following tradition, she dutifully followed him into membership in the nearest Methodist church. At first it seemed to be a suitable arrangement, but as they studied the Bible together and as their judgment and prayer led them to new levels of faith, they decided to change congregations. They chose the Chalmers Memorial Associate Reformed Presbyterian Church, a citadel of orthodoxy at the edge of Charlotte.

At home their life was largely taken up by hard labor. Frank Graham was a proud farmer. His three hundred acres were the tag end of a family estate ruined by the Civil War. During most of his life his farm made little profit, but he had faith in its possibilities. His dream was to own a dairy.

Morrow Graham did her share. She split wood for the kitchen stove and cooked and washed for her husband and for his brother. When they bought a dairy herd and established a milk route for the suburban homes that were spreading out from Charlotte, she scoured the pails, kept production records, and dispatched monthly bills. Every day began with breakfast on the table at 5:30 A.M. When Billy came, she accepted the additional burden of nursing him.

Later, when she could afford a maid, she bought a piano, and her singing and playing introduced a dimension of culture into the farm household.

Scraping together all her egg money, she paid for a complete set of *The Book of Knowledge* and read its gentle stories each evening to young Billy. The arrival of Catherine, eighteen months after Billy, added to her duties.

During her son's early years Morrow Graham told herself many times that he wasn't really a bad boy. The adjective she used was "maddening." She felt that motherhood was a sacred chore and all would be well if she could teach him enough of the Bible. The Scriptural command was clear: "And thou shalt teach them (God's words) diligently unto thy children, and thou shalt talk to them when thou sittest in thine house, and when thou walkest by the way, and when thou liest down, and when thou risest up."

This admonition from Deuteronomy was heeded from before dawn 'til dark, but in between she suffered a thousand pangs. One of the verses she taught him was "Thine ear shall hear a voice behind thee saying, this is the way, walk ye in it." Young Billy, it seemed, did not know how to walk; instead, he zoomed through the house like Tarzan, a character he sought to imitate.

"I came home one day," Morrow Graham told me several years ago, "and learned that he and Catherine had waged war over a simple can of beans. Catherine was eighteen months younger and a girl, but Billy Frank had pushed her so hard that she staggered backwards through two sets of swinging doors."

As her son grew older and bigger, balancing on his slim, strong legs, she learned to remove everything throwable or breakable from any place to which he could reach, leap, or climb. He became a bulldozer, a mountain goat, a tornado, and an angel in bewildering succession.

Over the weeks and months of growing, plates were pulled off tables, buckets of milk were spilled over the kitchen floor, eggs from the poultry flock were innocently scrambled, and once a passing motorist knocked at her door to inquire if she were the mother of the skinny blond boy who had slung a rock through his windshield.

A day came when her palpitating heart could no longer bear the strain and she hustled Billy Frank off to the doctor's. "Billy just isn't normal," she explained. "He's got too much energy. He never runs down."

The physician checked his squirming patient and handed him back to his parents. "Don't worry," he assured them. "It's the way he's built." His diagnosis was an augury of things to come.

Neither physicians nor psychologists have been able to agree on what span of years in a child's life are most important. A University of Chicago researcher has said that little of importance happens after the first year; a European psychiatrist claims that the first three years are all

72

meaningful; and the Jesuits and the Chinese say, "Give us the child for his first six years, and we care not who teaches him afterwards."

Certainly, Billy Graham's first six years were a fruitful period. His playground was the whole outdoors. His zoo was a barn full of milk cows and a woods full of tiny animals. His pets were two amiable goats. One was a small nanny that would butt the kitchen door until someone tossed her a stale biscuit. The other was a large brown goat whose favorite stamping ground was the hood of the family car.

Billy Graham's heroes were Tarzan, Babe Ruth, and such Biblical characters as the young David who killed the giant with his slingshot.

He was four years old when a truly memorable event took place. Frank Graham came home from town one day and announced, "Billy Sunday is coming to preach in Charlotte. I think we ought to hear him."

Now Billy Sunday was a colorful and mighty worker for the Lord. People said that he was the most famous preacher in the world and that his voice could be heard for a mile. He would preach, not in a Charlotte church but in a gigantic tabernacle filled with thousands of wooden benches, its dirt aisles carpeted with sawdust so deep that it got into everybody's shoes.

Sunday was also a great athlete and a former big league ballplayer. To Billy this last fact was the most important.

"He jumps all over the place," somebody said, describing Sunday's style of preaching. "He climbs up on the pulpit and even onto the piano."

The Grahams drove into Charlotte on the appointed day and, along with thousands of other pilgrims, entered the big tabernacle. Under the leadership of a skilled song-leader, they gave voice to old Gospel hymns. Billy recalls that the song service was vastly different from that of his parents' church, where they sang nothing but psalms. The hearty music-making made him feel good. Finally, evangelist Sunday began to preach.

"I was fascinated," Billy says. "The evangelist waved his arms and shouted. I still recall the thrill and the excitement of that meeting."

Young Billy, remembering his father's warning, behaved himself with remarkable sobriety. "You sit still when he preaches," Frank Graham had ordered, "or Billy Sunday will run you right out of his tabernacle."

Billy Frank believed him.

Afterwards, Sunday service at the home church was never quite the same, but churchgoing, itself was becoming a deeply imbedded habit. Frank and Morrow Graham attended faithfully, and they always brought Billy. Inevitably, he came to know the church building intimately, the result of juvenile explorations of which his parents were unaware. The fact that Uncle Andy Bailes was the sexton gave him a certain freedom. One Lord's day he absented himself so long after services that Graham senior had to delay his family's departure to hunt for him in the rambling building.

They found him in the sacristy, sitting among empty bottles of grape juice, happily drinking the leavings of that day's communion.

On another Sunday he suffered such a fit of squirming that both father and mother issued solemn warnings. Subsiding momentarily, he soon returned to heel-kicking and knuckle-cracking.

When the service was over, the Grahams marched out, red of face and short of temper. The father's control lasted into the vestibule. There he whipped off his belt and laid his son across his thigh. Perhaps he remembered the injunction, "Do not withhold discipline from a child. If you beat him with a rod, he will not die."

74

Frank Graham's belt became his rod. True to Scripture, Billy did not die.

The remainder of each Sabbath was as austere as the morning church service. Sunday belonged to the Lord. All of it. If games were played, they were Bible games. If reading was done, it was Bible reading. Sunday funnies were banned. And as the family grew in size, each new member was required to spend hours learning a doctrinal quiz called the Shorter Catechism. Billy could never understand why it was called short, for it contained over one hundred fairly difficult questions, from "What is the chief end of man?" to "What doth the conclusion of the Lord's Prayer teach us?" Nor could he understand many of the answers, though he could repeat them perfectly before his tenth birthday.

And so a character was shaped, not hewn by massive blows but patted into perfection by thousands of daily taps and admonitions. One can watch a child for six years or ten or a dozen and assume that not much is happening, but that conclusion would be wrong. What Billy learned in his childhood years appears often in his sermons.

"Take your child to church," he urges parents. "And don't you dare take them and leave them while you hurry off to play golf."

"Home was the first church," he says. "Home was the place where you heard the name of God for the first time. It was the first school. Nothing means more to me today, as I think of my own home, than the fact that my mother and father believed in God in their simple way and that they took us children to church. They never *sent* us to church, and they put something into our character that we'll never get away from."

Sometimes he contrasts his mother's attitude with that of a modern matron. " 'Why do I need a home?' a woman said some time ago. 'I was born in a hospital, educated in a college, courted in an automobile, and married in a church. I live out of a delicatessen, tin cans, and paper bags. I spend my mornings on the golf course, my afternoons at the bridge table, and my evenings at the movies. When I die, I'll be cremated and buried in a brass urn. All I really need is a good garage for my car.' "

Of discipline and whippings he says, "If I broke a rule, Father never hesitated. Off came his belt. Mother preferred a long hickory switch. I had literally hundreds of whippings. I think they were right to whip me."

He feared and loved his parents. He always knew that he was loved and where he stood.

The distinguished psychologist, Dr. Ernest M. Ligon, director of the famous Character Research Project at Union College in Schenectady, N.Y., says that the best formula for building a wholesome character was expounded by Jesus in the Sermon on the Mount. In a epochal treatise named "The Psychology of Christian Personality," Ligon points out that the principles put forward in the New Testament two thousand years ago are totally valid today in terms of modern psychology.

This is not to imply that farmer Frank Graham or his wife Morrow became psychological guidance counsellors in any conscious sense, but it is clear that the effect of their Scripture-oriented way of life was destined to create in their first son the model of an integrated Christian character.

The principles are worth examining.

"Here is the nature of character," Ligon says. "It consists, not in forms of external behavior or negative ethics, but in strength and unselfish action. It is not inherited, but must be developed. Its motivation is not fear of punishment, but the desire for self-realization and love."

But first there is the newborn infant, self-centered, pul-

76

ing and enigmatic to all but his parents. In the beginning he lives by instinctual impulses, striking and grabbing or whining and chuckling according to whether his environment gives him pain or pleasure. But presently the child begins to notice people. One easily imagines the infant Billy looking up from his cradle or from the buggy in which he slept in the yard beyond the kitchen door to see the ebony face of the dairy foreman or the blue eyes shining from beneath the blond mop of his father's hair or the roundness of his mother's strong body. And soon he began to turn joyously toward the sound of their approach and to lift his tiny hands. And this was the beginning of love.

"At this point character begins," Ligon says. "Unless parents can inspire such affection for themselves in a child that he gets pain from hurting them, they cannot develop character in that child. Even the physical punishment which parents give their children finds its greatest effectiveness in this motive. When a boy's mother is whipping him, he is faced with the fact that, for the time being at least, she does not love him. This is the worst part of the punishment."

The coin has another side. If the child hates his parents, punishment will have the effect of turning him vengeful and obstinate rather than obedient. "It follows," Ligon reminds us, "that physical punishment should never be inflicted upon a child except by someone he loves."

Surely, the young married Grahams understood this, and in the selfless manner which was their way of life and which had already motivated thousands of Southern boys into useful self-realization, they added to their own daily regimen countless acts of unconscious love.

And so they saw how swiftly their son began to blossom.

I remember visiting the Grahams at the old home place during the 1958 Charlotte crusade. By that time Charlotte's city limits had advanced far enough so that the Grahams had a city address—4501 Park Road. Though the barns still stood, they were not being used. The once green pasturage was covered by the asphalt of the Park Road Shopping Center, and a high-rise Standard Oil office building stood in the old cow pasture. In three directions seas of roofs proclaimed real estate developments.

The Charlotte *News* described the homestead: "It is shaded by a score of large, old trees which Frank Graham himself set out thirty-five years ago. To the right is the city limits and the Park Shopping Center, its neon lights casting red and green patterns over the arbor of scuppernongs that Billy planted as a kid. To the left, just a couple of hundred yards away, is the low, white frame building in which he was born."

Until recently, brother Melvin continued to live in that cottage, using it as headquarters from which to manage the other farms he and Billy own in partnership and to supervise the suburban real estate into which the Graham acres have turned.

During that visit I was invited to roam across their fields and through the rooms the family occupied when Billy was a child. Standing by a weathered arbor, I was able to imagine a younger Frank Graham sweeping up his first son and carrying him on a tall shoulder through the steamy milk shed, holding him so that he could pet the soft nose of a heifer or setting him astride a farm horse for a ride through the meadow.

In the house the Graham children used the two back bedrooms . . . the two boys in the room nearest the barns so they could hear any disturbance, Catherine and Jean in the other.

After all her offspring had married, Morrow Graham rearranged her house to accommodate her grandchildren. She redecorated the old dairy office on the first floor, turning it into a family bedroom. Upstairs, her old bedchamber became a special room for guests. The day I was there its most recent occupant had been her celebrated son, and he had left several mementos. On the dresser I found notes for a sermon, two worn Bibles, and five new golf balls.

Mrs. Graham made her famous tea for me. The recipe is known all over North Carolina: "Take the juice of two lemons and two oranges and strain it. Then make a half-gallon of tea. Mix in the juice. Add one small bottle of ginger ale. Serve quite hot."

She calls it Russian tea, but she did not know why. A few days earlier she had served it to some unexpected guests. A delegation of Tennesseans had come to look at Billy's birthplace. She saw them standing outside and invited them in for tea. They were delighted to accept, all 187 of them.

While we sipped and chatted, Frank Graham sat in a straight chair, ready to answer my questions. He was tall and thin, like his son, and every inch a gentleman. Morrow Graham sat in her rocker, ever on the alert to discover an unsatisfied wish that a guest might entertain.

"You've raised a famous son," I began. "Do you think any of the things he learned here on the farm helped him in his evangelistic work?"

Frank Graham answered. "Yes, Billy gets a lot of attention, and he's a pretty fair preacher, but my boy, Melvin, he's made a study of farming until I reckon he's one of the very best farmers in this state."

I said, "Billy got up early and milked about twenty cows, I'm told. That must have taught him something."

"Yes, he was pretty good at it, but Melvin would come

79

along and milk thirty cows. He loves farming, he loves the earth and raising things. You just can't find anything wrong with that boy."

Obviously, the senior Graham had *two* famous sons, and his face glowed as he talked of their achievements.

Morrow Graham spoke up, chuckling. "Billy was really kind of famous a long time before he began to preach. We used one of his baby pictures to advertise our dairy, and it was printed everywhere."

Frank Graham said, "I started with a Model T truck. By the time Billy could drive, we had a Chevy. Billy liked trucks and cars. He liked speed. . . ."

And their memories began to stir.

Billy had hung from those trees in the yard, screaming like Tarzan, frightening the wits out of passing horses and drivers. "I think maybe that yelling helped develop his voice," his father said. "When he came back from college and held his first meeting here in Charlotte, I was worried that nobody could hear him. But he did all right. He could preach real loud."

That upright piano in the corner of the room? His mother said, "He came back from some conference or other, determined to learn to play it. He begged me to teach him. I guess he'd been inspired by some boy who'd got all the attention."

Frank Graham said, "More likely he'd been inspired by some girl."

We went into the kitchen, which was presided over by a pleasant Negro woman who had worked for the family almost two decades. The room was large and orderly, and one side of it was filled by a gleaming electric range of heroic size. "That was the second electric range in this county," Frank Graham said with pride. "We still use it."

"Billy always liked to eat with the smell of coffee, but

80

he'd only drink a few sips," his mother remembered. "His favorite food was ham and grits and red gravy."

A kitchen calendar hung on one wall, a Bible verse printed under each date. About forty such calendars have hung in that kitchen, and every day through all those years the verse of the day has been discussed and its meaning probed. Very often it was memorized.

"Goodness knows how many hundreds of verses the children learned before they left home," Frank Graham said. "Billy was a slow learner at first, but he got better. After he went off to school, he really began to learn his Bible."

Even then, discussing their memories of Billy's up-bringing, they had little enough knowledge of the discoveries of scientific psychology; instead, they thought it only common sense that the wisdom of the world's greatest book, the Bible, should be shared with one's children and that the best way to do this was to have the young ones memorize a verse or two every day. Then there were the stories to be read about Jesus who was born in Bethlehem and visited by the wise men. Such tales were published in much of the literature to be found in the Graham home, and I doubt that they knew they were following a very trustworthy, scientific principle—or was it a divine law?—when they gradually transferred the youthful Billy's admiration from his powerful and loving earthly father to a heavenly father who was ever so much more powerful and loving.

But that is what happened in as orderly a fashion as if that country house on the red-dirt farm was the world's finest psychological laboratory. And the new idol of Billy's was a hero of titanic proportions, talked about in church and Bible school and prayer meeting and at daily worship.

Was this transfer of hero worship important to the young

Billy Graham? Let parents listen! Doctor Ligon says, "His whole future depended on it."

Can it happen to other youths today? The questions must be answered. On what nourishment can Christian character feed in the average modern home? Or in what church? Is it in the sermon that preaches of Viet Nam and freedom, of tithing and bazaaring. I doubt it. Is it in the Bible class conducted by a frequently unprepared Bible School teacher? I doubt it. Where then do the boys and girls of this generation receive their injections of worship? I shall return to this topic presently.

But now, imagine young Billy at table, at play, at small tasks, learning from his elders that the world is good and governed by God, with its proper time for sowing and reaping, for grazing and milking, and that six days of work are succeeded by one day of rest and thanksgiving.

But every day during those formative years, the boy was assigned his full share of chores, which were often astonishingly difficult. He did not mind. Doing his work well was a way of growing up. Weekdays he roamed the fields with his father or the hired hands or with children from nearby farms. Mostly, their backgrounds were similar to his, but some were much less fortunate. Too often their parents exhorted them to rectitude by making them memorize codes of commandments. Theory held that such a course would build character.

They were wrong. A powerful character must be composed of solid traits cemented together by love for others. Young Graham learned this without knowing he was learning it. His farm routine of small chores revolving about pasturing, feeding, and milking the family herd provided the natural matrix of his future.

"A child must learn to give, sacrifice, suffer, and deny himself," Ligon says. "He cannot be made to do these things. He will do them only for those he loves. If no

82

opportunities are provided, he will grow into a selfish, spoiled individual. Many sincere mothers make slaves of themselves and deny the child his best gift, which is character."

I once asked Frank Graham, "In those early years were you conscious of trying to shape Billy's life?"

He said, "I guess I was always shaping it with my tongue or with my belt, but not because I thought I was doing something unusual. There's only one right way to live, and it's laid out in Scripture. That's how I've tried to live, and that's how I wanted my children to live."

Young Billy learned from what his parents told him, from what the Bible said about Jesus, and from what his parents did with their own foursquare lives. And he sprouted upward like a willow.

Chapter Eight

At the core of Christian education there has always been firm discipline. The mother of John Wesley, the founder of Methodism, said, "The first thing to be done with children is to conquer their will, teach them to fear the rod, and to cry softly."

In her day the initial schooling session was exacting. A child was allowed six hours in which to memorize the entire English alphabet. On the following morning he was given his first reading lesson, beginning with the first verse of the first chapter of Genesis.

A more leisurely pace prevailed in America, but not much. In *In His Steps* Charles Sheldon told how his family gathered after breakfast for worship. Each person had his own Bible. His father opened to where they had left off at the previous session and read two verses. His mother read the next two, the oldest child read the next, and so on. They followed this pattern for five years, never missing a morning. Sheldon said, "I think I am the only man living who has heard the complete Bible read aloud five times."

Billy Graham's day began with a farmer's breakfast: plenty of milk, homemade bread, butter, hot cereal, fresh eggs, sausages, and ham. Frank Graham, who had been up since 2:30 A.M., came from his work in the dairy barn and asked the blessing. Afterwards, he opened his Bible and went to work on Billy Frank's memory.

The usual assignment was to learn a psalm, one verse per day.

"All right, recite."

Billy repeated all the verses he had learned thus far.

"Now read the next verse out loud."

Billy took the Bible and read the new verse.

"Copy it down."

He scribbled the words in his cheap copybook.

"Be sure you know it tomorrow."

Then Frank Graham rose and went back to his chores. Morrow Graham began to pack a lunch for Billy to take to school.

Billy recalls those instructional periods as among the most important of his life. They implanted in him a love of Scripture and a yearning to be acquainted with all of it. "I wanted to be saturated with the Bible," he says.

Later, as he groped toward a way of preaching that would reach into the hearts of people, he began to call up from his memory many of the verses he had learned at that breakfast table. Today passages of Scripture are an important element in his sermons. "The Bible says . . . he declaims, holding aloft the Book. "The Bible says . . . the Bible says . . . the Bible says. . . ."

"The Devil can't stand up against Scripture," he believes.

His formal education began in the usual way. (The Mecklenburg school system, however, consisted of eleven grades instead of the regulation twelve, a custom in many southern states.) On his first day a school bus stopped at his corner at 7:45 A.M. and carried him to the Sharon Grammar School, a rural institution poorly supplied with everything except pupils. When he finished that first bus trip, he walked into the building with a pounding heart. The great adventure of extending his horizon beyond the limits of his own family was beginning. It would involve many

85

changes, frequent crises, and some shame. Fortunately he suspected nothing.

About mid-morning of that first day he had made his first mistake. His mother had handed him a lunch box and told him about the noonday break. "Eat your lunch then," she said. When a bell sounded and the classroom emptied, Billy Frank assumed that this was the anticipated pause. Alone at his little desk, he stuffed himself.

But it was only the morning recess, and when the real lunchtime arrived, his lunch box was empty. Full of hunger and chagrin, he sat through a miserable noon hour, watching his classmates gorge themselves.

That same afternoon he made his second mistake. When the class was dismissed, he joined the rush to the door. Suddenly his teacher loomed over him, caught his ear in a painful grip, and gave it a yank that lifted the frightened child to his tiptoes. Then he shoved him through the door. The unexplained punishment filled him with dread and pain. To this day he does not know what he did wrong.

"How was it at school?" his mother asked.

His response was not enthusiastic.

"Did you have fun?" sister Cathy said.

"No."

A few days later he ran into another problem. For some reason now forgotten, Billy shook his fist at a second-grade boy. Apparently the gesture was the same as a declaration of war. The other party happened to be large, rough, and the class bully. He cornered Billy and began a personal vendetta.

"He gave me the worst beating of my life," Billy says.

After several subsequent attempts to defend himself, after collecting black eyes and scraped shins and loosened teeth, Billy made a discovery. He learned he could outrun the larger boy. Eventually, his adversary gave up the chase.

By 1928, when he was ten years old, Billy had become

the tallest and probably the least studious boy in his class. But he liked school, and he was discovering that he liked girls. The announcement that the entire fourth grade would be transferred to another and larger building, because of overcrowding, delighted him.

The new school was named Woodlawn, and it contained both grade and high school classes. Predictably, its regular students considered themselves superior to rustic "transfers" from that country place down the road.

So Woodlawn scholars and Sharon fourth-graders glared at each other, and then the fight began. Young Billy, the tallest boy in his class, was the advance guard of every skirmish and the victim of every ambush. This happened not by choice but because his height attracted attention. The civil war endured for several months until both sides were exhausted. "Looking back," he says, "it appears that I spent an unseemly amount of time in combat."

His elementary schooling made him proficient with his fists; unfortunately, his brain was not equally exercised. All available records show his indifference to book learning. He says, "My father was a farmer who left school in the third grade. My grandfather was a farmer. It looked like I was going to be a farmer, I reasoned, so why should I waste my time with a lot of books?"

His class behavior reflected this attitude. One teacher wrote his parents that she had to chase him around the desks and whack him with a ruler in order to settle him down.

Of book learning he absorbed little, but this is not to say that his education stopped. Education concerns "people learning," too, which has its own importance. And "people learning" involves not only classmates and teachers but also one's status in the family.

At home the Grahams continued their habit of working and worshiping together, giving little time to play. Frank Graham did occasionally sit with young Billy, talking of

87

fishing and hunting trips they might take, but they never materialized. The father knew how to work, but he had never learned to play. To a great extent, his son has followed the same path.

Each of the Graham children had chores. Morrow Graham's green thumb was famous, and Billy became her helper. Mulching shrubs, pinching back blossoms, he became a competent gardener. At corn-planting time he was transferred to the fertilizer detail, with the duty of carrying one aromatic load after another to the cornfields and pouring them into the distributor tank. On return trips he frequently came home through the woods, bringing his mother bouquets of wild flowers.

One season he dug in some grape seedlings, wondering if the red soil would nourish them. Thirty years later his mother was still making grape jelly from those hearty vines.

He was seven when he got a bicycle. It absorbed every atom of his concentrated attention for an entire day, during which he mounted and fell off, mounted and capsized, mounted and crashed—with time out only for lunch and dinner—until he was able to ride triumphantly from house to feedlot and back. He learned a lesson then that has since turned up in several sermons.

"I found there was one thing I had to do on that bike if I wanted to stay on it," he says. "I had to keep moving forward. If I stopped moving forward, I would fall off and hurt myself. A Christian must learn that," he adds. "He must keep moving forward in his faith."

Another possession was even more cherished. This was Billy, a large and opinionated goat. Billy Frank and Billy the goat made an inseparable team. He cut down a pony harness and taught Billy to pull a small wagon. Loading his vehicle with vegetables, he would truck them from garden to storehouse or cold cellar. Melvin says that his very first

88

memory is of Billy Frank driving Billy the goat up a path, followed by a small white nanny, followed by a collie dog, followed by a flock of chickens.

When the goat tired of the game, he would turn around in his harness and lie down, concluding the matter. His action posed a problem that Billy could never solve.

The shaping of character is an interminable and often agonizing procedure. Ruskin has written, "One man is of agate, another of oak; one is of slate, another of clay. The education of the first is polishing; of the second, seasoning; of the third, rending; of the fourth, moulding."

And some men are made of all those materials, as was the young Billy Graham. Every experience taught him something.

One day a hired hand pulled out a plug of chewing tobacco and cut off a "chaw." "It's time you learned how," he said. "Want to try it?"

"Why not?" The invitation to show his burgeoning manhood was irresistible. He took the proffered bite and rolled it on his tongue, cringing at the unfamiliar taste.

"Spit it out!" His father's shout came from behind, harsh with anger.

Billy spat. His father stripped off his belt and bent his son across a hard thigh. The leather descended. "No son of mine's going to chew that filth," he said. The belt flailed away, emphasizing every word.

When he had delivered the full message, Frank Graham turned on the hired man. "You're fired. Get out."

Frank Graham had never heard that he might be wounding his son's ego, so he went on to his next chore with no worry whatsoever, and Billy never chewed tobacco again.

Father Graham set the major goals with respect to ideals, but Mother Graham arranged the details, which was the part that needed maternal wisdom. A mother always knows her son's readiness better than anyone else.

Once a babe leaves his high chair, a father is apt to assume that he is ready for firearms and farming. A mother's intuition is more accurate. It was Morrow who saw that young Billy's responsibilities were always commensurate with his capacities. Thus tragic failures were avoided, and each small triumph coalesced with the next to build ever-increasing self-confidence.

"Set no purpose beyond your child's ability," is advice that all mothers should memorize. It embraces the wisdom of Solomon's Proverbs and the compassion of David's Psalms, and it provides a foolproof escalator to heightened self-realization at any age.

So in North Carolina common sense preceded modern science with astonishing fidelity, holding that if a child fails too often, he retreats into a world of fantasy and achieves his goals only in daydreams. Or perhaps he retires even totally and becomes that misunderstood oddity called a schizophrenic. A mother's intuition therefore must stand up straight against a father's impatience.

In other respects Frank Graham was as scientific as any other dairyman. Take the matter of the best way of milking. To young Billy's delight his father switched one day from hand to machine milking. But his cows grew gaunt, and their udders became diseased, so he resumed the old-fashioned method. Three more times he tried to persuade himself that machines were better than men, and each time he found them deficient.

"Four failures were enough to convince me, because I had to go back to hand-milking every time," he told me. "If you're selling whole milk, there's just nothing better."

In 1928, he supported another cause, and his involvement made a lasting impression on his son. That was the year in which the Democratic party nominated Governor Al Smith of New York for the Presidency. The Republican candidate was Herbert Hoover.

Because the elder Graham could not accept the notion of a Catholic in the White House, he campaigned hard for Hoover. His defection from Democratic ranks caused much comment among relatives and friends. On the other hand, Billy's schoolteacher went down the line for the regular party ticket, working for it with extracurricular enthusiasm. The students, however, mostly followed their parents.

When it was announced that Al Smith had been defeated, the victorious rebels, with Billy among them, did a snake dance through every classroom. But even as he rejoiced, Billy sympathized with his vanquished teacher. "I can still see him sitting there, looking so unhappy and miserable," he remembers.

A Southern farm boy is constantly in contact with Negroes, and at the time of Graham's youth there was little apparent strain between the races. Billy played with Negro children and worked in the dairy with Negro "hands." The association led him to understand and respect a colored person exactly as he respected a person of his own race. Reece Brown, his father's competent Negro foreman, became a close friend and benefactor.

As Billy's long muscles thickened and as he learned to hold his own against other farm hands, Brown took over his practical education in dairying. Years later, Billy tried to describe him.

"He was the highest paid man on the place. He'd been a sergeant in the army. He was one of the strongest men I ever saw. He had a tremendous capacity for work and great intelligence. I felt there was nothing he didn't know. He had a profound effect on my life in its earliest years." He became like a second father.

When Graham took the lead in bringing unsegregated religious services to the South, thereby stirring up a storm of criticism, it was his memory of Reece Brown that helped him hold his course.

91

So the polishing and seasoning, the rending and molding of those years shaped the things he would say in some unimagined time and place and also helped to dictate what he would do in a future home of his own.

"We had strictness, and we were happy with it," he once told me.

Weak parents are his special concern. He finds his standards in the Bible. " 'Train up a child the way he should go, and when he is old, he will not depart,' " he quotes. "Modern parents have made a mistake in letting their children have too much freedom. Parents are actually afraid of their children today. I was in a home and the father told his little six-year-old son to close the door. The little boy stamped his foot and said, 'No!' The father shrugged and said, 'What can you do?' I know what I would do if that boy were mine. I'd put him in the door-slamming business."

He believes that every parent has a sacred obligation to train his children, and he believes the surest plan for a Christian recruitment is to start with the very young. Evangelist Billy Sunday held the same opinion, saying:

"If you want to lick the devil, hit him over the head with a cradle."

Dr. Nelson L. Bell, Graham's distinguished father-in-law and a former medical missionary, wrote these words in a recent issue of *Decision* magazine:

"We are careful to train our pets, trim our trees, and weed our lawns and gardens. Why, oh, why do we so often leave our children to their own devices. . . ? 'Folly is bound up in the heart of a child, but the rod of discipline drives it far from him.' "

Dr. Bell believes that discipline is a grace, that the surest foundation of a sound family is for a child to know where he stands and to know also that the good are rewarded and the bad are punished. And that after punishment there is forgiveness. "Discipline your child while there is hope. . . . Let him know, as God has permitted his children to know, that the offender will be punished and *forgiven*. This is the Christian principle."

In Graham's home today evidence abounds that these principles are followed. Much of the time Ruth Graham must serve as both father and mother, rejecting invitations to accompany her husband to crusades. The tragic example of the wife of a once-celebrated evangelist supports this resolution. She had followed her husband during his globe-trotting days, helping devotedly with his mission, but she had lost contact with her children, who grew up to careen from one personal misfortune to another.

"What a pity it would be, what a tragedy it would be," Billy says, "if I were to travel so much around the world that I would lose my own family."

In the Graham home today, as in his youth, Sunday is a day specially reserved for the Lord—all day long. They go to church together, walking, stair-stepped from tallest to smallest, down the aisle of the Presbyterian church in Montreat. At home they play Bible games and tell Bible stories. And Sunday is treat day. Such goodies as candy and soft drinks are unrestricted.

And sometimes they take a very special walk up a lofty trail, look out over the Blue Ridge mountains, and feel very close to God. Graham once told me this beautiful story:

"I was up at our little place with my daughters," he said. "We had walked to the top of the mountain behind our home and were looking out over the peaks and valleys of the Appalachian chain. I said to the older one, 'Honey, do you realize that perhaps the man you are going to marry one day is already a little boy about twelve or thirteen years old?' She said, 'No, I hadn't thought of that.'

"I said, 'Well, he's out there somewhere. Why don't we

93

say a prayer that God will bless him and his father and mother as they rear him and keep him straight and clean and honest?' And we got down on our knees right there and prayed for that little unknown boy somewhere who some day may be the husband of my daughter."

That twig was bent long before, not only on the Graham farm but across the Atlantic and down the centuries, by pious Scotch families on their knees together, by fathers punishing with birch rods or leather belts, and by parents practicing forgiveness.

No one has found—no one is likely to find—a better way.

Chapter Nine

Billy Graham was in North Carolina, preparing to leave for a crusade in Australia; I was in Connecticut. We were talking long distance about a magazine article to be called "What Young People Ask Me About Religion."

It would attempt to answer four letters he had received, asking these questions:

If I become a Christian, will I still get a kick out of life?

Will it make me unpopular?

Will it hamper my business opportunities?

Will it bring me happiness?

I asked, "When you were a teenager, did questions like that bother you?"

He said, "I think adolescents are all alike. They think they want fun and popularity, success and happiness. Yes, I wanted them. I wanted them so hard that frustration made me bite my nails to the quick."

"Was this the most critical period of your life?"

"It's critical for everyone. I very nearly went the wrong way."

Billy Graham's sympathy for youth and his involvement in their problems have given him insights which enable him to attract more young people to his services than any preacher in history.

More than 50 per cent of his crusade audiences are under twenty-five years of age. His "Youth Nights" are the biggest of the week. He says the reason for this is that "youth wants a cause to believe in, a flag to follow, and a song to sing!"

While working on that story, I learned much about Billy Graham's own earlier years. I also learned of principles of behavior which, quite possibly, are of supreme importance to all mankind. The science of psychology has made vast strides during the last few decades, and it is startling to observe how the exploration of our last frontier of science, which is *inner* space, is rediscovering many of the ancient ethical and moral concepts of the Old Testament. Certainly, if parents today raised their children as did those Old Testament families, our world would be quite different.

On the strength of modern research, it seems probable that the prime interest of boys of the stone age was about the same as that of the twentieth-century adolescent. Graham's mother once described her son's taste like this:

"Billy liked girls, and girls liked him."

He would come to dinner many an evening, licking his lips and talking fast, saying, "I met a new girl today, and she is about the cutest girl I ever saw in my whole life." His "cutest girls" became a family joke.

Some persons seek leadership. Others have leadership thrust upon them. Regardless, certain qualities of body and mind must be present for success. Most character analysts agree, however, that the factor most important in developing a leader is the experience of leading.

Apparently, all these principles were to operate in young Graham's life.

First, he possessed admirable physical equipment. In high school he was an enthusiastic baseball player. Completing a double play at first base or hitting a two-bagger gave him a supreme sense of satisfaction. Psychologists say that such satisfactions are a powerful influence on the development of a youth's personality. But young Graham was not at all concerned with the why of life. He knew, with

96

the flawless faith of youth, that he loved baseball and girls, not necessarily in that order.

When Babe Ruth came to Charlotte, his father took him to an exhibition game. He and his gang got seats in the front row. Afterwards, his father escorted him into the great Babe's presence, and they shook hands. "I'll never forget the thrill," he says. "Babe was the idol of my young heart. I was envied throughout the school because everyone knew I'd shaken hands with America's great baseball hero. I didn't wash my hands for about three days."

In those early years he learned the importance of being competitive. His rival was a big boy named Red Mc-Knight. They both wanted to play first base for Sharon High, and they were as alike in talent as two peas. The showdown came when Coach Eudy set up a scrimmage game and sent them to bat alternately. "Whoever gets the first hit gets the job," he promised.

Billy got up and struck out. Red McKnight struck out. Billy struck out again. McKnight struck out again. In his fourth time at the plate Billy scratched a single through the infield. Coach Eudy said, "You're my boy."

"And that's the truth of how I made the Sharon ball team," Graham says. "Don't let anybody tell you I was a hot-shot hitter."

When he tried out for basketball, he was less successful. In Carolina, adjacent towns develop a bitter sports rivalry. Red McKnight was again his rival. Red had height and power, so he became the regular center while Billy rode the bench. Once, when Red's car broke down, Billy played through a whole game, helping to win a victory over Sharon's arch rival, Pineville High.

That evening held another surprise. A gang of Pineville bullies planned to beat up the victors from Sharon, and they lay in wait until Billy and his mates were on a dark street. Then they attacked. Surprised, the Sharon kids fought with any weapon they could find. Billy remembers, "I grabbed a stick and swung it hard at the fellow who jumped me. When he turned and ran, I could see the blood running from his head. I thought maybe I'd killed him."

So he won high school letters in baseball, basketball, and blood-letting. It was unusual training for Christian leadership.

During his last two summer vacations he played semiprofessional baseball when time permitted. Old newspaper sports pages carry his name and his batting average. It was always under .300. But he made real money: ten dollars when his team lost, fifteen dollars when it won. By his own appraisal, he was talented enough to dream of playing some day in Yankee Stadium and other big league parks. Checking up, I once talked with his high school coach.

"Sure, Billy had ability," he told me. "In the field he was one of the best. His weakness was at bat. If he'd kept at it, improving like he was, he might have gone to the majors."

Commentators have since called his big league ambition a peculiar aberration. However, he was really just conforming to his time and environment.

"It's hard for people today to understand the economic pressures of the depressed South," he explains. "Wanting to be a ballplayer was typical of all the boys who had any skill. It meant a good living. It meant a respectable living. You remember that boxing in those days was a decent sport. You had Jack Dempsey and Gene Tunney. Among young boys being a boxer was a very respected profession. And you made a good living.

"Today, a boy graduates from school and goes into industry and makes more money than he would in sports. In my youth it was reversed. Then, everyone played baseball, every boy that could walk. I guess more stars have come out of North Carolina than any other state. I loved the game, and I dreamed it, including the hope of playing in Yankee Stadium."

Eventually he played in several big league parks, but as an evangelist. In 1954, during his New York crusade, he held an outdoor rally at Yankee Stadium that attracted more than a hundred thousand persons who filled every seat and every foot of playing field except the roped-off diamond. And twenty thousand others had to be turned away.

Another day he sat in the Dodger Ball Park in Los Angeles with Mr. and Mrs. Walter O'Malley and saw his name up in lights. He was starting a crusade there, and the big scoreboard spelled out, "Welcome to Billy Graham."

If his physical preparation for leadership might be called precocious, his mental preparation can be called inadequate. During some school years he rarely cracked a book. To be sure, he got passing grades, but that could have been the result of his father's being on the school board. Jobs were hard to find in those depression days, and a teacher thought twice before flunking the popular son of a pillar of the community.

In his senior year he came under the influence of an inspiring teacher named Charlotte Hunter. She called him "a late developer" and tried hard to cultivate the fallow field of his intellect. "He was a wonderful boy," she remembers, "but as yet his mind had not awakened."

Billy gives her credit for arousing him from his long scholastic sleep. He began to study, to take as much pride in getting an "A" as in hitting a home run with the bases loaded.

But the person in Mecklenburg County who was happiest about this newfound interest in books was his single-minded mother. With extraordinary clarity she knew where she wanted him to go, and she knew that you can lead a horse to water but you cannot make him drink.

"My mother kept me going," Billy recalls. "Socially, she was at ease with every person. She could talk to anybody. She read a great deal, and every night before our nine o'clock bedtime she would read a story before we had our prayer.

"I loafed at school, but I wasn't permitted that pleasure at home. Most people think of Mother as a gentle person, but she became gentle only after her great spiritual experiences in the early 1930's. Before that, she had a rather quick temper, and she never hesitated to spank us. I had hundreds of spankings, and I thank God for it.

"What did I learn from her? I can't separate my mother from my father, because they both taught me integrity. In out little world the worst thing you could do was go back on your word. They must have taught me character, too, because I did not commit sexual immorality when the opportunity was so available. In their idealism they expected me to be clean. They never doubted I would be. They trusted me."

Once he overheard his father tell another man, "My Billy Frank's a mighty good boy. I've never really had a day's trouble with him." Billy swelled with happiness, promising silently to be worthy of such praise.

But now and then a wave of impatience with discipline would engulf him. It flared highest when he was lectured, after some picaresque adventure, about his religious commitments. True, he had affiliated himself with his parents' church at the age of twelve, but he felt nothing; he accepted no responsibility for behaving in any but the normal style of his gang.

At Sunday School, at church, at young people's meetings, at prayer meetings, and at revivals he heard religious instruction which seemed mostly designed to prevent enjoyment of his youth. "I was full of rebellion," he says. "Some

100

persons try to force religion down their children's throats, and it makes them sick. I'm not sure that my parents gave me too much, but I know I was rebelling against religion."

On occasion they invented other capers, manifestations of youthful friskiness as common to their age as acne. In some enigmatic fashion their hell-raising contributed to the wonderful process by which God turns a boy into a man. Billy has confessed some of his pranks.

"If somebody had seen me as a teen-ager in Charlotte," he has said, "I'm sure they would have thought I was crazy, off the beam, and going to hell.

"I probably was.

"I remember driving my father's car through the middle of town on the sidewalk.

"I remember turning it into the square with a policeman shouting, 'You can't do that,' and I said, 'I think I can.'

"I remember standing up in the back seat of a convertible with my girl friend, ringing a cowbell, right in the middle of town. I did all those things and a lot more."

"By today's standard what we did would be considered very tame. In my community it was called wild. We didn't destroy property. My wildness, I'd say, was mostly cutting up, but nothing destructive. On Halloween we fellows would walk through town with our arms locked and bump into everyone; other fellows would do the same, and we'd have some action when we met. But it was all in good fun."

Forgotten today, the return of beer with the repeal of the Volstead Act was a monumental event in many states. In North Carolina, boys who had sampled nothing stronger than Bevo and other beery imitations discussed its imminent availability with drooling relish.

Frank Graham, Sr., admittedly a stern father, was also a smart father. One published story says he brought home a case of beer, set it on the kitchen table, and forced his two oldest children to drink the stuff until they were physically ill. "And they never touched a drop again," is the happy ending. It happens to be true in spirit, untrue in detail.

He brought beer home, but only one or two bottles. He called his children into the kitchen, opened a bottle, and said, "This is the stuff you've been hearing about. I think it's pretty nasty. I hope you'll think so, too. Now I want you to taste it."

Billy remembers taking one swallow. He gagged and choked. The taste was unbelievably bad, and he spat it out. One of the girls did the same thing; he thinks it was Catherine. Nobody got sick, but there was the same happy ending: they never drank beer again.

Today his attitude toward drinking is remarkably relaxed. He once told me, "I don't feel that the Bible teaches abstinence. I think Christ drank wine; I don't think that was grape juice. I think the Bible teaches that wine, if taken at all, should be taken in moderation. On one hand there's the Nazarite vow, which Samson and certain others took, that forbade drinking; and there are Scriptures that discourage it. On the other hand I can find no place where we are told to observe total abstinence, except where there is the danger of causing someone to stumble. I like the story of Doug Judson, who helped me for some time. Doug, before his conversion, was a heavy drinker. In fact, he was converted with a martini in his hand. One day my wife asked him if it had been hard to quit after drinking heavily for such a long time. Doug looked at her thoughtfully, then shook his head. 'No, Ruth,' he said. 'No. I found something more important.'"

In view of Billy's frenetic escapades and experiences, it is pertinent to inspect the family influences that shaped him in relation to the measures which social science believes to be effective in modifying behavior. I turn again to the researches of Dr. Ligon.

He postulates that a mother must recognize that she will often find herself playing the roles of both father and mother.

Normally a father provides the strong family leadership and is the family hero, at least in the eyes of his children, and so transmits to them, without even knowing it or understanding it, their basic philosophy and their level of moral integrity. Some readers may disagree with this finding, but the Ligon statistics prove that it is usually so.

Father is also the practical man about the place, the programmer and executive against whom most mothers cannot compete. But when it comes to understanding each individual child and relating individual ability to either a heady challenge or a difficult task, mother is a genuine genius.

As for emergencies, science says father must stay out of the picture. He operates effectively only when he knows "what is going to happen and is ready for it." To mother, another emergency is merely dull routine.

Ligon says also that tradition establishes the father as a stern disciplinarian, but "our evidence comes out the other way round. It is mother who must exhibit firm discipline. It is she who must never compromise her standards."

In the matter of teaching social skills she is the mentor par excellence.

Finally, every child craves love and respect from his parents, but he alone judges when he is receiving it without really realizing that he is judging. At such a time words must be replaced by empathy between mother and child and by a silent dialogue composed of feeling and intuition, which provides an inner language that is always changing and which the mother must study everlastingly.

The above paragraph will sound like Greek to fathers, Ligon promises, but it is scientifically correct. And so he summarizes his research in these words:

"When you try to picture all this in a sort of living painting, you see father out in front of the family, leading the way, first braving the dangers but also challenging to high adventure, seeing the realistic forces operating about them, growing in wisdom as well as in stature.

"Mother brings up the rear guard, helping each child in his efforts to follow Dad's lead, coaching Dad a bit from time to time on child psychology, binding up hurt feelings, encouraging the faint-hearted, resolving the countless interpersonal conflicts, and keeping the child growing in favor with God and man."

Thus the family grows both inward and outward. Billy Graham's concern for America's family life is often expressed in his sermons about the family. One of them is built around both his memories and his study of the Bible. "The Bible says, 'Set thy house in order,' he explains. "Today I ask you—is your house in order?

"An orderly house finds both husband and wife professing Christians. The Bible says, 'Be not unequally yoked together.' I do not think there can be genuine love between two people outside of Christ."

In an orderly house neither spouse will divorce the other. "God never meant that we were to break up. Only death can us part," he declares. "God says only one thing can break a marriage vow, and that is adultery."

In an orderly house the wife submits to the husband. "The Bible says, 'Submit to . . . be subject to . . . be in subjection to . . . be obedient to . . . reverence and love. . . .' God said that the husband is to be the head of the home. That has never been changed. It has never been revoked. It is taught all the way through the Scriptures.

"In an orderly house no one is superior in his God-given place. But the Bible teaches that the wife is to fit into the world of her husband. If not, the Word of God is blasphemed and your prayers can be hindered."

Discussing day-to-day problems, he tells women, "Be attractive. When John comes home from a hard day's work, don't yell from the kitchen, 'Is that you, John? Shut the door.' Instead, you dress up in a fresh dress, greet him with a big kiss, and welcome him home. Make him feel like he's somebody. He may faint, but you try it anyhow.

"Try to keep up with your husband's interests.

"Keep up with his work. . . .

"Keep the house clean. . . .

"Curtail unnecessary expenditures. . . .

"Don't nag and don't complain. . . .

"Give your life to Jesus Christ. In the parts of the world where Christianity has not made an impact, the woman is little more than an animal. She's a beast of burden. . . ."

In the same sermon he flings these injunctions at all husbands:

"The Bible says, 'Husbands, love your wives even as Christ also loved the church and gave himself for it. . . .'

"The husband should *remain* a lover. . . . How long has it been since you greeted your wife with a kiss? I'm not talking about a little peck on the cheek. I mean a *kiss*. . . .

"Do the little things, thoughtful everyday things. If you go away, write her a card or letter each day. . . .

"Be a gentleman with her. Before you were married, if you came to a mud puddle, you'd take off your coat and put it down and say, 'Walk on it.' Now, if you come to a mud puddle, you say, 'Jump, lady. I think you can make it.'

"Don't be a tightwad. I don't think there's anything lower than the man who keeps all the money to himself. . . .

"In God's sight, the man and the woman are partners and all you have is half hers. . . .

"You husbands are to forgive your wives. . . .

"Now, I want to tell you something I've learned in reading many books and through experience. You can never understand your wife, so don't try. You will never understand a woman. A woman is not meant to be understood; she is meant to be loved. Even psychiatrists can't understand them. . . .

"Take God into partnership. There ought to be a family altar in your home. God holds the man responsible for the spiritual life in the home. You are the preacher in your home. You are to set the example. If there is no altar, if there are no prayers, and if no grace is said at the table, it is the man's fault. . . ."

Graham's texts come from the Bible, sometimes from the King James Version, but often from the Revised Standard Version, the English New Testament, or the Phillips translation. But his picture of a family in which Christ can truly be said to live comes straight out of his boyhood in North Carolina.

Frank and Morrow Graham held such deep convictions that they once moved quietly from their home church to a more conservative one when a new pastor advanced doctrines with which they could not agree. Until Frank's death in 1962, he and Morrow lived a full and joyous life on the same farm to which they had moved after their honeymoon.

By the final months of the Hoover administration in early 1933, the nation had collapsed into an economic tailspin. Everywhere banks were closing. Farmers in the West were losing their acres. Hoovertowns were springing up on city fringes. Families in Charlotte were withdrawing their savings from banks and putting their cash in a sock. Frank Graham had saved four thousand dollars, and it was on deposit in the Farmers and Merchants Bank. It represented a lifetime of hard labor.

"What do you think, Frank? Reckon the bank is safe?" friends asked.

"Safe as Gibraltar."

Then Franklin D. Roosevelt became President and declared a bank holiday, closing every financial institution in the nation. When the holiday was over, the Farmers and Merchants Bank failed to open its doors. The lifetime savings of Frank and Morrow Graham were gone.

The blow almost deranged Frank Graham. He could understand hail or tornado or drought, which were God's doing, but he could not comprehend the loss of his life savings. For a while he lived in a state of black discouragement.

Billy recalls, "He had to start over from scratch. Eventually he got it all back, but at the time it was a terrible blow."

No wonder that a company of sorely pressed Christians, with Frank Graham among them, soon turned to God in the privacy of a forest grove, where their spirits were free of masonry and ritual and where nature's glory mollified despair. The depression was at its deepest when these men were wont to fall on their knees beneath God's trees, praying from early morn until sunset.

They were a hardy band, part of a group that had originally enlisted in the cause of Christian evangelism following Billy Sunday's Charlotte campaign many years earlier, the same series of meetings to which Frank Graham had taken young Billy. For several years after, they had held revivals in the old 18th Street mission, but gradually their enthusiasm waned, and ultimately they disbanded.

In 1932 they came together again, convinced that the hour for revival was at hand. Conferring with their local ministerial association, they got no encouragement. "The time is inopportune," they were told.

But Christian laymen are a stubborn breed, to the greater glory of Protestantism, and this group refused to abandon their ideals. They met again, twice, in a grove on Frank Graham's farm. Hidden in the copse, they prayed, meditated, and planned.

By 1933 they had bought a tent, hired an itinerant evangelist, and conducted a rousing revival at the corner of Charlotte's Graham and 5th Streets.

That same season a Reverend Mordecai Ham was jousting spectacularly with Satan in nearby Augusta, Georgia. Ham was of the old school, lambasting sin and tongue-lashing sinners. Neither rank nor riches intimidated his spirit or diminished his thunder. He loved to pick on the high and mighty and to carry a fight to a brawling finish. The men who met in Frank Graham's grove sent him an invitation to hold a meeting in Charlotte in 1934.

With his acceptance in hand, they gathered to lay the groundwork for a revival that was destined to change the course of Billy Graham's young life. Frank Graham attended the meeting, and so did T. W. Wilson, Sr., father of T. W. and Grady Wilson, Billy's friends who were later to become key members of his evangelistic team.

The revival would be held in a tabernacle built of raw, unpainted pine. No cheaper material was available. It would be outfitted with benches and chairs from funeral parlors. The evangelist and choir would sit on an elevated platform at one end. Shavings and sawdust on the earth floor would keep dust or mud to a minimum.

The announcement that Reverend Ham was coming to Charlotte sent the religious community into an uproar. Some of the clergy disapproved. William G. McLoughlin, Jr., says, "Mordecai Fowler Ham was a rural edition of Billy Sunday, an itinerant revivalist who had won a reputation among pious folk for his fiery denunciations of sin and his success in producing renewed religious enthusiasm among cold church members. Ham was especially noted for his ability to bring recalcitrant young people to the anxious bench and break them of their adolescent rebelliousness."

Significantly, many members of that organizing committee were the fathers of children in their teens. Ham confessed later that Frank Graham had once pointed out Billy

Frank and suggested that special pressures might be in order.

Young Billy had earlier come under the influence of an upstanding Scot named Albert V. McMakin and his three sons. Returning home from his eighth-grade class one day, he had found his father and a husky stranger in deep conversation.

"The McMakins are going to run the farm on shares," Graham, Sr., explained. "I'll take care of the dairy, and Al will raise the crops."

Choosing McMakin as a partner was a stroke of genius. His three boys were solid, muscular, chore-hardened types. Each was a good farmhand, yet each had a mind of his own. When Billy learned that the father was a baseball fan and could name the batting and fielding averages of all the big league players, he was in seventh heaven.

Being younger, Billy followed the McMakin boys wherever they went. He copied their mannerisms and their speech. Their high moral ideals reinforced his already powerful idealism. Their active minds prompted him to study affairs beyond the borders of Carolina. Summer days they worked together in the fields; nights they settled down to good talk or good books.

Billy McMakin, the youngest, became a close friend and confederate in a thousand projects. Without planning, in an apparently aimless way, young Graham's intellect began to stir.

"I had no purpose until they introduced me to ideas about the world that I'd not discovered even in school," he says. "They had a remarkable effect on my life." When the spirit of rebellion flared inside him, it was usually moderated by the example of the McMakins.

Old acquaintances remember that Billy was open, friendly, and popular enough to be elected president of the young people's group in his church. He was reliable because of the code he had learned at home. He was against spectacular sin for the same reason. That he personally refrained from sinning, he recalls, probably should be attributed to the fact that working for his father kept him too tired, yet within his secret heart he felt not one jot or tittle of genuine Christianity. He attended church to please his parents and to prevent arguments, but he was not yet ready to surrender his inner world.

To him Evangelist Ham's arrival in Charlotte was merely an added aggravation. Why should an outsider be brought to town to tell everyone what they already knew? Why should busy people be expected to spend hours each evening, sitting on hard benches, listening to a windmilling preacher? The town talked about it, argued about it, and some of the original backers fell away.

Frank and Morrow Graham decided to wait and see. Morrow's dedication to Christian service needed no outside stimulation. She was already studying the thoughts of some of the great teachers of that generation: Dr. Harry Ironside, Dr. Donald Barnhouse, and Arno C. Gaebelin. Their devotion to a religion that sought out sinners and assigned salvation to faith instead of good works or ritual excited her. She shared her knowledge, going about the county to talk before Bible study groups.

So the Ham revival of 1934 began, conducted by a rustic facsimile of Billy Sunday in a town which largely did not want it and for a people many of whom thought they did not need it, including young Billy.

True to prediction, Ham immediately stirred up trouble. His unerring nose knew exactly where to look for sin in the boiling pot of a Southern city. His huge voice named dates and places, his flailing fists pounded sensitive spots, and his big feet stepped on tender toes.

A report flashed through the town that he claimed to hold proof that the students of Central High School were indulging in immorality. The student body marched on his tabernacle, shouting they would run him out of town. Fortunately they did not find him. Newspapers published the story, whetting interest.

One day Billy's baseball coach made a coarse jest about Ham's noisy evangelizing, and Billy's laugh was the loudest and longest. He felt he had to declare himself, so he crowed, "If that man walked in right now, I'd smack him square on the nose."

Antipathy for the evangelist in some quarters was matched by admiration in others. Day by day, comment about the preacher's fearlessness increased. Audiences grew and then overflowed the wooden tabernacle. One of Billy's uncles had been "soundly converted," as the local saying was, and he spent long hours talking religion to Frank Graham, Sr. "Brother Ham is God's man, Frank," he insisted. "You ought to support him."

Billy heard both sides, and his curiosity mounted. One night Albert McMakin, Sr., said to him, "Billy Frank, why don't you and I go down and hear that fighting preacher?"

Billy had recently told the McMakin boys, "Religion is sissy stuff," but the idea of a two-fisted, red-blooded, name-calling parson appealed to him. A visit to his tabernacle might be fun. "Let's go," he said.

What was he like, this non-Christian youth of sixteen on the eve of his visit to the Ham revival? To understand what he became, we should summarize what he was.

His brother Melvin describes him: "He was tall, growing up to six feet and two inches. He was thin . . . about 140 pounds. He had a laugh exactly like mine. Our voices are pretty much alike, too. Sometimes, when I go over to mother's, the phone will ring and I'll answer it. Somebody says, 'Hello, Billy. I didn't know you were at home.' He was always in good shape physically. Delivering milk and forking hay took care of that. His muscles were hard,

111

and his hands were very strong from milking. I remember he could make a baseball jump when he threw it. I was six years younger, and I guess I was a hero worshiper. I never did find anything wrong with him."

The foundation on which Graham would presently erect his career was solidly built, the result of hard work and play. A scientist has written, "Physical activity provides periods of involvement in integrated activity which can lead to a clarification of the self-image, the enhancement of self-esteem, the development of self-control, and an increased sense of security."

Those qualities are universally needed in a world of increasing tensions. Another psychologist says, "A boy's attitude toward his own body is directly related to what he feels regarding another person. I don't think you can respect your neighbor unless you first respect yourself."

Physically, young Billy was as ready as a boy can be for mature experience.

Mentally, he was beginning to awaken, spurred by his mother, the McMakin boys, and one or two others.

Morally, he was clean but given to hare-brained escapades.

Spiritually, he was zero.

Chapter Ten

When Billy reached the tabernacle and first saw the immensity of the structure, he was startled. Most of the seats were already full, and the choir section behind the minister's platform was packed. They found benches just as the service began. After hymns, and Bible reading, and a powerful sermon, Ham walked to the front of the platform and said in a voice that shook the rafters, "There's a big sinner here tonight." Billy remembers thinking, "Mother must have told him I was coming."

Throughout the sermon he had felt an increasing sense of guilt. It seemed that Ham was preaching directly to him. "The words came straight at me," he says. "And I thought all those thousands of people were watching me." To avoid the evangelist's accusing glare he moved to another seat, behind a woman with a big hat.

"I don't recall what he preached about, but I was spellbound. Something new began to speak in my heart," Graham has told me. "The next night all my father's mules and horses could not have kept me from attending."

He became a regular but uncomfortable visitor. He always felt that the evangelist was watching him. Finally, to avoid the evangelist's eye, he volunteered to sing in the choir and was given a seat *behind* the pulpit. Young Grady Wilson sat in the next chair, and introduced Billy to his big brother, T. W., and they talked of baseball and girls and hunting. Grady was short, an intellectual type; T. W. was

huge and gangly, a hell-raiser type. The trio often sat together, watching their friends go forward and calculating
the enormity of their own sins. Billy shook his head in bewilderment. Why did they do it? He was still full of
rebellion.

The campaign wore on, and church members were sent
into the audience to help herd reluctant sheep into the fold.
A family friend named J. D. Prevatte was one of these.
He urged Billy to go forward, but the boy clung to his seat.
Already a church member, a leader in his church young
people's club, his sins could not be *that* serious. He shook
his head.

Prevatte asked, "Billy, have you ever really surrendered?"

"I don't know."

On another night a cousin named Crook Stafford reinforced J. D. Prevatte, adding the weight of his urging, but
Billy fended him off. While he clung to his seat, other personal workers moved efficiently among the people, pausing
here, praying there, sending a man, woman, boy, or girl
to join the group standing before the evangelist's pulpit.

Each nightly service became a separate battle. On the
strength of good reports Morrow Graham and her husband began to attend a revival Bible class. They were concerned for Billy, but they did not press him. He knew they
were praying for him.

One night he could hardly stand it. He sat glued to his
seat through four verses of "Just As I Am." Then they sang
"Almost Persuaded," and J. D. Prevatte came and knelt
beside him.

Billy found himself on his feet, in the aisle, walking forward. His mind had not willed it. He had not meant to
respond. His legs carried him without conscious guidance.

Graham remembers, "I simply stood up and walked forward. I showed little emotion outside, and I shed no tears,
and I felt like a hypocrite when I saw so many around

114

me who were crying. Then without warning, all my worries vanished, and I was filled with a deep sense of joy and peace."

Standing before the altar, while Evangelist Ham pronounced a benediction, Billy had one last rebellious thought: "I'll bet it doesn't last," he said to himself.

When he reached home, his parents already knew what had happened. They told him of their joy, they knelt together on the kitchen floor and prayed.

When he went to bed, he fell asleep the instant his head touched the pillow.

Next morning, he recalls his room was flooded with the brightest sunlight he had ever seen. He walked to the window. The sky, the trees, the fields, and all things seemed changed. The foliage seemed so much greener that he inspected it with special care. Still not trusting his eyes, he glanced at the flowers blooming in his mother's neat beds. Their colors were almost painfully bright. Their beauty, he thought, was created just for him.

Many years earlier another evangelist-in-the-making named Dwight Moody had been converted in the back room of a Boston shoe store. When he awakened next day, he, too, saw a new world. "I thought the old sun shone brighter than ever before," he wrote. "I thought it was just smiling upon me alone. As I walked up Boston Common and heard the birds singing, I thought they were all singing a song just for me."

Young Grady Wilson, Billy's companion through many tabernacle evenings, had gone forward with him. Several services later, Grady's big brother, the terrible-tempered T. W., began to feel pangs of conscience.

Describing his personal struggle, T. W. says, "I was sick of religion and puritanical ideas. That night a man sitting two rows away looked as if he was coming over to speak to me about my soul. I said, 'If he comes any nearer, I'm going to get out of here.' He started toward me, and I left. I ran out into a big open field behind the Charlotte bus terminal. But I was so miserable, I felt I'd rather die than go through another night like this one.

"Well, the Spirit of God started to work. I called on the Lord to forgive my sin. Kneeling, white trousers and all, in the dirt, I forgot all about everything, and I took Christ for my savior. Then I went home. Next morning I was so happy, I couldn't sleep, so I came downstairs and began to read my Bible. Mother came in quietly and discovered me. She said, 'Son, have you been converted?' and I said, 'Yes, Mother, I have.' I don't know whether she started laughing or crying, but of all the prayer meetings I've been privileged to attend, that was the greatest, at 5:30 in the morning, with just my mother and me."

All three boys, Billy, T. W., and Grady, are ministers today.

That first day following his conversion Billy caught the school bus, wondering what his classmates would say. Their banter was what it had always been. "Maybe they don't know about me," he thought. He went from one class to another, acutely sensitive to their attitude. He imagined that one old friend turned away when he entered a room. A remark, "Here comes ol' Moses," drifted from another group. Now and then the subject seemed to be changed hurriedly.

Later he tried to summarize the difference in his life. "When I walked down that aisle and gave my life to Jesus Christ, some of my friends thought I was crazy," he said. "Some of the fellows didn't quite know what to think. A few dropped me. Trying to live for Christ cost me something. I wasn't quite so popular at parties."

One reason was his candid determination to live according to his new code. The parties enjoyed by his group were

116

usually given over to games and sociability. One night a classmate shouted, "Let's roll up the carpets and dance." The gang assented, and the floors were cleared. A family phonograph was cranked up and loaded with records.

Billy knew that his parents opposed dancing. He did not fully agree with them, but he wanted to respect their wishes, so he told his date, "I think we'd better go."

"The fun's just starting," she said.

"We better go," he repeated.

"But why?"

He wavered for a moment. Psychologists report that the resolution of such a dilemma is critical; a person either succeeds or fails, sometimes forever. "I don't think it's right," Billy told his girl.

Her eyebrows arched, and she turned away. "Then run along to your Sunday School. I like it here."

He was embarrassed and chagrined, and yet he was proud that his moral strength was great enough to support his judgment. He walked across the porch, hearing laughter and a girl's voice chirping, "There goes Moses."

Trying to sleep, he churned his bedclothes into lumps and knots. If God was all-wise and all-good, why did he sometimes reward goodness with so much pain? He would wrestle with that problem many times during his life.

More immediately, he tried to practice his new-found faith. A person converted to Christ is a person who is "turned around." The Bible told him, "Except ye be converted and become as little children, ye shall not enter into the kingdom of heaven." He studied that verse, and it became his pole star.

Growing slowly in maturity, young Billy discovered a strange new interest in improving his grades. Charlotte Hunter was his eleventh-grade teacher. Her encouragement helped him to surmount his rougher experiences. His scholastic record was a disaster, but she would not give up. They began to race the calendar, hoping that industry and luck would enable him to graduate with his class.

With each passing week he felt stronger in his conviction of being converted. Every day it became easier to practice what he was beginning to preach.

One day a tire on his father's Plymouth went flat. Steering it carefully to the garage where his father's trucks were serviced, he asked for help. The mechanic had apparently got out of bed on the wrong side that morning. He grunted, "The way you wild kids drive, it's a wonder you don't come in with four flats."

He went to work on the crippled wheel, muttering imprecations. Billy felt a twinge of sympathy and was about to offer help when the mechanic's tire tool slipped and he fell, bellowing oaths.

Billy faced him, white-cheeked. "You stop cursing," he commanded. "You stop taking the name of Our Lord in vain."

The mechanic picked himself up, incredulous. "Are you tellin' me to shut up?"

Billy said, "I forbid you to desecrate the name of Our Lord." It was a phrase he had heard Ham use.

The mechanic's face purpled, and his angry eyes grew smaller. "Listen to me, you punk. I'll use any blankety-blankety language I want."

"Not fixin' my tires, you won't," Graham said.

The mechanic spat into the dirt and raised his tire-tool. "Get outta the shop. Get outta here 'fore I lose my temper."

Something moved Billy forward, jaw out-thrust. Something put words into his mouth. "If you don't stop swearing, I'll ask my father to take his business somewhere else," he shouted.

They stood eyeball to eyeball, each gulping deep breaths, and then the garageman backed off. "Crazy kids," he mum-
118

bled, returning to the faulty tire. "Crazy, loony screw-balls. . . ."

He finished the job quickly, and he did not swear.

Billy's pursuit of virtue moved presently from the sublime to the ridiculous. For some time he and Grady had been rivals for the affection of a charming young lady. As born-again Christians, they were embarrassed by their rivalry. Each privately made a decision to step aside.

Billy, his face aglow, said, "Grady, she's yours. She's the cutest girl in the world, but I want you to have her."

Grady, overcome with brotherhood, said, "*You* are my true friend. I hereby give her to you."

Billy was a foot taller and accustomed to getting his way. He leaned over, belligerent, "Now you looky-here, Grady Wilson. I've made up my mind, and you're gonna have her."

The dialogue extended for weeks, neither making a move toward the young lady. And the gentle belle who caused it all sat at home undated, wondering what she had done to discourage the attentions of her Lotharios.

The new mode of life was reinforced by meeting other revivalist ministers, mostly young graduates of Bob Jones' remarkable college in nearby Tennessee. In practicing Christian hospitality, Frank and Morrow Graham often offered bed and board to itinerant evangelists, and two of their guests that season were young Jimmie Johnson and Fred Brown, both vigorous, athletic, and articulate.

Billy envied their broad shoulders and sturdy legs. Fred Brown had been a well-known football star. He could have gone on to an athletic career, but he chose to preach instead. Billy followed the young ministers around, absorbing their attitudes, imitating their manner. "I developed a deep hunger to know more about the Bible," he recalls. "I tried to be courteous, kind, and loving to all those around me."

The visting clergy were a new experience. They were

not long-faced and bluenosed. They had fun. One day Billy said, "We got a pretty good ball club. How about coming out for practice?"

They came and slammed the ball about like professionals. "You could make a pro team easy," Billy said. "How come you're preachers?"

Brown answered, "I think the Lord needs the biggest men he can find. Remember your Bible? Simon and Andrew were big men."

"I didn't know that."

"You're going to be a big man when you fill out, Billy."

"Oh, yeah? Well. . . ." He shrugged, unable to find words.

Jimmie Johnson was a powerful man, but he also possessed a fine brain, which he used to compose sermons that attracted large crowds. Soon Billy and Grady and T. W. Wilson became his unofficial escort, following him around like puppies. If he wanted a chore done, they fought over who would do it. They polished his car, carried his briefcase, and mailed his letters. They became his chauffeur, his valet, and his bodyguard. In turn, he fed their minds with his simple trust in God's plan.

They were lucky to be converted in their youth, he told them. Spokesmen in biblical times had frequently admonished their audiences to remember God while they were still young. He stressed the necessity of the new birth, and he explained that it never came to two persons in the same way. It might come to some like a thunderbolt, as it did to Saul of Tarsus, or it might come like the slow rising of the sun that changes darkness to light. But when the line of change is crossed, when a man experiences that, then conversion claims everything he is.

Conversion demands a changed way of thinking, so that the self is pushed to one side to make Jesus your guide, he said. No desire can exist except the desire to serve Him.

120

This change and others must be made before the Holy Spirit can enter your body to take up residence in your heart.

Jimmie could not prove these claims. He admitted cheerfully that he did not really understand them. But they were scriptural; of that he was positive. And you became a new person, in whom God lived, created by the new birth.

Later Billy would wrestle through similar discussions with other young people who asked, "What is a Christian?" The answer he liked best, and which still serves him, is: "A Christian is a person in whom Christ dwells."

Normally outgoing and jolly, Grady Wilson grew silent after those discussions, as if meditating a problem. Finally he announced, "I'm going to be a preacher. I'm going to Bob Jones College next year and study for the ministry."

Billy told his mother of Grady's decision and went about his chores, not noticing the hint of pain in her eyes. Years later she confessed the reason. Following his conversion she had set aside a quiet time to pray daily that he would lift up the Cross of Christ and go into His ministry. She was to pray that same prayer day after day and year after year until it was answered.

Soon it was May, 1936, and Billy's name was on the list of Sharon High School graduates. The achievement surprised several competent observers, including most of his old teachers. Billy has given credit to his father's being elected to the school board. Actually, he would have passed anyhow. It was a nip-and-tuck affair, but the diploma was honestly won.

Boys in his gang were talking about colleges. In September they would scatter to the four winds: to Wake Forest and Chapel Hill, to Duke and Emery. T. W. Wilson and Grady, following Jimmie Johnson, the stalwart evangelist, were going to Bob Jones College. Everybody was asking, "Where you going, Billy?"

"Somewhere, I reckon."

"You oughta know now. Maybe you won't get in."

"I'll get in."

Before making up his mind, he was to take another long stride toward his future by means of an experience that told him much about himself he had never suspected. For three hot, exciting months he became a door-to-door peddler of Fuller brushes.

Albert McMakin, Jr., had left Frank Graham's farm to take a job with the Fuller Brush Company. The pay was good, better than farming. Recruiting salesmen for the coming summer, he invited the most promising youth he knew. Billy was seventeen years old, thin as a beanpole but full of enthusiasm. He lay awake, thinking it over. Selling was easy, Albert had said. You knock on a door and give the lady a present. You come back later and take her order. Usually it worked in apple pie order. A good salesman could make enough money to pay for most of his college expenses.

Billy told Grady and T. W. about the opportunity, asking if they would join up. They were enthusiastic. He went to his parents for advice.

Frank Graham warned Billy, "Selling is a hard life. You travel. You're never home." He was citing the very qualities of the new job that appealed to Billy's venturesome mind.

"I can learn it," he replied. "Al says what you have to do is all written out in a book."

"You're a good hand in the dairy. Maybe you can be a good salesman, too. Go ahead and find out."

McMakin took his protégés into South Carolina and trained them in two talk-crammed days. Then he called them into a hotel room. "You're ready," he said. "You'll compete against each other and against me. Whoever sells the most brushes gets a bonus."

They drove into a town, rented furnished rooms, and canvassed their assigned areas. They would rendezvous each night, and McMakin would appraise their successes and failures. Billy learned how to pacify an angry dog, how to stick a foot in a door without being noticed, and how to talk his way into a busy housewife's kitchen. Sometimes he failed. One woman raised a second-floor window and told him to go away. He kept on talking, praising his product. She dumped a bucket of water on him.

"Never give up," his instruction book said. "Show faith in your product. Believe in it. Be sincere." He bought a Fuller toothbrush and used it six times a day.

It wasn't long before he added a wrinkle of his own. He began to pray. Later he talked about it in these words: "Being gangly and shy, I had a hard time meeting people. One day I decided to say a prayer before each door. When my sales were counted that night, to my amazement I found that my business had almost doubled. The same thing happened day after day. I had learned the secret of a great and wonderful power."

If that sounds as if he were using prayer to feather his nest, what really happened is exactly the reverse. "It goes back to your personal encounter with Jesus," he told me. "It goes back to your conversion. When you encounter Jesus, you commit yourself to Him, you promise to trust Him in everything, and then you *receive* Him. Trying to sell my brushes, I suddenly became aware that I had left God out of my work.

"So it occurred to me that I might tell customers about my God as well as about my brushes. I wasn't sure about it, not at first, so I began to say a little prayer each time I knocked on a new door. I didn't pray to sell brushes. I only prayed that God would use me."

In this way he began to talk to those housewives, not so much of brushes but of a person's need for God. Predictably, the appearance of a handsome youth who talked religion and offered brushes broke down sales resistance. When his commissions zoomed, it merely proved that whatever a man did could be done better if God were an acknowledged partner.

Years later, when he returned to the Carolinas to conduct crusades, he met many old customers. Mrs. Bernard Farley, of Florence, South Carolina, was one of them; she had rented him a room and then bought his brushes. "He was a good boy and didn't go to shows," she says. "We often discussed religion together, but I didn't dream he would ever be a preacher."

Billy saved his pennies, which was one reason for not going to movies. His ancestry was Scotch, and his natural instinct demanded frugality. Besides, he remembered years when cash was so rare in the family treasury that only a few coins could be scraped together. "We weren't always mouse poor," Billy says, "but I knew we weren't rich either, because Dad could never afford to buy us kids a cone and a soda both in the same week."

That summer also supplied two other experiences which jostled his narrow concepts of the world. After a day of selling brushes in a strange town, he and Grady recognized the familiar face of a man from back home, a pillar of the community who had been a personal worker during the Ham revival. The man was sloppy drunk.

They tried not to believe their eyes, but the fact was obvious. Their friend was besotted and revolting. They wondered how any decent person could act with such deceit. They were disturbed that a man so respected could behave so distressingly. It was their first close look at human weakness. The sight ushered them into the real world where people often fall from grace and need help to rise again.

A few weeks later their path crossed that of Jimmie Johnson, who was preaching among the sinners of South Carolina. Jim invited Billy to accompany him on a visit to a near-by jail.

Billy accepted, partly from curiosity, partly to enjoy the company. Jimmie was already an effective evangelist, with flashing dark eyes and a bag full of oratorical surprises. At the jail he exhorted the prisoners to embrace a better life. Billy let his mind wander. Suddenly the sound of his name brought him back to the smelly cell block. Jimmie was saying, "Take Christ as your savior and you'll know what I'm talking about. Young Billy Graham has learned the truth. He gave up sin and accepted Christ, and his life changed immediately. You listen hard, because he's going to tell you how wonderful it feels. Billy, you go ahead!"

Billy swallowed hard. Others could witness to their faith, fellows like Grady, but paralysis always gripped his tongue. He enjoyed listening to Christian testimony, but the idea of standing up and giving it scared him. He saw a dozen pairs of eyes staring through the gloomy air. The silence lengthened, interrupted only by the knocking of his knees. He lumbered to his feet. If only he were selling brushes. . . . A good salesman had to convert his prospect to a certain way of thinking and then persuade him to buy. He thought, "Maybe bearing testimony is about the same." He began to talk slowly, but with singular earnestness, of what Jesus Christ had meant to him. Looking into their eyes, he told them a story from the Bible in which a jailor had asked his prisoner, "What must I do to be saved?" And Saint Paul had answered, "Believe on the Lord Jesus Christ." Billy's face glowed with his sudden hope that the same thing might happen here. "Just believe, just believe, right here and now," he urged. Exhausted, he dropped onto his chair, hearing Johnson's quick voice exhorting the jailbirds. He relaxed, feeling good. He had done it. He had made his first religious talk. Boy, that was something. He had done it for the Lord.

After the service Jimmie said, "You did right good with that witness."

"You sure took me by surprise."

"You ought to work up a testimony and practice it."

"What in thunder for?"

"Well, you might give it in meetings. Who knows, one day you might even want to preach."

Billy said, "Not in a thousand years! I'd rather be an undertaker."

Frank and Morrow Graham were proud when their son came home. It was already common knowledge that he had broken all sales records and become a star salesman. Old men, whittling in the sun, remembered him as a kid in knee pants. "That Frank Graham's boy, I hear he's done right well."

"Sold more brushes than anybody ever. Even beat his boss."

"He's got a big offer to stay on, I hear. Wonder what he'll do?"

His parents wondered, too. When they looked at his fair face, each parent saw a different man. Frank Graham, to whom money had always come hard, saw a budding dairy farmer. Morrow Graham, with deeper insight, saw a crusader in the making.

Old friends, noting his new assurance, said, "Billy, you've changed."

It was true. For the first time, young Billy Graham had a goal. Surprisingly, it was to acquire an education. Having tested his wings, he had discovered the glory of flight. Having tested his knowledge, he had discovered its limits. He thought a good college might erase some of his inadequacies.

Bob Jones College had trained his friend Jimmie Johnson. Grady and T. W. Wilson had already signed up. The great Bob Jones himself, a powerful preacher of the dramatic school, had visited Sharon High School in Billy's senior year and fascinated the students with his wit and his electrifying personality.

Billy knew nothing about his institution, but he liked its products. Ma Sunday, wife of the celebrated Billy Sunday, served on its board of trustees. Its literature was keyed to adventurous preaching. "Our preacher boys not only learn to load the Gospel gun," it claimed, "but they learn to fire it."

His mother made a mild dissent. She wanted the best for her boy, and she suspected that greater scholars, if not more dedicated men, existed in some of the old line schools up North. Mothers were like that, always entertaining extravagant dreams of what their sons could be.

Her choice was Wheaton College in Illinois, but it was many times as remote as Bob Jones College and three times as expensive. Only a foolish mother in the year of 1936 would have dared to think of sending her son, undistinguished in everything except selling brushes, to a great Northern school or to implement her dream with a daily prayer.

Chapter Eleven

Before the decline of mass evangelism Bob Jones had been a famous Southern preacher. Like other campaigners, he had next turned his talents and energy to establishing a college for the sons and daughters of "like-minded" Christians. His was a college of one book: the Bible. His was a college with one purpose: to increase the number of Bible-trusting preachers, Sunday School superintendents, missionaries, social workers, and evangelists.

The full story of Graham's initial collegiate experience is both complex and interesting. It begins the day Frank Graham, Sr., packed Billy and the two Wilson brothers, plus luggage, into the family Plymouth and headed toward the Appalachians. Cleveland, Tennessee, then the site of the Bob Jones campus, was a day's drive west. The excited youths watched the passing countryside with bold, eager eyes. Well-muscled and self-confident, they saw no reason to doubt their ability to attain any objective.

Always a planner, Billy had a special vision. "Let's organize the freshman class and get ourselves elected to offices," he suggested.

"Just the three of us?"

"We can do it if we stick together."

T. W., oldest and most practical, asked, "What you got in mind?"

128

Speeding toward the Blue Ridge foothills, Billy outlined his project. "They'll have a meeting to organize things, and I'll make a speech nominating Grady for president. Then Grady can make a speech nominating me for vice-president. We'll run the whole shebang." The hump of massive King Mountain soon rose out of the plain, reminding them of the thousand Carolinians who stormed the heights and defeated a superior Redcoat force at the peak. To a young tarheel anything was possible.

The engine's song began to change as they started to climb toward the hairpin curves of the Blue Ridge highway. Tang of balsam, spruce, and fire cherry filled the air. The Plymouth struggled up the last ridge and stopped. The world dropped away, tumbling and splitting in crazy planes and parabolas. Colors rioted in groves strewn about "balds" and crags. An early frost had plated a billion leaves with gold. The boys absorbed the scene as Frank Graham spoke quietly. "You just can't look down on all that beauty and not believe in God," he murmured.

They drove on toward Hickory Gap and Asheville, where the road bent southward to the Tennessee border. Then they arrived in Cleveland, red dust on their tires proclaiming their strangeness. Cleveland, Tennessee, was a sleepy town, but on that day it buzzed with the voices of returning scholars. In its center the Bob Jones College was a beehive of confusion. Frank Graham deposited his passengers and began the lonely return trip.

They registered, meeting youths whose religious background was as Bible-centered and as evangelical as their own. They went to the meeting to organize their class with Billy's plan carefully rehearsed.

The session opened with a prayer. All meetings and all classes at Bob Jones began with a prayer. A temporary chairman called them to order. "Do we have nominations for the office of president?" he asked. Billy leaped to his feet. He named Grady Wilson, an honor graduate in high school, a ministerial student, a young preacher who already had two years' experience in soul-winning. Responding with undemocratic haste, his classmates voted Grady into the presidency.

Billy sank back, his job well done. Swollen with youthful pride, he enjoyed the prospect of claiming the two top offices. According to plan, Grady would now nominate him.

President Grady took the chair and asked for nominations for the vice-presidency. A gabble of voices rose, offering names. Grady accepted them one by one. Billy waited.

"I move the nominations be closed," a voice said.

Billy sat upright, trying to catch Grady's eye. The motion was seconded and carried. In quick succession the class elected a secretary, a treasurer, and a sergeant-at-arms, but none was named Billy Graham. He sank back again into his seat, this time, however, convinced that his pal was a traitor.

Grady tried later to explain. "We forgot to read *Robert's Rules of Order*. After I got elected, I remembered I couldn't nominate my own vice-president. I had to preside 'cause I was president."

"But you promised. . . ."

"I had to preside over the meetin', Billy. How could I do anything else?"

Graham's first disappointment was followed quickly by others. He discovered that the college had no baseball team. To a youth still dreaming of playing at Yankee Stadium, the blow was almost a knockout.

But worse was to come. For the first time in his life, he found himself boxed in by rules and regulations imposed by an authority to which he could not appeal. A sign in every room said, "Griping is not tolerated." If your ceiling leaked, you could complain to the college officers and ask for repairs, but you could not talk about it to a fellow student. That was griping.

Bob Jones himself was a formidable character, and he dominated the college. Never one to lack for words, he spoke at chapel almost every day and preached at church on Sunday. He had a gift for homely expressions, and he took pride in using them. "If the Devil's going your way, ride the Devil," he told his students. The students loved and feared him.

As the weeks passed, Billy began to feel increasingly uncomfortable. On campus you were not permitted to speak to girls except during certain hours. You were not allowed to loiter. You could not leave the campus unless you signed a book. Upper classmen might have cars, but they could not drive them on Sunday. Violations were mysteriously reported and demerits awarded. If you got enough black marks, you were confined to the campus. If you got so many more, you were shipped home in disgrace. To a youth who had spent a summer as a successful salesman with full responsibility for every action, such supervision was irksome.

Another trouble galled him. The Bible was used to settle every dispute. It was the ultimate authority. Billy had always accepted the supremacy of the Bible, and he had no wish to change now, but insistence on the precise meaning advanced by the school became a heavy cross. One day he violated a rule by crying, "Don't we ever have the right to figure things out for ourselves?"

For that he was marked down as a problem student and given a bunk in a room with an older youth named Wendell Phillips, who was supposed to provide a steadying influence.

Phillips, a brilliant graduate of the Moody Bible Institue in Chicago, did all he could, but Graham's unhappy momentum carried him from one crisis to another. In substance, Billy's lack of efficient study habits betrayed him. He was simply not prepared to understand college-level subjects. So his nerves grew raw, his stomach rebelled, and his mind refused to concentrate.

Hoping that the therapy provided by a little preaching might afford some relaxation, Wendell Phillips caused a country church to ask Billy to talk to their young people. Billy rose to the challenge with a determined effort, choosing as his subject, "If Christ Had Not Come, What?"

Stanley High, who wrote the first serious biography of Billy Graham and whose stories in the *Reader's Digest* helped to spread his fame, obtained a first-hand account of that sermon from Phillips himself. It seems they had to walk to the church because school rules did not permit the use of Phillips' car on a Sunday. And they walked home, too, covering, in all, a distance of eleven miles.

"Billy started in the easy, casual way he always uses," Phillips said, "but suddenly, as he went along, I realized that I had heard this sermon before, or at least had read it. A few weeks earlier I had sold some Moody colportage books to several of the students, and here, before my eyes, was one of those sermons coming to life. Billy went right down the line in the outline and did a terrific job. But in his desire to be dramatic he gave me an awful scare. He stood in that pulpit and declared as forcefully as he knew, 'The coming of Christ was foretold, centuries before the Messiah came, by type, by symbol, and by prophecy. The smoke from every Jewish altar was an index finger pointing to the Lamb of God who would take away the sins of the world. One thousand years rolled by and still no Messiah. Two thousand years and still not Christ. . . . Three thousand. . . . Five thousand. . . .'

"Right there I began shaking my head. He saw me, looked a bit perplexed and quickly switched to another thought. After the meeting he said, 'Wendell, why did you shake your head like that?' I told him, 'Billy, I was afraid you wouldn't stop, as you rolled the centuries back, short of fifteen to twenty thousand years, and those dear Bible-loving people—who put 6000 B.C. as the date of Creation—would never invite us back again.' "

As therapy the effort failed. Young Graham continued to be jittery, unhappy, and shockingly uneducable. Finally, he was called to the faculty office. "You're failing in almost every subject," his advisor said. "Your attitude indicates that you don't care."

"Sir, I do care," Billy interrupted.

"Your grades don't show it."

"I just can't settle down."

"You've skipped classes. . . ."

"I won't do it again."

"You've got practically no chance of passing your next exams."

Billy sensed that he was about to be "shipped," the ultimate disgrace. "Sir, I'll catch up," he promised solemnly. "You give me a chance, and you'll see."

Possibly aware of a quality he had not suspected, the advisor changed his mind.

"If that's a promise, you've got one more chance," he said. "But it means digging hard every single day."

"You can count on me, sir!"

Billy hurried to his room, his collar turned up against the wind. The autumn had been raw and foggy, unlike the pleasant weather of his native Piedmont. His pulse was pounding, and moisture made beads on his skin. Within twenty-four hours he was in bed with influenza.

"My real trouble began with that flu," he remembers. When he judged that the attack was over, he got out of

133

bed and pitched into an orgy of study that exhausted his strength. Flu bugs attacked him again, and his fever returned.

That blow was a coup de grâce. He concluded that God did not intend for him to be at Bob Jones College. When he went home for the Christmas holidays, he told his parents of his unhappiness and his search through prayer for God's will. "I want to quit school," he said.

They agreed he could do so. One formality remained— a final interview with Bob Jones himself.

At the designated time Billy was ushered into an impressive, book-lined room. The old pioneer had made up his mind that Billy belonged under his tutelage and that his future would be served best by returning for the spring session. Graham was equally determined to escape.

Bob Jones finally let him go with this ungraceful valedictory: "You've been nothing but a failure here," he said. "If you're a misfit at Bob Jones College, you'll be a misfit wherever you go."

"With his pronouncement of doom in my ears," Graham recalls, "I left for home."

Chapter Twelve

The Charlotte doctor tapped Billy's chest, inspected his pale skin, and delivered this prescription: "Your boy needs a lot of sunshine. Get him south where he can be outdoors and do a lot of swimming."

"We want him to go to college," his mother said.

"I know the place," Billy interrupted. "It's called the Florida Bible Institute."

Wendell Phillips, his former roommate and mentor, was already enrolled in the Florida Bible Institute, having transferred from Bob Jones. "It's heaven. The sun shines all day," he wrote. "The school is in one wing of a resort hotel surrounded by palm trees and a golf course."

Again Frank Graham packed his suitcase and drove his son to college. Liking what he saw of the flowers and palm trees and the school set spectacularly in the bend of the Hillsboro River, he started back north to give a good report to his wife.

Florida Bible Institute was a strange sort of establishment quartered in one wing of a slightly moldy hotel that had seen better days. But its teachers were an exceptional group of men, all ministers of Tampa churches. Its founder was a saintly gentleman named Dr. William T. Watson, minister at a Christian and Missionary Alliance church.

The good doctor called an emergency meeting soon after Billy's arrival. The faculty and ninety boys and girls assembled in a capacious room that served as a chapel. Already young Phillips, who knew everyone, had introduced Billy around, and the latter was able to take his place among several new friends. Everybody was relaxed, he noted, which was a surprise in the light of his experience in Tennessee.

Doctor Watson asked for careful attention and then stated calmly that financial straits were upon them again. Recent contributions had been light and expenses high. He said the school had to raise ten thousand dollars by the end of the week, or it would close its doors. So this was to be a day of prayer and fasting, a devotional effort by everyone in the school to seek the Lord's blessing.

Billy knew that prayer was powerful, but his mind boggled at raising the sum of ten thousand dollars. As men and boys and girls sank to their knees, the room became hushed until the only sound was a multitude of murmurings. The prayer meeting lasted into the late afternoon.

Later that day a telegram arrived from a man in the North who said that a strange but powerful compulsion was urging him to send a contribution to the school. His check, he said, would come by the next mail. It would be for ten thousand dollars.

When the gift arrived, Doctor Watson called a meeting of thanksgiving and read a passage of Scripture: "If ye abide with me, and my words abide in you, ye shall ask what ye will, and it shall be done unto you."

"*Ask what you will, and it shall be done. . . .*"

Graham recalls, "It was experiences like that which began to strengthen my prayer life and deepen my sense of the reality of God."

Excitedly, he pitched into his newly assigned duties. Every student worked, and Graham became a dishwasher. Board, room, and tuition cost one dollar per day, which his labor would pay off in five hours. Soon word spread that a new speed record was being set in the kitchen, with the new boy Graham washing dishes so fast that he kept five driers busy.

In his spare time he invaded the other wing of the hotel and sought out guests who wanted shoeshines. On weekends he caddied at the adjacent Temple Terrace golf course, where the tips ran from twenty-five cents to one dollar for a round of eighteen holes.

Any youth worth his salt must work off excess energy when he leaves home for the first time. Billy and his case of Fuller brushes had toured the Carolinas, but that was so close to home that he could have turned a corner and bumped into old friends and acquaintances. At Bob Jones he was so tightly yoked to rectitude that kicking up his heels was an impossibility. Now, at age eighteen, he found himself unexpectedly a part of the life of a boom town in a playground state.

It was a stimulating experience. Each trip into Tampa or across the bay to St. Petersburg stimulated his eyes and ears with new sensations. By now the depression was broken, and a feeling of hopefulness pervaded the land. Sleek yachts rode at anchor in the harbor, and big cars rolled endlessly along Bayshore Boulevard. As he paced along the seawall and gazed through high iron fences that guarded pink and white palaces, his thoughts must have turned to the future.

Fifty years earlier, in another city, but in a similar situation, young Dwight Moody was equally unaware that he would become the world's foremost soul-winner. He wondered instead how he could make a million dollars. That was the great American dream, and in nineteenth-century Chicago many men were realizing it. Moody expected to fill his purse and *then* do good works.

In early 1937 Billy Graham swam in warm Florida waters, wandered through lobbies of ornate hotels, and dreamed. Bookstore windows displayed John Steinbeck's *Of Mice and*

Men. Newspaper headlines talked of a new labor technique, called the "sit-down" strike. In England King George VI was crowned. In Chicago Joe Louis knocked out Jim Braddock to become the second Negro world's heavyweight champion.

Billy seemed to be an average boy, possessing none of the characteristics of a "Holy Joe" or mother's pet. Boy? He was a young man who towered over almost every person he met. As yet, though, he had not found himself.

The man who helped Billy Graham most during that first year in Florida was the college's dean of men, Rev. John Minder. Billy recalls, "He was a giant of a man, redheaded, and a bachelor who took time with every student. He was to play a decisive role in my early years."

Under Dean Minder's guidance Billy gradually adopted the remarkable mental attitude of the student body. Not mansions and yachts but careers of service were the substance of their daydreams. Minder's system of guidance was neither hortatory or admonitory. Instead he was kindly, understanding when things went wrong, and, most important, always available.

He had one inflexible requirement: his students had to know their Bible. "I had the Scriptures ground into me," Billy once told Harold Martin of the *Saturday Evening Post*.

The grinding process did not preclude healthy fun. One of Billy's first acquaintances was a lanky blond youth named Roy Gustafson. Coming from Boston, he was naturally acclaimed as the school intellectual. When he offered to sell Billy a book about Paul's letter to the Romans for only one dollar, the Charlotte youth was overwhelmed by his kindness and gladly made the purchase. He discovered soon enough, however, that he had been tricked, for the volume had been written by a seventeen-year-old boy and was entirely useless.

138

When Gustafson joined the Graham evangelistic team many years later, he would tell audiences how he had "cheated" Billy Graham of a dollar when they were both school boys. "And it's been a heavy load on my conscience ever since," he would add, taking a bill from his pocket. "Here, Bill, here's your dollar back."

Graham had his first contact with outstanding Christian leaders. Gipsy Smith, an English evangelist, came to the institute and told great stories of soul-winning. So did Rev. W. B. Riley, the grand old Baptist, whose church was in Minneapolis, and Homer Rhodeheaver, a famous song leader for Billy Sunday.

Letters came regularly from Grady and T. W. Wilson, still attending Bob Jones College. They had chosen their course; they would preach the Gospel. Indeed, they were already preaching at village churches at every opportunity. Reading their glowing reports, Billy felt like a backslider.

All spring long he studied hard to work his way through the Old and New Testaments. As yet he had no conviction that he should become a minister. One cannot read his nineteen-year-old mind, but one reason might have been that he felt some concern over his conversion.

Down the years conversion has meant many things to many ages. In the last century when people in England fell under a religious conviction and began to shake, shudder, and collapse, they became known as Shakers. This kind of conversion, when it happened, was clearly visible. In nineteenth-century America, especially in camp meetings, conversion was thought to be a sort of "possession" or "fit" that involved jerkings and threshings and shoutings. Yet when Billy had responded to Mordecai Ham's summons in Charlotte, he had merely felt uplifted.

Even his father, he recalled, had passed through a much deeper experience. Three ex-Confederate soldiers turned evangelists were holding a Charlotte meeting when Frank

139

Graham was a youth. Their church was a plank meeting house three miles from the Graham farm. Their sermons had stirred up the countryside until everyone was talking of nothing but heaven and hell. "If you don't want to get religion, stay away from there," visitors warned.

Frank had to find out for himself what was happening, so he went to a service. The hymns began, followed by mellow and joyful Scripture. Then came the traditional sermon emphasizing God's punishment, for which the only antidote was repentance and God's redeeming love.

Upon invitation, Frank Graham went forward, but he had many questions to ask. When he departed that night, his heart was aching. Those preachers had healed neither his doubts nor his fears. Atonement and sanctification were difficult concepts for a young farmer who had not been to school since the age of ten.

For many nights he attended the revival, listening and yearning but unable to feel the physical cleansing which signified the arrival, in his body, so he thought, of the Holy Spirit. Not eating, he lost weight. On the tenth night, in a miraculous manner, the light suddenly broke through, and he felt that he now comprehended the mystery of how Christ, by dying on the cross, had atoned for his, Frank Graham's, sins.

Later he liked to tell of driving up to the meeting house that night. "My face was changed," he said. "It was so different that everyone noticed it. Brother Coburn, the preacher, saw it, too, and he called me up to the front. He asked the audience to look at me real good, and he made one of the sorriest predictions in history. He said, 'Brothers, we all know this boy and we love him. Some day, I think, we'll all hear Frank Graham preaching Christ.' " God had other plans, however.

Young Billy Graham, thinking of many matters, including his own conversion, while he attended his daily classes, could not believe that God, as the saying went, had yet laid his hand on him. Years later he would speak often of his time of uncertainty and illustrate it with a story.

"Maybe I was a lot like the farm boy who saw two big letters in the sky: P.C. Thinking it over, he decided that the heavenly signal meant for him to 'preach Christ.' So he left the farm and enrolled in a Bible school and began to preach. Well, he was so bad that his audiences began to complain, so he had second thoughts about that P.C. Finally he quit school and came home again.

"They said, 'Jimmy, why aren't you out preaching? What brings you home?'

"He said, 'You know that big P.C. I saw in the sky, the letters I thought meant for me to preach Christ?'

" 'Sure we remember.'

" 'Well I found out what that really means. It means "plow corn." ' "

After the school's commencement exercises in May, Graham returned to his father's farm to deliver milk and help get in the harvest. The Wilson boys were home from Bob Jones College, and they talked freely of their ambitions. In their minds the future was settled: they would get a church somewhere, like hundreds of other devout Southern boys, and become faithful shepherds to community flocks.

"What about you, Billy?" they asked.

"Before I make up my mind I've got to know more."

"Have you asked God to help make a decision?"

"I'm not prepared to preach. I don't know enough."

Each morning at half past two, Billy and T. W. started on their milk route. At six, after four hundred deliveries, they would return home to eat one of Morrow Graham's ham-and-grits breakfasts. Between preaching engagements Grady would drop in for a meal, telling such glowing tales that Billy was envious. Publicly he shook his head when his future was discussed, saying "Two things I'll never be: an undertaker or a preacher."

That fall Dean Minder welcomed him back to the Bible

Institute like a long lost son. That splendid teacher had talent for bolstering timid egos. He had no idea what this gawky country lad might become, but he knew that time given to him would be well spent. Under Minder's tutelage Billy finally began to discover the techniques needed for efficient study.

Because everyone else in the school was doing it, he spent some of his free hours preparing the outlines of several sermons. The study began as practice in organizing materials. Then he began to embroider his themes with proof texts and illustrations. Quickly getting the knack, he began to enjoy the exercise. Soon he had four complete sermons in his mind.

About this same time he began to hike along the Hillsboro River and its adjacent swamps until he reached a broad tree-filled depression. In his mind's eye it would become a cathedral. He climbed onto a stump, took out a sermon outline, and preached. He had read of Paul preaching on Mars Hill and Luther before the Augsburg Confession and John Wesley in the meadows of England. How did he compare, he wondered, with their great voices? His own voice was high but powerful. The parakeets and blue jays, the snakes and crocodiles fell silent.

Once, three hunters came into view and paused to listen. Perspiration suddenly dampened his palms. He wondered if they would make fun of him or report him to the authorities or take a shot at him to see him dance. His young voice echoed among the dead trees, blending with bird calls and the rustle of the river. After a while, the hunters went on, and he climbed down to solid ground, trembling yet exalted. "They didn't laugh at me," he remembers, "so I concluded that my message must be getting home."

Chapter Thirteen

Early the following spring, Billy drove north with Dr. Minder to a property the dean owned, 150 acres of woodland used each summer for Bible conferences. The grounds needed cleaning, and he looked ahead to a weekend of hard but satisfying physical labor. Rev. Cecil Underwood, pastor of a church in nearby Polatka, drove down to help.

That was the day he asked, "Billy, could you preach for me tomorrow night?"

Graham was appalled. "I've never preached a real sermon in my life."

"I'm responsible for the service at a Baptist church up in Bostwick. I wish you'd do it."

"But I'm no preacher." Billy was distressingly aware that he had never really heard God's call, that he was not prepared, and yet an urging within pushed him toward it. He had developed four sermon outlines, and he had practiced them. He sought God's will in a quick prayer. "Okay, I'll do it," he said.

That night he could not sleep, and his trembling shook the bed. "I studied and prayed for hours," he says. "Next day I practiced and prayed."

That night he drove up Highway 17 to the hamlet of Bostwick. This was historical country, populated by some of the first families to follow their fortunes down the nearby St. Johns River. He chuckled, recalling that the river rose in a spring-fed lake called Hell and Blazes.

His audience consisted of only forty persons. During the hymns he suffered every possible anxiety. Perspiration dampened his shirt, and his tongue seemed to grow larger. He looked at the pulpit, and it appeared to be a mile away. When he was introduced, he rose and walked toward it, grateful that his feet did not get tangled up. Grasping the pulpit's edge until his knuckles showed white, he began to speak.

His first sermon spun off his tongue and was quickly replaced by the second, then the third, then the last. When he had exhausted all four, he licked his lips and backed away. He had preached for eight minutes.

During the closing hymn, Billy asked if anyone wanted to accept Jesus Christ as Lord and Savior. When several persons raised their hands, he asked them to come forward for a prayer together. One burly woodsman raised his hand but remained in his seat, so Graham left the pulpit to speak to him.

As he approached, he saw the woodsman's lips curl and heard his voice sneer, "You don't need to think you're so smart. Just because you're going to that school down there, you don't know everything."

Billy halted, searched his mind for words, and found it empty; then he turned away and fled back to the platform. Distress darkened his thoughts for days because he had not known how to respond to the countryman. Finally, Dean Minder applied a psychological poultice. He reminded Billy that he really had no call to go down into the audience to single out the man. "And maybe God was using him for a purpose. You were swinging along, thinking what a soul-winner you could be." Minder added, "Maybe God thought, 'I'd better take this boy down a peg.'"

That evening he learned two lessons. The first one tested his talent and the second one his capacity for humility.

That summer, when the annual student exodus took place, Graham faced a dilemma. He could go home to the farm with its long hours and its warm associations, twilight baseball, and sodas in Pineville, or he could stay in Florida. Dean Minder had invited him to help at the summer meeting place on Swann Lake and to work around the hotel grounds. Lawns and hedges required cutting, and the work was doled out to deserving boys.

"I'll stay," Billy agreed.

It was a fateful decision because it sent him to the Swann Lake conference at a time when exciting personalities were teaching and speaking and when musical groups from Tampa were providing sacred entertainment.

One such unit—three of Graham's classmates from the Florida Bible Institute—blended their voices in evangelical hymns, imitating the famous Boswell Sisters of radio. As musicians, they were a great success, and one of them, without half trying, captured Billy's heart.

The cycle of courtship began. Letters to his mother, to Grady, to Wendell Phillips immediately said, "I've just met the sweetest girl in the whole, wide world. . . ."

The experience was overdue. From the time he left home, the cords binding him to his high school friends had been stretching and breaking. His last home-town romance had gone bankrupt because of his feeling that the girl he favored did not observe her religious commitments with adequate fervor. In an odd requital, she sent back portions of his love letters, cut apart, classified, and pasted on sheets of paper, supporting all the arguments he had used while attempting to persuade her to greater dedication.

Now he was in love again. Her name was Emily. When classes began that autumn, he pursued her with a single-mindedness that has since been successful in many other enterprises. The late Stanley High, one of the first newsmen to get to know Billy Graham well, says that she was devout and beautiful and that both of them were in love. "By the end of the semester—during which she had first lien on Billy's time, thoughts, and limited funds—they were unofficially engaged. Finally, to put something of an official seal on it, Billy—when the time of the annual class party came around—instead of sending her a twenty-five-cent corsage customary for such occasions, went all-out and bought her one for fifty cents. She never wore it."

Instead, she faced the love-lorn Carolinian and explained why she was giving him up. He was not, she indicated, much more than a religious "ne'er-do-well." He had not announced himself as either a minister or a missionary. He was meandering through life, dilly-dallying with God's precious time. She liked him well enough, but she did not like his superficial outlook and his rudderless drifting. Her coup de grâce to love's young dream was the revelation that she had just pledged her heart to another —one of Graham's college friends—who *was* going into the ministry, who *was* going to a theological school, and who *was* going to amount to something.

Stumbling home, Graham recalled scraps of Scripture used by his mother in times of stress, by his father, and by Mordecai Ham. None of them provided the balm he needed. It was midnight when he knocked on Dean Minder's door.

Time and humility are needed to explore the mystery of God's plan. On their knees, the minister and the stricken youth sought understanding. It would not come.

Billy wrote to Wendell Phillips, who was home, on sick leave, "All the stars have fallen out of my sky. There is nothing to live for."

Phillips wrote back, "Read Romans 8:28."

Saint Paul had told the Romans, "And we know all things work together for good to them that love God. . . ."

Today Graham is reluctant to discuss that premature romance, not because it reminds him that he was jilted,

146

but because he does not want to embarrass the girl with public attention. True to her pronouncement, she did marry a youth who became a minister, who did go on to a theological seminary, and who did truly amount to something. Today, he is one of the high-ranking officers of the Army's chaplain corps. Both he and his wife are warm friends of Billy and Ruth Graham.

In succeeding days only a few close friends sensed that a steely determination had taken hold of Billy's heart. His letters to Grady reflected it. One day Dean Minder conducted before the student body a service that quite possibly was tailored personally to persuade young Graham to select his vocation. "Young men, I urge you to give yourself completely to the service of your Lord. Let the words of Matthew and Mark become your North Star," he said, looking at his protégé. " 'Go ye, therefore, and teach all nations, baptizing them in the name of the Father, the Son, and the Holy Ghost. Go ye into all the world and preach the Gospel to every creature.' "

As if he had been waiting for that charge, Billy burst from the assembly, knowing that his time of grace was over. At once, he was required to take a stand. Would he become a preacher? If so, he should proclaim it and set his feet on the path. The thought made him weak. He remembered a verse from Hebrews:

"Lift your drooping hands and strengthen your weak knees, and make straight paths for your feet so that what is lame may not be put out of joint but rather be healed."

"I had fought that call for weeks," he says. "Just before commencement I went out under the stars one night at Temple terrace. Our school was surrounded by an eighteen-hole golf course. The trees were loaded with Spanish moss, and in the moonlight it was like fairyland. I remember sitting on the edge of the eighteenth green, looking up at the moon and the stars. A soft breeze was sweeping in from the south. I recall getting on my knees and saying, 'O God, if you want me to preach, I will do it.' Tears were streaming down my cheeks as I made the great surrender to become an ambassador for Christ."

Graham feels that a minister's "call" is essential to the vitality of the church. Only after receiving a "call" will a man feel compelled to broadcast the good news to all the people. That night young Billy wanted to shout his decision to the skies, but he remembers feeling unprepared and no match for the tasks. He felt both bold and fearful, triumphant yet afraid. He felt like Moses, he says, who told God he was too slow of speech and tongue to lead the Jews. But God had said, "Go! And I will be with thy mouth and teach thee what thou shalt say."

Under the vastness of the night sky, his thoughts marched across the continents, his imagination roamed, even as he felt his unworthiness. Jeremiah had felt unworthy once, protesting, "I am a child." Billy closed his eyes, bringing close the presence he felt about him. "God, here am I! Send me!"

He heard a voice replying, "Be not afraid, for I am with thee to deliver thee, saith the Lord. I have put my words in thy mouth. Go and tell the people." He says he remembers it clearly.

Later he tried to compose a suitable message to his parents. Words were inadequate, he discovered. He finally settled on a single sentence: "I feel that God has called me to be a preacher."

Now the days were too short; already he had become a student leader, holding class offices. He moved with the dynamics of knowing where he was going. From early morning until after midnight, he guided his overflowing energy into the task of becoming a good preacher.

Dean Minder gave him a formula. "Know your message, believe your message, and speak with conviction."

148

Ruth Graham and her evangelist husband arrive at Southampton, England, to begin the Greater London Crusade of 1966.

Billy's boyhood pal, Grady Wilson, who is now one of the mainstays of the Graham organization.

The advance guard of the Greater London Crusade of 1966, Walter Smythe, Bill Brown, Lane Adams, and Robert Ferm.

Cliff Barrows, principal song leader at the Graham revivals.

Great singing at Billy Graham meetings is provided by George Beverly Shea.

Volunteers from church choirs sing night after night during the crusade held in Montgomery, Alabama.

Billy Graham faces his public.

A crusade counselor has the job of following up the work of the pulpit.

A typically responsive Graham audie

one in the Boston Garden.

Billy Graham meets the press—England, 1954.

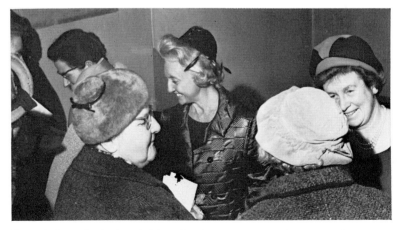

One of the principal activities of volunteer women is to organize prayer groups prior to crusades.

During a crusade, usually two services per week are held for young people.

Billy Graham preaching to a Spanish-speaking audience. Man at his right is making a simultaneous translation.

Problems addressed to the Billy Graham Evangelistic Association in Minneapolis are always given individual attention.

A scene from the film, *The Restless Ones.* The movie's Gospel message has caused tens of thousands of young people to accept Christ.

A French housewife reads Billy Graham's magazine, *Decision,* a publication delivered to millions of homes in a dozen countries.

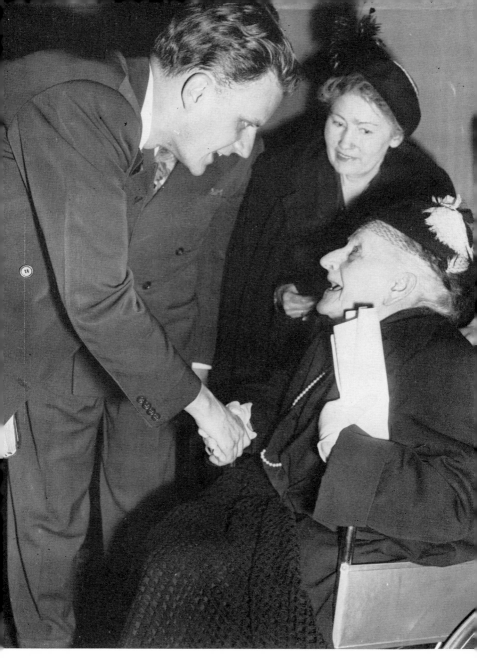

Billy Graham has always been known for his devotion to the frightened and lonely, to the ill and the aged.

"I'll learn how, even if it kills me," Billy vowed.

Minder said, "You learn to preach by preaching. Go to a mission. Stand on a street corner. Preach God's word and be on fire for it. Then maybe you'll kindle a fire in your audience."

His mother had once given him several books on Bible subjects. He had deliberately left them behind, so now he sent home an urgent plea. The college library with its stock of volumes about dead evangelists became his study hall. He read every book he could find about John Wesley, George Fox, Charles Finney, Dwight Moody, Billy Sunday, and many others.

For the first time, he became aware that evangelism had its techniques, its history, and its abuses. To be sure, many Protestant journals asserted that mass evangelism was dead, but Graham's research began to persuade him that the lackluster worship he had found in some churches was out of step with current needs. Evangelism might be the answer.

As he studied its techniques in the diaries of evangelist Charles Finney and others, he became aware of the importance of the spiritual change brought about by conversion. Reading widely, he found writings reflecting early Christian experiences. Some evangelists, with no other objective than saving souls and preparing them for the Kingdom of God, thought that conversion included a violent physical transformation. They cited the Book of Acts, which told how Saul of Tarsus, seeing a light and hearing a voice, fell to the earth, trembled, and lost his sight.

John Wesley, who founded the Methodist Church, wrote in his diary, "While I was speaking, one man before me dropped as dead and presently a second and a third. Five others sunk down in a half-hour, most of whom were in violent agonies."

George Fox, the young Englishman whose beliefs barred him from orthodox churches, went into the fields and

149

preached to hearers who then suffered seizures of trembling and shaking.

Billy paid close attention to the paragraphs in which Reverend Finney gave specific instructions on how to bring about conversion. "To win souls, look into Hell and hear them groan," he had written. "Then look at Heaven and see the saints in their white robes, with their harps in their hands, and hear them singing the songs of redeeming love."

Graham learned that preaching was only one element. Dwight Moody, the layman who became an international evangelist, had organized a complicated attack on sin by forming thousands of church workers into committees of ushers, doormen, choirs, prayer leaders, and door-to-door visitors. When Billy Sunday came along, he adopted and improved the same devices with such success that his critics claimed he had turned revivalism into Big Business. Graham tucked a thousand such facts into the back of his mind.

The Temple Terrace golf course sloped toward the swampy banks of the Hillsboro River, and Billy often retired to it to practice the new things he was learning. He would sometimes carry a book of famous sermons and read them aloud, acting out parts. Standing on a stump, he tried out gestures and inflections.

"Many times, surrounded by darkness, I called out from that cypress stump and asked sinners to come forward and accept Christ. There were none to come, of course. But as I waited, I seemed to hear a voice within me saying, 'One day there will be many.' "

In a short time he had memorized fifteen sermons. He was not yet twenty years old.

The Florida Bible Institute was famous for its musical talent, and one of its free services to nearby churches was to supply them with a gospel team, a student preacher and a vocal or instrumental trio.

One Sunday, Graham read the Bible lesson to a small Methodist congregation. His subject was "The Feast of Belshazzar," a theme that would play a large role in later crusades. As he read his text, he came to the words, "Mene, Mene, Tekel, Upharsin. . . ." Suddenly he knew that he had forgotten how to pronounce them. He stumbled ahead, mangling them. A man's laugh cackled behind him. Its source was a student preacher named Roy Gustafson, who, obviously, did know how to pronounce them. To this day, Billy remembers that laugh, its stinging quality, and its implication of his inadequacy. Yet Roy Gustafson is one of his close associates and a member of his team.

Chapter Fourteen

Dean Minder had counseled, "Get out and preach." It was easier said than done. Weeks passed, and no church invited him. He grew discouraged. His fifteen sermons began to tug wildly at their moorings within him, seeking an outlet.

He dogged the steps of the Reverend Corwin, an elderly missioner from Tampa who came regularly to the campus to invite some young preacher to deliver a weekly message at the mission he supervised. Billy's pursuit was in vain; Corwin always chose another.

He began to wonder if some divine purpose lay behind this apparent failure. Maybe God did not want him to preach. His perplexity became a kind of blind fury. One day he was mowing the grass of the golf course when he saw the distant figure of Reverend Corwin. He prayed that God would give him his chance. He thought, "Lord, if he doesn't pick me today, I'll just give up trying."

He continued mowing, trying to look very tall and capable. Finally, the old gentleman saw Graham and headed toward him. Billy's heart leaped. Waiting, he wondered what other work he might do if he were passed over again. The farm needed another milker. His return would please his father. He could sell brushes. A very big moment was coming up.

Reverend Corwin plodded down the long slope, inspecting every line and angle of the young man's face and body.

At last he called out, "Mr. Graham, would you mind coming to our mission Sunday?"

When God called Amos, he was plowing a field. Amos was a farmer, too. Graham's first reaction was a sense of absolute unfitness. But he was not about to miss his opportunity.

"I'll be there," he said.

Next day, he preached to thirty Spanish-speaking children. It was the launching of an unprecedented career.

"I talked almost as loud to those children as I do now in a stadium," he says. "Apparently Mr. Corwin was impressed with my loudness and earnestness. I'm sure my sermon was weak in content, but he asked me back the next Sunday."

After his second visit, he was so fired up that he cornered the gentle reverend with an urgent question: "Would it be all right if I went right out on the street and preached?"

"Go ahead."

That day he preached seven sermons on seven different street corners. The experience multiplied his enthusiasm for the pursuit of sinners. On subsequent weekends he preached often at the Tampa City Mission on Franklin Street and in the streets before bars and cabarets. "There were many wonderful conversions," he says. "Recently I met a Baptist minister who told me he was converted in one of those street meetings."

One day a gang of street bullies leaped on Graham from behind, threw him to the ground, and rubbed his face in the gutter. When they tired, he thrust out his long jaw and finished his sermon.

As word about the resolute young student spread, other invitations arrived. After preaching in a United Brethren church one day, he was handed a small envelope. It contained $2.25, his first pay as an evangelist. He carried it

153

with him for days, wondering how to send it back; it seemed sacrilegious to take money for telling the good news of the Gospel. Ultimately, he consulted his friend, Dean Minder. The resourceful dean read parts of the ninth chapter of First Corinthians:

"Know ye not that they that minister about sacred things eat of the things of the temple, and they that wait upon the altar have their portion with the altar. . . ."

The language could have been more explicit, Graham thought, but it eased his conscience. He kept the money.

Letters even came to the school office, asking for the "boy preacher." He accepted a week of meetings arranged by his old friend, Rev. Cecil Underwood, at the West Polatka Baptist Church in Polatka, Florida. The building was tiny, with pews for about 150 persons. Each night the townsfolk filled it, and Graham effected many conversions.

Occasionally he faced an unexpected crisis. In Polatka he was plagued by a group of young people who whispered, laughed, and cut up during his sermon. One night he interrupted his message to say, "Now you all behave yourselves. If you don't, I am coming back there, and I'll throw you out of this church."

One roughneck scrambled into the aisle, shook his fist at the pulpit, and clumped out, slamming the screen door. Billy's face reddened with indignation. The insult was to God. He shouted a warning, "I can do other things besides preach. If that fellow ever does that again, I'm going to give him the whipping of his life."

He later repented of his intemperate statement, worrying that his roughness might have driven the boy further from God's kingdom. But he had no more trouble. At the week's end, eighty-two persons had professed their conversion to Christ.

As he preached and gained experience, he came to feel

154

that a minister was not really a minister unless he was winning men for Christ. Any service which won no souls was a painful failure. If several such services fell together, he withdrew into himself, totally miserable.

One springtime he was attacked by an epidemic of troubles. His sermons seemed less fruitful, and his grades were down because he had devoted too much time to preaching. Not knowing how to pace himself, he was trying to do everything: study, preach, practice, work, play, all at a headlong pace. By night, he could hardly sleep. By day, he could hardly stay awake. It was the beginning of his lifelong battle with insomnia.

Fatigue finally sent his mind into a tailspin and he began to question whether or not he had really been called by God. His depression became so deep that he launched a canoe and paddled alone up the wild Hillsboro River. He soon found a spit of land and beached his craft so he could rest and meditate. Cranes waded nearby, and birds sang, and the sun was a blessing to his restless mind, but he could perceive no guidance. Again and again he rephrased his simple query: Oh, God, am I doing your will?

Paddling homeward, he begged God to give him a sign. This was a new venture in faith, this request for a personal revelation—somehow it seemed to be almost a breach of faith—but his desperation for certainty demanded it.

So he did as Gideon had done thousands of years earlier. He put out a fleece. When Gideon was seeking to save Israel from her enemies and needed God's help, he asked for the sign described in the sixth chapter of Judges:

"Then Gideon said to God, 'If thou wilt deliver Israel by my hand, as thou hast said, behold I am laying a fleece of wool on the threshing floor. If there is dew on the fleece alone, and it is dry on all the ground, then I shall know that thou wilt deliver Israel by my hand, as thou hast said.' And it was so. When he rose up early next morning and squeezed

155

the fleece, he wrung enough dew from the fleece to fill a bowl of water."

Billy Graham told the story of his first—but not his last —fleece in the brief autobiography he wrote for *McCall's* magazine. "I rowed back toward the campus," he said. "A stranger stood on the shore. 'I'm looking for a fellow named Graham,' he said. I told him I was Billy Graham. He said, 'We got a meeting down the road, and our preacher didn't show up. Can you come preach for us?' And I did." He had his sign.

Recently he told me, "That river was a sort of sacred place to me, and I had some of my most thrilling spiritual experiences there. It was wild in those days. It was way out of town and full of alligators, snakes, and beautiful cranes. I would sometimes pull up to a stump, tie the canoe, and just sit there thinking and praying. My struggle was —is my life pleasing to God? Is what I am doing what He wants me to do? I asked that question quite often. I still do."

So his nagging uncertainty disappeared. His calling, he now felt deeply, was by divine appointment.

So the strange power of evangelizing that rises in some man of God and commands the world's attention every forty years or so began to fill young Billy Graham. A Baptist congregation invited Dean Minder to conduct its annual revival. He persuaded them to listen to his protégé every other night. That first week, they took turns. On Sunday, the dean said, "Billy, these people don't really want to hear me. They want you. I'm going back to Tampa. You'll have to preach this next week by yourself."

Billy thought, "I'll run out of sermons."

But he preached every night, and the crowds came. When Minder returned for the final service, he found loudspeakers strung up outside among the pine trees.

"What's going on here?" he asked.

"So many people can't get inside the church," Billy said, "it seemed like a good way to let them all hear the Lord's word."

Back at school the whirlwind of his energy spun endlessly, consuming the days and storing their values for the future.

During the remainder of his time at Tampa, he preached often enough to consolidate his rising reputation as a "boy preacher." Vacation time he went home to Charlotte and preached some more. One season he held a week of meetings in the Old Sharon Church he attended as a boy. Recalling his inability to express himself in public, his parents entertained doubts about his staying power and wondered if even an audience of home folks would come out to hear him. On the first night, he preached for ninety minutes. His sermon was, "God's Program for This Age." That week the church overflowed with the largest attendance in its history.

Frank Graham could still recall his pleasure and surprise many years later. "He had a Bible class during the day, and he preached each night," he told me. "He was about as good then as he is now."

Brother Melvin says, "I thought he was quite a fellow. He preached about twice as loud as he does now, and he still preaches plenty loud."

On another visit to North Carolina, he was asked to preach at a home for delinquent girls. Full of zeal, he addressed the inmates of the corrective institution. One of them was a girl who had lived with her family in a tenant house on the Graham farm. He remembered her, and her presence in the home shocked him deeply. He had a single five-dollar bill in his pocket, and he gave it to her.

In Tampa a fellow student minister asked him to hold a full-scale protracted meeting in west Florida. Billy was

157

thrilled. It would be his first full-length revival on his own. Grady Wilson tells the tale of subsequent events with ill-concealed glee.

In the flush of anticipated success, Billy ordered a set of posters and mailed copies to his family and friends. They read, "Billy Graham, evangelist, will hold a meeting in the First Baptist Church." It named the date and the town, Capitola, Florida.

By now Grady Wilson had gained considerable experience as a preacher, and he decided to pay a surprise visit to his old pal. Having little money, he and another youthful minister hitch-hiked to Florida.

They ran into trouble in Tallahasee; nobody had ever heard of Capitola. Finally, an ancient cab-driver said, "Wait a minute. I do believe there's a community named Capitola out that away. It's right close to Shay."

But Shay was served by neither train nor bus that day, so they talked their way aboard a lumber truck which dropped them off some miles short of their goal. They finally came upon one unpainted crossroads store in which several men were playing checkers. Grady asked directions to Capitola.

"You're in the heart of the city," they said.

"But where's the Baptist church?"

"That's on down the road a piece."

"Aren't they having a meeting there?"

"Well, we did hear talk about it, but the young minister got called away, and they had to cancel. Nossir, there's no meeting."

It began to rain. Grady and his friend sloshed back to the railroad at Shay. A train was due that night, but it would stop only for a signal. They made a torch and borrowed matches. Taking turns at sleeping, they finally heard the distant train. It was three o'clock in the morning. They tried to strike their matches, but they had become wet. Miraculously, their last match ignited the torch, and the train stopped. They climbed aboard, sopping wet. The cars were air-conditioned, and they froze all the way back to Tallahassee.

Grady Wilson is an accomplished storyteller. When he returned to Charlotte after that expedition, he may have added a few flourishes to the tale of Billy's "first revival." Over the years, he may even have added a few more. He repeats it now whenever he feels that Graham needs taking down a peg. When Billy is asked about his first revival, he says, "My memory fails me. . . ."

"If the Lord will keep Billy dedicated," Grady Wilson says, "I'll keep him humble."

What did happen? The young pastor of the Capitola church had been unavoidably called to another situation, but Graham, who had asked so many for the support of their prayers, had forgotten to notify them of the change.

However, he again needed all the prayer support he could muster when his friend and mentor, Dean Minder, asked him to fill his pulpit at Tampa's Gospel Tabernacle for six weeks. The Minder church was a well-scrubbed edifice supported by a congregation of solid citizens. For six weeks, Billy would have a church of his own. The responsibility thrilled him.

First, Billy moved into the adjacent parsonage.

Next, he began to knock on door after door throughout the neighborhood, utilizing experience gained while selling brushes. Most local residents were of Latin descent, and many were Catholics. He invited them all to Sunday services.

He visited hospitals and sat with the ill and injured, praying for their recovery.

He visited the homes of ailing church members.

His person-to-person experience became the basis of a belief that still endures "I'm convinced that the modern

159

pastor does not make enough house calls and that the people in today's congregations have lost touch with their pastors," he says.

Each afternoon he slipped into the church's sanctuary to practice his Sunday sermon. A venerable custodian was his only auditor. The old man would occasionally make a suggestion.

On each Sabbath Billy ascended the pulpit and stretched out his long arm holding a leather Bible. His message was stark, and his belief in it was unassailable. "The Bible says . . . the Bible says . . . the Bible says. . . ."

As he talked, the difference in ages between the minister and congregation dissolved. With brightening eyes, they watched him move to right and left, leaning his taut body across the platform's edge, swinging his Bible like a mace. They always subsided to absolute silence, the sign of wandering souls coming to attention. Graham's professors had discussed the handling of an audience, pointing out that church fathers had written of the impalpable things that could occur on such occasions. Billy felt the warm flow of abiding truth and gave silent thanks to God. The process of evangelical growth was beginning.

This growth continued when he preached at the Peniel Baptist Church, south of Polatka. The sanctuary was filled each night. Baptist tongues buzzed as they discussed the earnest delivery of the "boy evangelist." The harvest of souls was mounting when, all at once, Graham came to a screeching halt the night the local pastor asked, "Brother Graham, what Baptist church are you a member of?"

With no notion of doom, Billy replied, "Why, I'm not a Baptist. I'm a member of an Associate Reform Presbyterian church in Charlotte."

"You're a—what?"

Billy sensed a crisis. At the Tampa mission his affiliation made no difference. When he preached on street corners, nobody questioned his credentials. Other churches, from Holiness to Methodist, had welcomed him. Apparently, his time of freemasonry was over. The pastor's furrowed brow was evidence enough.

"If my deacons learn you're not a Baptist," he said, "there might be such an uproar we'll have to stop these meetings."

An old idea returned to the young man's mind. The Baptist Church had fought historically for religious freedom and placed great emphasis on the separation of church and state. Baptists had no bishops but gave each church freedom to pursue its own course. This liberty had made Baptists one of the South's most powerful groups.

Graham had been baptized by sprinkling when he joined a Presbyterian church as a boy. He wondered if he ought to switch. But what would his parents think? More important—what was God's will?

"I want to pray about this," he said.

In his bedroom he put the matter squarely before the Lord, and soon he knew what he had to do. He telephoned his mother in Charlotte and asked her approval. He found the pastor who had challenged him and announced his decision.

Next night, standing in the Baptist pulpit, he told a star audience that he was a Presbyterian, but that he wanted to become a Baptist. And he hoped that this country church would accept him as a member and give him a Baptist baptism.

Now this was really something to talk about over the back fences of Polatka. Busy tongues spread the news: the boy preacher would soon be baptized at Silver Lake.

The crowd that witnessed the baptismal service was tremendous. Rev. Cecil Underwood, Billy's old friend, took him to a sloping beach and immersed him in lake water, calling out the name of the Father and the Son and

161

the Holy Spirit. Recalling his sensations for *The Houston Post,* Billy said, "At least three hundred people were along the banks and the sandy beach, but I was the only one baptized that day. I was not embarrassed or afraid. It was glorious."

Not all clergymen shared Graham's innocent delight in the changing of his denomination, accusing him of superficiality. He counters by telling the story of his second baptism to every large group of ministers to whom he speaks, especially Baptist ministers, saying that that immersion meant a great deal to him, being symbolic of being buried with Christ and of rising with Him. But then he adds his little joke. "Of course, it was kind of like a shotgun wedding," he admits, "but how else could the Southern Baptists grow to be the biggest denomination in the United States?"

"I've learned to appreciate and love and admire the warm and wonderful fellowship among the people of my denomination," he says. "I don't agree with all the things Southern Baptists do. I've not agreed on the race question with many of them, though some of the leaders of racial understanding in the South are Southern Baptists. All of them have meant much in my life."

One more step would formalize his commitment. He would have to be ordained.

Later that summer a convocation of pastors was called by the St. John's Baptist Association. Billy drove across Florida to sit at the feet of the Rev. Woodrow Flynn, once his roommate at Florida Bible Institute and now a young pastor with his own church. It was he who preached the ordination sermon.

About two o'clock that sunny afternoon Baptist ministers came from all over Florida to complete the ritual. After prayer, singing, and exhortation, they questioned the candidate. One of them posed a complex theological

162

question that momentarily threatened Graham's poise. Answering it would be both difficult and boring, so he replied, "Brother, I have been preaching in this area for nearly two years. You surely know what I believe and what I preach. That ought to be sufficient."

The reverend brother smiled and said that it was.

Finally, the visiting ministers laid their hands on Billy. The ceremony, described in the Book of Numbers, was as old as Moses, "And Moses did as the Lord commanded. He took Joshua and caused him to stand before Eleazar, the priest, and the whole congregation, and he laid his hands upon him, and commissioned him as the Lord directed."

Thousands of years later, the Apostle Luke would relate a similar event in the church at Antioch. "The Holy Spirit said, 'Set apart for me Barnabas and Saul, for the work to which I have called them.' Then after fasting and praying, they laid their hands on them and sent them off."

Feeling that "laying on of hands," Billy walked the last mile between his ambition and the churchly establishment to which he would devote his life.

From that moment on, he was an ordained minister, a status of considerable value to a youth working his way through college. Now he could conduct funerals and baptize and marry people.

He could also sign his mail: Reverend William Franklin Graham, Junior.

He was not yet twenty-one years old.

That springtime of 1940 he began to take stock of his future. His classmates had plans involving country pastorates, mission posts, or junior positions in community projects. Most of the girls were planning on marriage or missions. Letters from home told him that his closest friends, the Wilson brothers, were becoming successful pastors. "Get yourself a church," they urged. "It's a wonderful life." But Billy felt a strange restlessness.

Reading the daily papers, he could not forget the issues that were determining the future beyond his campus, beyond the South, and beyond the borders of the United States. He read of Hitler and Mussolini and of Stalin's Soviet Russia. Did the success of dictatorships, he wondered, presage the coming to America of fascism or communism? Hitler had easily crushed Czechoslovakia. He had conquered Poland in a fortnight. Now, with Europe locked in battle, the White House was proposing a draft law.

Nearer home, a host of domestic issues clamored for solution, and his Bible study provided no ready answer. Was it proper for Roosevelt to seek the Presidency for the third time? Was it just that the dust-bowl farmers in Oklahoma and Kansas should be forced to abandon their farms? Were race relations in the South only skin deep?

His future would be influenced by such questions, and he would need to know how to try to answer them. Advanced courses at a university would help, but the costs of higher education were beyond him. Fellows with good connections got jobs and worked their way through, but he had no connections.

One day a call came from the nearby golf club for a caddy. Billy responded and picked up the bags of a pleasant man from Chicago, who was staying with his mother in the other wing of the resort hotel. Conversation revealed that his brother was the president of a northern college.

At one point the man asked Billy, "What'll you do after you graduate?"

"I guess I'll get a church somewhere and preach."

"I heard you preach the other night," the visitor said. "I liked your sermon."

"Thank you, sir."

164

They played another hole, and the man asked, "Did you ever hear of Wheaton College?"

"Yes, indeed! From my mother."

Morrow Graham had prayed for years that Billy might complete his education at Wheaton College, one of the most highly regarded religious colleges in America.

The man said, "You've got possibilities, but you'll need more education. You can get it at Wheaton." Graham's heart began to pound as he sensed that the man was leading up to something. "If you'll go to Wheaton for a year, I'll take care of your tuition." He could hardly believe his ears. They finished the round of golf and separated with the understanding that they would talk again. Billy told several friends of the offer and met a wall of discouragement. They argued that empty churches were crying for aggressive, young pastors and paying good salaries. He thought of the four years spent in Bible study. Would one more year give him better tools for the Lord's work?

The Bible says, "When thou prayest, enter into thy closet and shut the door." Graham found it necessary to lay his dilemma at his Lord's feet. "The more I prayed, the more certain I became that God was leading me and that I must further my education at all costs," he says.

When his mind cleared, he called his parents and discussed his decision. Morrow Graham told me later that she will never forget the excitement in his voice or the joy in her heart when she heard the news. "Billy thinks he made up his own mind," she said, "but I tell you that boy was prayed into Wheaton."

A senior's life in any college is difficult. Graham's was complicated by the pressures generated by his own enthusiasms. He had agreed to hold summer meetings in the country around Toccua, Georgia, and York, Pennsylvania, having been invited by vacationing pastors who had heard his student sermons. Now, he had to pass his final examinations with marks high enough to assure acceptance at Wheaton.

Though eagerness to get on with the Lord's work filled him, he curbed his impatience each day enough to take a long, meditative walk, a practice he has continued all his life. Stanley High reports, "It was both exercise and devotion. The burden of his prayer was that God would make good use of his life."

What might the future hold? Graham says, "It is just as well I didn't know. If I had known, I might not have believed. What I did believe was that my time was in His hands."

Finally, the grades of all the seniors were posted. Billy was neither the best scholar nor the worst. In May his parents came for graduation, bringing his brother and sisters. A fortnight after Winston Churchill became Prime Minister of Great Britain and at a time when the world was shuddering with the hopelessness of Dunkirk and the surrender of Holland, Belgium, and France, Billy Graham heard his name called. He walked forward and received a diploma. He was twenty-one years old, entitled to vote in that autumn's election for either President Roosevelt or Wendell Willkie. He was also subject to his country's call to arms.

His parents thumbed through the school's yearbook for 1940 and found his lean face. It looked at them from above these lines:

Personal aim: evangelist.

Favorite song: "Faith of Our Fathers."

Favorite Scripture verse: "I exhort you that ye should earnestly contend for the faith which was once delivered unto the saints."

Ahead lay several weeks of back-country crusading. One Florida visitor had asked him to hold a summer revival in York, Pennsylvania. Billy had accepted gladly, hoping to test himself in a strange community, with a different kind of people. Also, en route he could visit Philadelphia, his first big city.

He chose a song leader from among his schoolmates, a young man named Ponzi Pennington. He bought a car to carry them, a nine-year-old Oldsmobile, for nothing down and the promise of ten dollars a month.

With Pennington, he started north: two immature men of God, prepared to save the world. Very soon they were struck by troubles that would have prostrated Job. Their merry Oldsmobile suffered blowouts, a leaky radiator, and snapped piston rods. It was a nightmarish trip, but they did make it to Philadelphia. Walking through the corridors of Independence Hall and the Betsy Ross House, they gawked like country boys. They took their first subway ride, noses pressed to glass windows as they tried to see the tunnels outside their speeding train. The day's big thrill came when they visited the Automat, an eating establishment where nickels in a slot open tiny glass and metal doors to a king's feast. They stuffed themselves and then drove on to York.

Their arrival was picturesque, their luggage-encumbered car spewing steam but held together by baling wire and faith. The York church awaited them. Billy noted that this country was hilly, the climate was chilly, and even the people seemed cold. He vowed to warm them up with the fire of his preaching.

He describes the results: "The people were strangely unresponsive. Then I learned that they could not understand me because of my Southern accent. For two tough weeks, I tried to sound more like a Yankee, but to this day I still say 'can't,' and it comes out 'cain't.' "

His corn-pone diction was only part of the trouble. Always a sharp self-critic, young Graham analyzed his sermons from opening announcement to invitation. Back in Florida, no Hillsboro river alligator had ever prompted self-scrutiny, nor had his audiences. But these Northerners, as the saying goes, sat on their hands.

Tearing his sermons apart, he found he was preaching with much sound, much fury, but little cohesion. He began to strip away all extra verbiage, to toss out every side excursion through the Holy Land. What remained was the elemental Gospel, as Billy saw it, that Christ preached in Palestine, and this was the message that he has preached ever since. Critics have complained that Graham always gives the same message. He admits it, saying, "I am consoled by the fact, reported by an eminent theologian, that Jesus repeated himself five hundred times."

His trial-and-error sermons soon began to reach the hearts of his York listeners. When he perceived they were listening gladly and responding to his exhortation, he resolved to avoid forever the complexities of doctrinal forensics. To this day, he extracts all the power he needs from the stark, unadorned message of Christ crucified and risen.

Chapter Fifteen

Billy Graham arrived in Wheaton, Illinois, in a second-hand car that would, within a few months, carry him to an important way station on his path to fame. He was almost twenty-two years old, an ordained minister, and as eager as a puppy to learn.

As he completed the details of his registration, college officials would glance at the open-faced, tall, blond youth and remark, "Why, you're a Southerner, aren't you?"

He always answered politely, "Yessir, but I cain't understand how you can tell."

The college sprawled over several acres of the prairie town of Wheaton, Illinois, twenty-five miles west of Chicago. It was a jolting change from the resort atmosphere of Tampa Bible Institute. Wheaton *looks* like a college, and some of its buildings, such as Blanchard Hall, are crowned by Gothic battlements that might have come straight from Oxford.

Founded before the Civil War by anti-slavery Wesleyan Methodists, the institution's first graduating class included a brother of Harriet Beecher Stowe, author of *Uncle Tom's Cabin*. It combined high academic standards with an exalted religious tone, and many famous scientists, physicians, and educators are among its alumni.

More than a thousand young men and women were on the Wheaton campus in the fall of 1940, each engaged in the complex task of adjusting himself to a Christian world in which a Nazi dictator and a fascist tyrant marched from one victory to another. Hitler and Mussolini had swept through Norway, France, Greece, and Africa. The Wheaton faculty, nondenominational but ardently conservative, dug deep in Scripture to explain these devilish triumphs.

On his first day the young man's ego received a rude jolt. "What course do you want?" they asked in the registrar's office.

"Anthropology, please. I'm a transfer from Tampa Bible Institute." He expected to be accepted as a senior or, at worst, as a junior.

"How many years were you there?"

"More than three."

"May we see your credits?"

They examined his diploma and his credits, shaking their heads over the inexplicable curriculum of the deep South. They broke the news brusquely. "We can give you credit for only one year of college-level work. You may enter Wheaton as a sophomore."

It meant extra years of studying and working at odd jobs to pay his way, but Wheaton offered challenge and opportunity. He said, "That'll be okay."

He recalls those next few weeks vividly. "They were among the most difficult of my life," he says. "My clothes were out of style, and I didn't have money to buy new ones. I was inexperienced socially and found it difficult to make friends. I missed the thrill of preaching. Also, I needed a job, but all the regular spots, such as waiting on tables and janitor work, had been filled. I began to wonder if I had made a mistake, but Christ had said, 'Once you put your hand to the plow, don't look back.' "

The tide began to turn when he met the Lanes, a Plymouth Brethren family with seven children, some of whom had been educated in Switzerland. Professor Lane taught

170

at Wheaton, and students trooped in and out of his big house at all hours. Billy became one of his regular visitors.

Through the Lanes he began to meet people and to make friends. Bustling Johnny Streater was one. This enterprising student intended to become a missionary and was working his way through college by running his own trucking business. He glanced at Graham's size and said, "You ever done any hard work?"

Billy showed the calluses on his hands. "Milked twenty cows every morning and helped with the farming," he said.

"What about last summer? What did you do?"

"I preached some and worked in my father's dairy."

Streater said, "I need a strong boy for moving furniture and stuff around town. I'll give you fifty cents an hour."

"You won't be sorry," Billy promised.

He became a truckman, attended classes as a sophomore, and braced himself against a way of thinking that was new in his experience.

Most Wheaton undergrads were serious-minded, but a few, as in any group, were frankly self-seeking. Billy's encounters with these types left him filled with amazement. In student confabs he talked freely about his work as an evangelist and the revivals he had conducted. It was a fact, although it did not occur to him, that he had saved more souls for Christ than most members of the Wheaton faculty.

It astonished and perplexed him when he heard other students say, "Why bother? Evangelism is dead."

"But the Bible isn't dead," Billy thought. "People will always need the Bible."

"These are new times," they said. "The auto, airplane, and radio have changed things. We must reach people in a new way!"

"I don't think people change," Billy argued.

His position was attacked by bright, ambitious minds.

171

"Why knock yourself out as an evangelist? You're a gypsy. You're not building anything up for yourself."

"I thought a minister was supposed to build up God's church."

"But you've got to eat. What's wrong with working up to a big pastorate?"

A dark, quick boy from the West said, "I've got it figured. You get a job as assistant pastor in a society church, and you hook a rich widow."

These were unpleasant moments. How could any man who followed the teachings of Christ be so concerned with material success? He read his Bible with fierce ardor, seeking the protection of its wisdom.

From the beginning Wheaton College was a broadening and, for a while, an unsettling experience. Hundreds of its graduates were stationed over the world as missionaries. Thousands of alumni occupied American pulpits. Most of the student body came from their churches, and some were children of missionaries and ministers serving in foreign fields. Billy heard about one Wheaton junior, a girl from China who was reputed to rise an hour before chapel each morning for private meditation. Campus gossip also said that she was beautiful and had been offered a Hollywood screen test. Interesting but unlikely, he thought.

Johnny Streater, also preparing himself for the mission field, already knew her. Her father was Dr. Nelson Bell, head of a big mission hospital in Tsingkiang Pu, China. She had attended high school in Korea and then come to Wheaton in anticipation of returning to a mission post in Tibet. Johnny told Billy, "She's the most beautiful and dedicated girl I've ever met."

One day Billy was in Williston Hall lobby with scores of other students when he saw Streater plowing through the crowd with two girls in tow. They were Ruth Bell and her older sister Rosa. Johnny said, "Billy, this is the girl I was telling you about."

Graham has mentioned that meeting in several sermons. "Our eyes met for the first time," he says. "I was impressed, timid, and bashful, but something, which I could never describe, went straight to my heart. The love bug had bitten me."

Fifteen years later he told me, "The most important thing that happened to me at Wheaton was that I met Ruth Bell. She was a campus queen and almost a legend. She was a junior, and I was a mere sophomore. She was a somebody; I was a nobody. I had no idea that God would ever give her to me. So I turned to prayer, seeking His help. For weeks I lacked the courage to ask her for a date.

"Let me tell you about Ruth. At home between crusades, I rarely awake in the morning but that I find her already dressed and reading her Bible. If only I knew one-tenth of what she knows. And she accepts her ministry of raising our children with the same happiness I do in preaching to crowds of people."

Today he has strong convictions about Christian mating. If you are a Christian, he holds, God has a person picked out for you, to whom you will make your way in due course as inevitably as swallows find their way back to Capistrano. His meeting with Ruth was foreordained by this same force.

I once asked him, "How can you be sure? How can the average young Christian boy or girl be certain that he is following God's will?"

He said, "If a man really knows Christ's will, he will know this; but it's difficult to explain to outsiders. There is a peace in your heart about it. There's a little voice that seems to say, 'This is it!' Everything else may be against it, but deep down inside you, there is a certainty

173

about it. You know this is the one God wants you to have."

In Wheaton, in 1940, he was far less confident that God was on his side. It took him a full month to work up enough courage to ask Ruth for a date. One day he found her in the library. He dropped into an adjacent chair. "Hi," he said. "There's a concert in the chapel Sunday. I think it's *The Messiah*. Can I take you?"

She accepted, and pretty soon the seriousness of Billy's intention became clear.

She recalls that he became bossy right away. One night he declared, "You can date me and nobody else; or you can date every man on the campus, and you don't date me." His long arms swept out and down in a typical movement later to be recognized by millions of people.

They began going steady. "I was in seventh heaven," he recalls. "Her slightest wish became my command."

Well, perhaps it was not quite his command, particularly her wish to become a missionary. After a suitable time, he proposed. He said, "Ruth, there's something very important that I hope you will pray about. I'm very much interested in you. Will you ask the Lord to guide us?"

She knew what that meant, and she knew she ought to tell him about her own plans. "How would you like to live in Tibet?" she asked.

It was the start of a long tug-of-war.

Date by date they exhausted one argument after another. "If God got me all the way from China to Wheaton, with a big war going on, he must mean for me to complete my education so I can be a missionary," she argued.

Billy started to point a long forefinger, a pulpit gesture of small use against a determined female. Recovering, he replied, "God got you to Wheaton, all right, but how do you know it wasn't for the purpose of becoming Mrs. Billy Graham?"

Her sister Rosa, in post-midnight consultations, had made

the same point. She counseled moderation in rejecting Billy's offer.

As the seasons changed, he and Ruth Bell had many dates, strolling along shady Wheaton streets, attending concerts, and going to church together. Others recognized them as a solid "twosome" long before they knew their own minds.

"Are you praying enough about us?" Billy demanded frequently. His question sobered her.

"I'm praying hard," she replied, "and I'll tell you the minute God gives me an answer."

He helped her by citing such Biblical passages as, "It is not good for man to be alone, and I will make him an help meet. . . ."

"I know," she said.

"But if God caused me to fall in love with you, isn't it clear that you're the helpmeet he had in mind?"

He piled up other arguments, impatient at her failure to recognize their command, demanding more prayer and self-examination. The Bible spoke clearly on the subject: "Whoso findeth a wife findeth a good thing." And "Wives, be subject to your husbands, as to the Lord, for the husband is the head of the wife as Christ is the head of the church."

"But we're not husband and wife," she said, "so they don't apply."

Another event of parallel importance to Graham's future, though he did not suspect it, was an invitation from the Christian Student Union, which sponsored religious services in a dozen or so small churches scattered across northern Indiana and Illinois.

"We want you to preach at one of our churches," they told Billy.

"Sure," Billy said.

"We'll send out a quartet for some special music."

"Good."

"You've got a car. We'll pay for the gas."

So young Graham, along with a quartet of gospel singers, drove off the following Sunday morning to deliver his first sermon since leaving the Southland. He was to learn later that he was chosen because he was the only preacher available who could provide his own transportation.

The Northern songsters brought back glowing reports. They had never been exposed to the pyrotechnics of Southern evangelism. Young Billy snorted fire and brimstone in the unrestrained manner he had learned down South and saw an answering glow come into the eyes of his small audience. When word of his success spread, invitations to preach piled up, but, motivated by a profound determination to give full time to his studies and get the best grades possible, he reluctantly declined all but a few.

At the end of the first semester, he sent home the best scholastic report of his career. His average grade was eighty-seven.

That spring he preached another key sermon. Wheaton's president had invited him to preach to the college congregation. He accepted and repaired to his third-floor rented room to beg God for help.

"I've never been a 'big brain,' " he told me once. "The preparation of sermons and articles has always been difficult. Even in recent years, when I am called on to give an address before a sophisticated or intellectual audience, I feel a sense of inadequacy and lack of preparation. I have to depend on God to help me. However, I find great strength in this dependency, and many times I've sensed that God is speaking through me, that it's no longer me speaking, but God. In a sense, I think this is what preaching really is: allowing God to speak through us."

The college audience included many professors and a few townspeople. Most of the professors were learned scholars and holders of doctoral degrees from great universities. On the appointed Sunday, young Graham faced them, his face shining, his whole being bristling with sincerity.

His sermon was not earthshaking, nor was it a failure. Helpful faculty members, recognizing a budding talent, were liberal with suggestions and compliments. And they paid him fifteen dollars.

At the end of his sophomore year, when he and Ruth separated to return to their homes, he was a marked man, knowing what he wanted to do, knowing that he wanted her to marry him, knowing that he must wait until she also was persuaded that this was God's will.

He departed, feeling confident of her eventual surrender. "I let God do my courting. I did not push or persuade," he says. "I was absolutely certain that if Ruth ever got married, I would be her husband."

He drove home to Charlotte and then on to Tampa, where he had promised to hold several meetings. As the weeks passed, Ruth and Rosa discussed her decision, covering the prospects of missionary life in Tibet again and again. Finally, her sister burst out with a powerful judgment: "You say God wants you in Tibet. Well, I doubt it. I don't think he wants you to be an old-maid missionary. I think he wants you right here in this country as Billy Graham's wife."

Ruth went to her desk and addressed an envelope to Rev. Billy Graham, Tampa, Florida. When she had written her acceptance, she walked out through the darkness to put it in a mailbox.

Billy opened Ruth's letter during a Florida revival campaign. He had no premonition that this letter was any different from others. But when he realized its import, he fell to his knees in thanksgiving.

That same month he answered a long distance call from Wheaton. It was an invitation to become the regular pastor of the college church. It met in a masonic lodge, it seated only three hundred, but it's congregation was lively, intellectual, and dedicated to God's work. He accepted. The small salary would help pay for his education. And perhaps by preaching to Ph.D's and listening to their criticism, he might absorb some of their wisdom.

That summer Billy arranged for his parents and Ruth to meet. The Grahams were attending a Bible conference at Blue Ridge, North Carolina, three miles from her parents' temporary home in Montreat. She went to the meeting, worried but calm. Frank and Morrow Graham pretended to be equally calm on that hot day chosen for the encounter. "I don't know what I was wearing, but I suspect it was a blue and white sheer organdy Swiss," she says.

They had polite words for each other, all of them knowing that much depended on this moment. The Grahams tested her Presbyterianism against their own rock-ribbed independence. They asked if she knew how to cook; they received a negative reply. Could she sew? She said, "I make all my own clothes." They tested her memory of biblical verses and found an amazing quantity of them packed into her pretty head.

When they separated, neither parent doubted that she was the ideal girl for Billy Frank.

The young evangelist-on-vacation next began a revival for his old friends and neighbors of the Sharon Presbyterian Church. The crowds grew night by night, and when the plate was passed on the final evening for a special love offering, it collected 165 dollars for Billy. He rushed to a jewelry store and bought a small diamond engagement ring.

In Montreat, Ruth's phone rang furiously. She expected no calls and answered it reluctantly. "I'm driving right over," Billy yelled. "Let's go for a ride."

When he joined her, he turned the car toward Asheville. After a while, he headed up a road to an Appalachian crest overlooking a tumbling world of forests and streams. He steered the car to the roadside and set the brakes. Without a word he took the ring from a pocket and slipped it on her finger.

"I pretended I didn't know what was going on," she says, "but I had a pretty good idea. Besides, I was absolutely thrilled."

That fall, he returned alone to Wheaton. Rosa Bell had developed a mysterious illness of the lungs—it was thought to be a kind of tuberculosis—so Ruth volunteered to skip a semester of school in order to attend her at a New Mexico sanitarium. The weeks passed slowly, though they wrote regularly.

That autumn of 1941, Billy's mind was pushing out in many new directions. The international situation, with its burden of human suffering and the prospect of America's entry into the war, overlaid everything. At the college, debate raged for and against isolation. A movement called "America First" was centered in Chicago, and it attracted many adherents.

In that atmosphere young Graham tried to rise each week to his duty of preaching responsibly to his college congregation. It was a stimulating and exhausting challenge, for he was coming up hard against minds which were broader and more experienced than his own. He soon learned to withhold an opinion until he had looked at all sides of the issue. He became aware of the impact of forceful declarations on persons without firm convictions. And he sensed the power a man could gain, in religion or in politics, by using emotional, superficial, and dramatic arguments.

Up to now he had known nothing of religious currents and movements outside the South, but nondenominational Wheaton was a cross section of geographical and theological interests. He heard, for the first time, excited talk about the Federal Council of Churches and its potential for good or evil. He learned, too, that wherever men try to work together, in business or in religion, tensions develop.

Jimmie Johnson, the young preacher from Bob Jones College, had also matriculated at Wheaton, and he and Billy roomed together. Johnson says it was a strenuous association, and it was made more demanding by Billy's recurring insomnia and his habit of practicing his sermons all night long.

Stanley High reports that Billy would frequently rout Jimmie out of bed, saying, "I've got to preach tomorrow night. You've got to help me." And Johnson would get up to help him with an outline. "And the next night I would go and hear him preach that same outline, and he'd do such a tremendous job, I'd sit there and takes notes on my own sermon," Jimmie reported.

Some of Graham's church members were Negro students whom he met in class and discussion groups. They were intelligent and dedicated Christians, and their presence began to give Billy some insight into the complex American racial question.

So now he was deeply involved in attempting to comprehend such diverse enigmas as the race problem, fascism in Europe, poverty in Chicago, and man's hunger all over the world. His room was littered with books and treatises. What with studying, preaching, and earning his living, he was under tension every night until the early hours.

He soon found he could not relax. In common with millions of other Americans, he became a chronic insomniac. We discussed it once in an Atlanta motel room.

"At Wheaton, that's the first time I really began to miss sleep," he told me. "I guess I'm built with tremendous nervous energy. It's like President Johnson. You can't be with him five minutes but what he's pushing. It's part of my personality . . . and of my physiology, I suppose.

"When I started traveling, I found that any change of

water or food or moving from one hotel to another ruined my sleeping and exhausted me in the daytime. I remember traveling with Grady or T. W. Wilson, and they could sleep at the drop of a hat. Next morning I'd be tired out, and they'd be fresh as a daisy.

"But I never took drugs. I just think I didn't know about pills in those days. The first drug I ever took was in 1954, while going to England. I couldn't sleep because of worry over a crisis that had broken out in Britain over my coming and because of the rolling of the ship.

"So the steward gave me Dramamine for motion sickness. I found it put me to sleep like a baby. When I got to England, I went to a chemist and bought some more. Later I had it analyzed, and I was told it was very safe but that it probably affected only about 10 per cent of the people in that way. So I still take some, though my insomnia has virtually gone compared to years ago."

At Wheaton his struggle to improve his mind exacted a price. But he developed successfully in other directions. For example, he smoothed down the cowlick in his blond hair, abandoned his habit of wearing high yellow shoes, and bought a new suit. The latter came about when a friend told him of bargains to be found on Chicago's Maxwell Street.

"But go early and bargain hard," he advised.

Billy scraped together a few dollars and drove into the big city. Maxwell Street was jammed with pushcarts. He found a clothing store and selected a suit.

"How much?"

The merchant asked three times its value. Billy offered one-third. They bargained continuously for sixty minutes during which Billy walked out three times. Finally, the exhausted merchant accepted Graham's offer, took his money, and pushed him out the door. Billy went back to school in triumph. His new suit had cost $4.95.

On Sunday, December 7, 1941, he retired to his room, as usual, to study his notes for the evening services at the Tab, as Wheaton undergraduates called their church. A friend came sprinting up the stairs. "The Japs have attacked Pearl Harbor," he announced.

Billy hurried to Professor Lane's home. All anyone knew was what they had heard on the radio. The Japs had thrown a "sneak punch" and caught our American forces completely by surprise. Already, half our Navy was disabled, and several thousand Americans were dead or dying.

It sickened him that war had come, but he shared the sentiment of the student body that the attackers should pay for their treachery. That night, he changed his text and preached on a subject that suddenly had a very special meaning. His talk was in three parts: Peace with God, Peace from God, and the Peace of God. "We can be in the midst of battle," he explained, "or in the midst of personal strife, but through God's love we can have peace in the heart."

Next day Dr. V. Raymond Edman, Wheaton's president, called an emergency meeting. Edman had been a doughboy in World War I. Better than any man there he knew the truth about war and what it would require of some of the students. He said, "I hoped this wouldn't happen, but we must give our loyalty and allegiance to our country and our flag. Many of you will be called. Some of you will die."

The meeting was emotional and nerve-racking. Many students wanted to enlist at once. Billy reviewed his personal qualifications. He was an ordained minister with considerable preaching experience. The chaplain's corps of the United States Army had already accepted several Wheaton graduates. He decided to apply for a chaplaincy.

The War Department responded with a counter suggestion: to win a commission, he must finish his college course and spend either one year in a church pastorate or three years in a seminary. When he was qualified, they would commission him.

His disappointment was tempered by Ruth's return to the campus for the spring semester. Together they planned their future as well as they could, considering the struggle in Europe and the Pacific. As the busy months passed, the scope of his activities increased: he was elected to the highest student office; he took over Streater's trucking business and its yellow truck; and he undertook enough outside preaching chores to become almost self-supporting.

Grady Wilson, with whom he had gone forward at Reverend Ham's revival in Charlotte, unexpectedly joined him as a Wheaton senior. He had resigned only a few days before his graduation from ultra-conservative Bob Jones College for reasons of conscience. The two North Carolinians now had a chance to renew their friendship while they studied and they also double-dated the two girls who would become their wives.

In January of 1943 Billy watched his friend win his degree, and a touch of envy pricked his heart as he realized that he had yet another season of grinding study. Outside Wheaton's walls of ivy the war in Europe was causing grief to many American families. A vast ministry called, and he yearned to get into it. When Grady began to preach, his unrest increased. When Grady married in nearby Chicago, Billy made a private decision. It was not too soon to think of his own wedding day. He and Ruth would graduate in June of 1943. If all went well, they could marry that summer.

That wartime commencement was a ghostly, unreal ritual. Members of the Wheaton graduating class, including Billy and Ruth, had other things on their minds. "Hail, Alma Mater" was being heard less and "The White Cliffs of Dover" more.

The effect of the war was everywhere. Allied forces had just won a bloody victory in North Africa, and the world was waiting for General Eisenhower's next move. An old friend would come home for a day or two, tanned and muscled in his soldier suit, and then vanish without even a good-bye.

Ruth and Billy, along with the others, accepted their diplomas, knowing that every male faced an undetermined number of years of military service and that every girl faced potential heartbreak. The big question was no longer how to earn a living; it was whether to marry now or wait.

Billy's personal plan was firm, by courtesy of the U.S. War Department. They would commission him as a chaplain after a year as a pastor. He already had the pastorate. It was a Baptist church in a nearby village called Western Springs, Illinois.

The congregation numbered eighty-five. The salary would be forty-five dollars per week. The arrangement was ideal, permitting him to take advanced anthropology courses at the University of Chicago and perhaps some advanced Bible study. The arrangement seemed ideal, that is, until he told Ruth about it.

The cause of the impasse they reached was simple. Ruth felt strongly that equal partners should consult each other in all important matters. Surely the location of their future home was important. In her view they should have discussed it, prayed about it, and settled it together.

Billy agreed wholeheartedly, but he had acted without thinking—a habit of young men not accustomed to double-harness—and now it was too late. He had given his word. Much prayer and large helpings of forgiveness were required to mitigate his offense. It was an object lesson he would never forget.

Eventually, they moved on to other vital matters: their wedding, for instance. Ruth chose Friday, August 13, 1943.

When she asked an old family friend if he would be free to perform a marriage ceremony on that date, he responded, "What fool is getting married on Friday the thirteenth?"

She said, "I am."

They were married in the Presbyterian resort community of Montreat, North Carolina, at a small stone church called Gaither's Chapel. By now the Bells had become prominent local citizens. Billy was merely the lanky boy from Charlotte that nobody knew, probably an odd ball, too, because it was whispered he had switched denominations, from Presbyterian to Baptist.

Billy says, "I remember their stares. Fortunately I had a clique of my own. My ushers were my old friends Jimmie Johnson, Grady Wilson, Roy Gustafson, and my brother Melvin. I stuck close to them, because nobody ever felt more superfluous."

It was an evening service, under a full moon. The Rev. Kerr Taylor, Ruth's lifelong friend, and the Rev. John Minder, Billy's mentor at Florida Bible Institute, read the ceremony. Andrew Yang, a Chinese friend, sang, and Sophie Graham, no relation of the Charlotte Grahams, played the organ. Bridesmaids were Jean, Billy's young sister, and Sandy Yates, an old schoolmate from China. Maid of honor was sister Rosa, now completely recovered.

Ruth wore a shimmering satin gown, not store-bought but made, with Ruth's help, by a local seamstress. To maintain its perfect smoothness, she *stood* as best she could in the back seat of her father's car during the drive between home and chapel, and it must be reported that no bride ever walked down an aisle with a smoother skirt.

When they had said their vows and been doused by showers of rice, they drove up the Blue Ridge Parkway to a honeymoon village in the shadow of Grandfather Mountain. Billy had sixty-five dollars for spending money. When it was gone, the honeymoon would be over.

Chapter Sixteen

By Labor Day, Billy and Ruth were installed in their first home, a small furnished apartment on the second floor of a house in Hinsdale, Illinois, four miles from his pastorate in the adjoining town of Western Springs. The walls crowded in on them, and the furnishings were threadbare.

"Any regrets?" Ruth asked.

"This is the greatest thing that ever happened to me," he said.

They drove to Western Springs to see "their" church. The structure was a weathered concrete foundation rising nakedly from yellow clay. No steeple, no walls, nothing but a basement foundation with a tar-papered covering on which a box, looking something like a doghouse, provided ventilation for the interior. The entrance was a musty passageway leading down to an underground door.

Billy said, "They built that foundation years ago and ran out of money. So they put seats in their cellar and called it a church. How do you like it?"

Any structure dedicated to God was to be honored, and any project in His behalf, no matter how difficult, would succeed through work and prayer. Ruth drew a deep breath and answered, "I think it's beautiful."

Several months earlier, Billy had suffered an identical shock. He had visualized a white steepled edifice rising above the rooftops of suburbia. This church had no steeple, no roof, no walls. But he recovered quickly and threw his extraordinary energy at every problem in sight. Committees were appointed to knock on doors and bring in new members.

"But we've got such poor accommodations," his deacons said.

"Christ preached in the fields and streets."

"We're only a neighborhood church."

"Then bring in your neighbors," he urged. "Knock on doors and invite people to come with you. We'll treat them real good."

"Our membership is so small."

"Christ started with only twelve."

As the weeks passed, his determination warmed his small band. Twice each Sunday he preached sermons that ended in a call for rededication and repentance. It was the way he had preached in the South, and he sensed an uneasiness in some of his flock. A part of every congregation believes that its pastor should speak reassuringly, run a good Sunday School, call on the sick, and do little else. A warning voice said, "Don't press these people too hard. They're accustomed to easy religion."

One day he met a hustling deacon on the street. "Why do you work so hard at your business?" Billy demanded.

"To make a living for my family."

"Then you're a sinner," Billy cried. "You're a sinner until you work *first* for the glory of God and *then* for the benefit of your family."

"Well, maybe I didn't say exactly what I meant. . . ."

"God comes first!" Billy said sternly.

He chided them with such warmth and so openly that none took offense, and many expressed agreement.

That winter he and Ruth lived on a budget so small that he often walked the four miles between apartment and church to save gasoline money. His path ran along a high

187

railway embankment where cinders blew in his eyes and down his neck, but neither these nor drifted snow impeded the flow of his planning.

"We'll have a men's club," he thought. "Every important church in Chicago is undergirded by a loyal band of men."

His deacons were skeptical. "We're so busy, Billy. We don't think we've got enough men to count on." A few said the idea was unsound and studded with difficulties and that heads of families would not give up one evening a week. Besides, where would they meet? Billy said, "Let's pray about it."

On newly printed church stationery, he wrote letters inviting famous generals, statesmen, politicians, scientists, and ministers to speak to his group at a dinner-meeting to be held in a famous Hinsdale restaurant called "The Spinning Wheel." Several acceptances came back. He worked them into a schedule, announced dates, and invited the entire community to participate. Before long, two hundred men were in regular attendance.

Within six years those same men would erect a beautiful, sacred edifice as a result of the impetus they received during Billy Graham's first year of leadership.

With Ruth as a working partner, he involved himself in one project after another.

He hurried out to the University of Chicago and registered for postgraduate work in anthropology, determined to earn his master's degree.

He recruited Sunday School teachers and began to build up his church school.

He agitated for new hymnals and more special music and invited visits from nearby Wheaton College quartets and soloists.

He reinvigorated a building committee. "We've got a roof," he said. "Let's get some walls under it and a steeple over it."

He started a savings account with five dollars from each forty-five dollar pay check. But it never grew.

And he never did find time to attend his anthropology classes.

Before marriage, most of his dates with Ruth had involved campus activities and church services. They really knew remarkably little about each other. Many problems of adjustment and mutual accommodation arose, were faced, and resolved. Their formula could well be copied by today's young newlyweds.

Ruth once told me how they divided their chores, telling a story about a farm couple. "A farmer asked his wife to help him plant corn one day," she said, "and while she was planting, he noticed that she was dropping too many kernels in a hill. So the farmer said, 'Woman, don't waste my corn like that.' To which she replied, 'I'll do as I please.' And the farmer said, 'No, you won't! You'll do as I say, because this is my territory.'

"Well, she gave in, and they finished the day's work and walked into the house. She said, 'Henry, have you wiped your feet before you tramped into my clean kitchen?' He said, 'No, I ain't.' And she said, 'Well, you git right out there and do it now.' And the man did, because that was her territory."

Any young couple faces periods of trouble and disagreement. Considering this situation healthful, Ruth repeats an aphorism she once heard: "If two people always agree, one of them is unnecessary." Measured by their early disagreements, both Ruth and Billy were *very* necessary. They did not fight, but both were outspoken about their principles.

Billy says, "We came from entirely different backgrounds. She was born and reared in China. I came from the South. I don't think we could have made it except that our marriage was built on a spiritual basis. When we faced a problem, we faced it in prayer.

189

"Very soon we realized that this year in Western Springs would be hard for both of us. Ruth's heart was still in Tibet, and mine was in evangelism; and there we were in that little church basement all because I had to get a year's experience before the army would make me a chaplain. My deacons understood this—I'd made it very clear—and they were wonderful about it."

Of course, Ruth's sister Rosa Bell, close by in Wheaton, was a frequent visitor. On special occasions, if they had spare money, they would all go to dinner at The Spinning Wheel. At home, the cupboard was mostly bare. "We never hurt," Ruth says, "and compared to most of the world, we were sitting pretty. But I tell you we didn't eat steak."

Billy would occasionally be invited to preach out of town by old Wheaton or Tampa friends. If ticket money was at hand, he would accept because it broadened his experience and his vision of religious work. Once he went out to Elyria, Ohio's First Baptist Church, and arrived with twenty-one dollars, a twenty-dollar and a one-dollar bill loose in his pocket, enough for a return ticket.

During the service the usher passed the plate to the ministers—something Billy had never experienced—and he had to reach hastily into his pocket for a contribution. He pulled out a bill and put it in the plate, almost simultaneously realizing that it was actually his twenty-dollar bill. Now he was left with only one dollar, not enough for his ticket home. To make matters worse, he had left Ruth in a hospital, recovering from a sudden illness, and she would be there, with a mounting medical bill, until he returned.

He says, "That twenty dollars was not a very cheerful gift. Reluctantly, I committed the money to the Lord, reminding myself of his promise that it would be returned manyfold. At the end of my visit, those good church people

190

handed me a railway ticket back to Chicago plus a check for ninety-five dollars."

In a remarkably short time, the Grahams came to what must now be one of the most remarkable partnerships in the history of marriage. As testimony, this is Graham's description of Heaven: "When people used to ask me what Heaven was like, I tried to describe it as pictured in the Book of Revelations. Now I think . . . it is like being married to Ruth."

He gives the credit to God. "If you're a Christian, I think God has the ideal person picked out for you. And if you don't wait for God's choice, you get his second and third best. I feel that God had Ruth picked out for me long before we met. And this means that, whether or not we loved each other or agreed on everything, we knew that our marriage was God's will, and that's the greatest seal against separation or divorce you can have. If you know you have that, you don't need to know any more."

The newsman in me had to ask, again, "But how does ordinary Joe Doakes know?"

"Well, it's hard to explain . . . it's so subjective. There's that little voice that seems to say, 'This is it.' Deep inside, you *know* it."

I reminded him of Oscar Wilde's quip, "A man can be happy with any woman so long as he doesn't love her."

He said, "I believe that marriage can be built on the spiritual level and that it provides the strongest possible tie. Before we were married, we didn't have any wild, passionate love for each other. Ours was a spiritual thing; we had found an affinity for each other. We knew we'd be partners for a lifetime. The ecstacy developed after marriage. Now our love has deepened because it was built on the right foundations. We've never been unhappy one day since our marriage. Never once has either of us given a thought to leaving the other. We know with certainty that we were God's choices for each other."

One slight problem remained unsolved, however, and it is still not settled. Glenn Daniels discusses it in his little book, *Billy Graham, the Man Who Walks With God*. The Grahams were at dinner with Dr. Torrey Johnson, a prominent Chicago minister who had taken an interest in the novice pastor. Johnson had organized a mushrooming Midwest Bible Church on Chicago's North Side, and established a popular religious program called "Songs in the Night." He asked Billy what he meant to do after the war.

"Billy said, 'Whatever the Lord wants me to do. I expect he'll let me know as time goes on. . . . When the world settles down, I'd like to go to theological school. There's so much I've got to learn.'

"Johnson considered it. 'Theological school? I wonder about that, Bill. I've heard you preach, and it seems to me you've already got plenty to say. The pulpit—that's where you belong. Stay there and preach.'

"Billy shrugged, not wanting to make an issue of it at the dinner table. He tried to make a joke. 'I ought to learn some theology. I'm married to a woman with a degree in theology, and I ought to be able to hold my own with her. . . . The trouble is that she's a Presbyterian theologian.'

"Johnson was surprised and amused. 'Presbyterian, are you?'

"Ruth smiled and nodded, wondering where the conversation would go.

"Billy said, 'Before I had a church of my own, we used to alternate, going to a Baptist church one Sunday and a Presbyterian church the next, just to keep peace. I haven't got any money, but I'll pay a hundred dollars to the person who can persuade Ruth to be baptized by immersion.'

"Johnson looked at Ruth with open affection. 'I don't think you'll ever have to pay out the hundred, Bill. But
192

then a fiery Baptist needs a cool-minded Presbyterian on his team. There shouldn't be too much trouble in your house.' "

For many years Graham has felt that arrangement is ideal. "It's really an asset," he says. "When I was starting out, it gave me contact with Presbyterians, and people began to see that I wasn't just a narrow be-dipped-or-be-damned Baptist and that I had a broader concept of religion if I would allow my wife to remain a Presbyterian."

One evening during that first year at Western Springs, Billy got a phone call which, in his words, "was destined to be a turning point in my ministry."

It came from his old friend Dr. Torrey Johnson.

He said, "Billy, I'm doing too many things, and I've got to slow down. Would you and your church consider taking over my radio program?"

The offer startled young Graham, but he thrilled to its possibility. "How could we swing it? We're still under a hundred members."

"Well, you think it over, and we'll talk again."

He discussed it with Ruth. Two problems bothered him. Could they raise the money? Was he sufficiently seasoned to become God's spokesman to a large audience scattered over many states?

"I'm afraid I'm not ready," he reported to Johnson.

"Who says so?"

"It's my own decision."

"Will you discuss it with your board of deacons?"

Chairman of the deacons was the young publisher, Robert C. Van Kampen, who had talked Billy into accepting the Western Springs pastorate. Billy reminded him, "The air is already full of preaching. Our competition would be powerful."

"But your preaching is different. I think thousands would listen."

They hurried to a special meeting of the board. The other churchmen listened to their story and asked, "How much would it cost?"

"Air time costs $600 a month," Billy said.

They laughed loud and long and voted "no."

Afterwards, Billy remembered that long-ago prayer meeting at the Tampa Bible Institute in which students and faculty had prayed all day long for ten thousand dollars, and how the mail had brought it. He argued with himself:

"This offer is against common sense," he said, "but it's real. Something led Torrey to this church, out of the hundreds he knows. Goodness knows, we could use extra money to increase our building fund and put a first floor over our basement. If this program could bring in contributions, it would be a Godsend. Maybe . . . maybe this is really God's hand at work."

Refusing to be discouraged, he visited his board members one by one, presented his thoughts, his arguments, and asked if they would help with a pledge for the first month. He was soon able to call Torrey Johnson and complete the deal.

The prospect of preaching from a radio pulpit both humbled him and brought on two important decisions. First, his delivery would be different from the weary voices heard on some religious broadcasts. Second, he would use a simple, short message.

Preparing his first sermons, he wrote them around this outline: the Bible says that God is a God of love. In order for there to be love, there must be an object to love. So God created man.

Then God gave men the freedom of choice. Wanting man to love Him of his free will, He told him there was a fruit in paradise which he should not eat. If he did, he would die. Man ate the fruit, rebelling against God. That rebellion was sin.

Sin is a disease of the soul. Man's soul is his intelligence, and it will live forever. The Bible says that it was created in the image of God, but that sin separates it from God. Despite man's hunger for God, he cannot contact Him because of sin.

One day, God looked down from heaven and saw all the trouble in the world. Loving men, He wanted to do something to help, but He was too big and men were too small for them to talk to each other. So He did an astounding thing. God became a man named Jesus Christ who walked among us and spoke our language.

After a while, having explained God's way for men to live, Jesus went to the cross to die. He did this to take onto His shoulders all the sins of mankind. He suffered and died for all men. He was buried in a grave, but He did not stay there. In three days He rose again to sit at the right hand of God, where he waits to intercede for anyone who comes seeking Him.

Though Christ took the hell that men deserve, a man must still do certain things for himself, if he is to enter the Kingdom. The first thing is to *repent*. The Bible says, "Unless ye repent, ye shall likewise perish."

The second thing is to *receive* Christ. One receives Christ by inviting Him into his heart as Lord, Master, and Savior.

The third thing is to *obey* Christ. One obeys Christ through living by the Ten Commandments and the Sermon on the Mount, and by reading the Bible, spending time in prayer, witnessing for Him, and being faithful to His church.

Repent . . . receive . . . obey!

The same message has since been poured into the ears of uncountable millions all over the world.

Having decided on his message, Graham thought out its delivery. Not big words, not soft sentiment, not the holierthan-thou tones of some radio ministers—these were barred by his concept that religion was exciting and significant. Listening to news programs, he found that the most commanding voice belonged to Walter Winchell. Winchell spoke with electric energy, throwing his words like punches, fast and hard. Billy decided to use a fast, punchy radio style.

He also needed a singer, a man's kind of singer with a deep, virile voice. Only one person in Chicago qualified, and his name was George Beverly Shea.

While still a Wheaton student, Graham had heard Bev Shea sing on WMBI, the famous station of Chicago's Moody Bible Institute. One night when John Charles Thomas came to the campus to give a concert, Billy sat a few rows behind Shea and admired his he-man bigness. He also admired his voice, even preferring it to that of the famous visitor.

In 1943 Shea was program manager for WMBI, a busy, important, hard-to-see man. Young Billy set out to land him for his "Songs in the Night" series. What transpired is perhaps as classic an example of why Billy Graham achieves his objectives as will ever come to light.

He went to Shea's office and was received by an efficient secretary. Did he have an appointment? Well, no. . . . What company did he represent? Well, none at all. . . . She was explaining how busy Shea was and how he had no time for unscheduled appointments when the big man's door opened and was left ajar for a few moments. Billy had sold brushes to reluctant housewives, and it occurred to him that this reluctant secretary could be handled in the same way. He put his foot in the door.

He says, "Then I walked in and asked Mr. Shea to come to our little church and sing on our new program."

Startled but impressed by the zealous youth, Shea put him off. Billy argued with him, face agleam with urgency,

Southern charm dripping from every pore. It's not a thing he turns on or off, it's an atmosphere in which he moves and lives, causing many persons over the years to agree to a wide range of improbable projects.

In the end Shea agreed that he would attend the first of the "Songs in the Night" broadcasts.

Graham says, "And Bev Shea and I have been together ever since."

Results from the first month of broadcasts were not spectacular, but they did enlarge his audience. People in eighteen states began to write letters and send small checks of appreciation to Billy Graham, Western Springs, Illinois. One night, in a fit of appreciation, he added a benediction to his broadcast, saying, "May the Lord bless you real good."

And the mail response increased. By the end of their second month, the program was self-supporting.

Thus, the precursor of a much more famous program was born. Currently, Graham's "Hour of Decision" girdles the globe. It presents the songs of Bev Shea and a fast-talking Billy Graham, though in recent years he has modified the headlong pace of his sermons. And people continue to write letters and send small checks of appreciation. Last year their contribution amounted to many millions of dollars.

Among Torrey Johnson's reasons for unloading his "Songs in the Night" program was his great concern for the thousands of footloose soldiers, sailors, and airmen who were roaming Chicago's streets each weekend. Already, his mind was working on a program to give them something better to do than frequenting dance halls and looking for pickups. A day would come soon, he knew, when the war would be over and millions of young men would be thrown back into civilian life in strange cities.

Elsewhere, other leaders were worrying about the same problem, and many of them began to organize fun nights for young people. In New York a Christian orchestra leader named Jack Wyrtzen was filling a Times Square auditorium with happy servicemen. In Philadelphia a youthful pastor named Walter Smythe was building up a following. In Minneapolis George Wilson, a young layman connected with Northwestern Schools, had assembled an active group of thousands. Their rallies were frequently different in the means used to attract an audience, but all were alike in their Christian emphasis.

Torrey Johnson decided that the need in Chicago was so great that he could not wait for a finance committee to solicit funds. Instead, he called together a group of ministers and laymen, mortgaged his home to raise cash, and hired Chicago's famous three-thousand-seat Orchestra Hall. The project was called "Chicagoland Youth for Christ."

Again the phone rang in Graham's small apartment. Johnson told Billy about his plan to reach servicemen and other young people who were not churchgoers. "I want you to be our first speaker," he said.

Billy was astonished. He was a rank beginner with no "name" value to attract people to a rally. He had never talked to more than a few hundred persons at once. "What kind of talk should I give?"

Johnson said, "I want you to preach a sermon, give an invitation, and win people to Christ."

Billy began his preparations with prayer and meditation. Soon the grapevine told him that Johnson was being criticized. Chicago had many famous pastors any one of whom could draw a crowd and deliver a stirring message. Johnson retorted that he wanted an evangelist. Critics asserted that evangelism was dead. Billy offered to withdraw, but Johnson stuck to his guns.

On the appointed night every seat in Orchestra Hall was filled, and Billy Graham was gripped by the worst stage fright of his life. He had never seen so many faces or tried to talk in such a large hall. He had preached to brush arbor and streetcorner crowds, and he knew how to make those audiences listen to God's message, but these thousands were different. Most of them had never heard an invitation from the pulpit. They were the "un-churched." Would they recognize Christ's urging?

After hymns, patriotic songs, and Scripture, Billy was introduced, and he began to preach with that mixture of apostolic fervor and country-boy humility that would become his trademark. Folding his leather Bible into a club, he banged out his points, punctuating with his long arms, striding about on his long legs, until every young face paid him rapt attention.

He says, "My sermon was about the feast of Belshazzar. It was a pouring out of thoughts which seemed to establish their own sequence by themselves. As my nerves relaxed, I felt again that I was merely a mouthpiece. Soon I forgot all about the audience. When I gave the appeal, forty-two young people responded."

Newspaper reporters were amazed at what a band of organized young people could do, and their stories brought large audiences to subsequent meetings. Suddenly, Youth for Christ chapters were springing up all across the country, holding Saturday night services, most of which were a cross between a revival and a hootenanny. Billy spoke at many of them.

In Europe and Asia the war was calling for more soldiers. Billy could not forget that he owed a personal debt to his country. When he finished twelve months as pastor in Western Springs, he applied again to the War Department for a chaplaincy. They accepted him, gave him a physical examination, and handed him a military commission. He bought an officer's uniform and a lieutenant's insignia. Thus, in July, 1944, he was a member of the Army of the United

States, soon to be assigned to a regiment, probably one going to the South Pacific. He would first attend chaplains' school at Harvard University.

Waiting, he flew to Providence, Rhode Island, to address a conference of young people. He had never visited New England, never seen the Atlantic Ocean. It was a memorable meeting at which he received compliments and was treated with deference. In a way he was becoming favorably known, thanks to his radio program and his appearances at youth rallies. His euphoria and good cheer lasted through the onset of pain which began on the way home.

He has told the story of his sudden collapse in *McCall's*. "Ruth took my temperature when I reached our small apartment, and it was 102 degrees. The doctor came and gave his verdict. I don't know which was worse, the pain or the embarrassment. I was twenty-five, a commissioned officer, a reverend pastor of a growing church, and I had the mumps."

He was desperately ill for six weeks.

One night, with his fever at 104, his mind wandered into such a disordered state that he began to describe the scenery. Ruth recognized enough of his talk to know that the vision in his mind was heaven. He described it in such great detail that she concluded he was dying, but his strong constitution and a resilient nature slowly fought off the infection.

However, as he recovered, he found that his plans were in disarray. He was as weak as a newborn puppy and almost as helpless. His weight was down so that he looked like a walking skeleton. His lieutenant's uniform hung from his broad shoulders in grotesque folds. In a few days he was expected to join his chaplain's class at Harvard. At the same time, his physician assured him that recuperation would require rest and quiet for several months. And Ruth, having served as wife and cook and nurse day and night for six weeks, was exhausted.

He laid out a careful program, keeping it simple, amenable to the attention of a man who could take only one weak step at a time.

First, he must postpone his army service.

Second, he must take Ruth away for a short vacation.

He wrote the Chief of Chaplains in Washington, explaining his collapse, and he received a response that unburdened his heart. They would cancel his school assignment until he was entirely recovered.

He looked into his savings account, searched through old pockets, and estimated the amount of money he could raise toward getting into a warm, restful climate. "Fly now, pay later" had not yet become an American transportation policy. Then the unbelievable happened.

Throughout his illness "Songs in the Night" had gone on the air regularly, presented by helpers and associates. Naturally, Billy's illness had been mentioned, and his condition was being followed by thousands of concerned listeners. One of them was a businessman who lived in the next town, La Grange, Illinois. He sent Billy a note: "I want you and your wife to take a vacation in Florida." And he enclosed a check for a hundred dollars.

"How strange and mysterious are God's ways in our lives," Graham says. But for that illness, he might have gone into the armed forces as planned and risen to high rank, as many of his friends did, or he might have perished on Okinawa, Leyte, or the Rhine.

Instead, his attack of "epidemic parotitis," usually called mumps, led him to Florida, to another conference with the ubiquitous Dr. Torrey Johnson, and to his participation in a globe-girdling scheme to evangelize the world's youth. In turn, this would lead to the "team" concept of spreading the Gospel and eventually to his memorable barrier-breaking revival of 1949 in Los Angeles.

But we are getting ahead of our story.

Ruth and Billy Graham motored to Orlando, Florida, and called on an insurance executive named Don Mott whose house guest was—Torrey Johnson.

Their visit was brief and social—old Chicago friends getting together in central Florida—but they made a date to meet again in Miami Beach. Torrey's manner was a little mysterious, they thought. "He's up to something," Billy concluded.

The folklore that has grown up around the evangelist relates that he and his wife moved into a Miami Beach hotel, that they found themselves by accident in the same hostelry as Johnson, and that Johnson told Billy, "You're just the man I'm looking for." The truth is more interesting.

Actually, they took a three-dollar room a few blocks away from a 79th Street hotel where Johnson was quartered. When Billy telephoned him, Torrey said, "Glad you're here. I want to take you fishing."

"When?"

"Right now."

It was a fishing expedition like none other, an "old pro" minister fishing for a "rookie" minister, using a line that would eventually reach across oceans and using a hook baited with God's grace.

On the tossing Gulf Stream, Johnson painted a vivid picture of the social dislocation that was bound to grow in America the moment the war ended. Mothers who had worked in factories would lose their jobs. Teenagers who had expected to go into the army would find themselves unwanted and on the loose. Farmers who had gone to work in war plants would shift to other jobs or return to the farm.

Johnson's remedy was a coast-to-coast pattern of Saturday-night rallies conducted by young pastors and laymen. He thought he could get his own church to let him work half-time at organizing a national body. He planned to raise money and open a central office in Chicago.

He looked Billy in the eye. "Will you come in full time as evangelist and organizer?"

"I was immediately enthusiastic," Graham recalls.

But three practical problems interfered. He was committed to the Army. He had a full-time job in his Western Springs church. And he had Ruth, a wife whose expectation of married life included spending some time with her husband.

He set about resolving them, and the effort most likely speeded up his recovery. A letter to the Chief of Chaplains, couched in the most persuasive phrases he knew, told of the mobs of rootless, mischievous youths to be won for maturity and good sense and perhaps to the worship of Jesus through young people's rallies built around a revival sermon. Where would he be of greater service, in a regiment—with the war all but won—or helping to pick up the pieces of lives broken by war and confused by peace? He asked for an official decision.

Another letter carried the story to Robert C. Van Kampen, chairman of his Western Springs board of deacons, asking if the church would release him. He even recommended a replacement, a former Wheaton roommate, Lloyd Fesmire, who was available.

And Ruth helped Billy write these letters. Together they pored over their Bibles, always at hand, and searched for the solution to their dilemma through its pages. What now was God's will?

Scripture told them that God endows men with different kinds of talent. "And he gave some apostles and some prophets and some evangelists," they read.

For over five years, as Ruth knew, Billy had steeped himself in the lore of evangelism. One of his favorite Scriptures was, "Preach the word; be instant in season, out of season; reprove, rebuke, and exhort."

They discussed the Bible's clear endorsement, how evangelism was mentioned fifty-two times, how Paul and Philip were evangelists, and how all the original disciples, on being driven out of Jerusalem, "went everywhere preaching the Word."

Many great evangelists had come not from theological seminaries but from humble circumstances. John Wesley was an Anglican priest, Paul himself was a tentmaker. Dwight Moody had been a shoe salesman. Billy Sunday was a ballplayer and a YMCA worker. Young Graham felt qualified by origin and training. And he believed that God had given him an evangelist's talent.

He and Ruth remained in prayer in their three-dollar room. If the Army would release him, if his church would release him, then Ruth, too, would release him to evangelize wherever God pointed, and she would patiently await his return with faith and steadfastness and love.

Chapter Seventeen

"What do you know about a go-for-broke outfit called Youth for Christ?" The man on the phone was Dr. Kenneth Wilson, managing editor of *The Christian Herald*.

I said, "Billy Graham helped start it. I think he's still a vice-president."

Wilson said, "I've got a report they've pulled ten thousand teenagers into Washington, D.C., for a national convention, and they've held over 250,000 rallies in their fifteen years. That sounds like a good story."

My research into the origins of Youth for Christ, Incorporated, and my talks with men who had known Billy Graham when he was its only full-time employee at the outset of his career gave me insights into his maturing, without which I would never have understood much of what he has done.

Long ago an Irishman gave Graham and his young YFC associates the name of "God's Commandos." They have certainly earned the title. Today Youth for Christ is diversified in its program of youth activities, but its early velocity and subsequent impact can be attributed to Torrey Johnson, Billy Graham, and the other first leaders.

At Graham's request, the Army gave him an honorable discharge, as did his Western Springs church. Ruth says, "We broke up our Hinsdale home with no trouble, no heartache. We tossed our pots and pans into the back seat of our car and drove off. We didn't own a stick of furniture."

She knew that he would be traveling continuously for many months and that he would not spare himself. She moved into a second-floor bedroom in the home of her parents in Montreat, North Carolina.

When Graham and Johnson started Youth for Christ as a national organization, they were facing up to one of the saddest oversights in present-day Christendom. As a YFC president, Dr. Ted Engstrom, would say later, "Our churches were crowded with children and adults, while the teenager remained the forgotten man in Christ's great commission."

A survey revealed that three out of four teenagers had never read the Bible.

Rev. Louis Evans, pastor of the First Presbyterian Church of Hollywood, said, "Twenty-seven million youths in this land are as destitute of religious training as though they were born in the South Seas."

Billy recalls, "The year was 1945, and I stood on the threshold of a religious and social revolution. The world was changing, and I was changing. When I walked into our Youth for Christ office that first day, it was still without a desk or chairs, but I experienced an unprecedented excitement. Somehow I knew this was where I belonged."

As Billy and Torrey walked down Wells Street to their newly rented quarters, their immediate problems were these:

Will money come in to support us?

Will young people respond to our invitation?

Can we persuade leaders in scores of cities to cooperate with each other to turn Youth for Christ into a great national force?

Can we pioneer new ways of reaching young people?

Will our effort result in teenagers being "re-born" and turned around to become practicing Christians?

Torrey said, "We're sure starting on a shoestring."

Billy pulled his thin coat around him. His Florida tan belied the weakness in his knees. "I've always lived on a shoestring. But this I promise: we're gonna grow fast."

"Your salary's guaranteed by a good friend who believes in our work," Torrey explained. "Another man promises to pay all your traveling expenses. Beyond that, it's up to you."

They turned into a doorway and went upstairs to a room so airless and ancient that even the paint appeared to be sagging. Billy's eyes saw dust and cobwebs and dirty windowpanes.

"This is it," Johnson said. "What's your first order of business?"

"First thing is to buy a bucket, some soap, and a mop," Graham said. "After that, we'll tackle the world."

It is time to scrutinize the folklore surrounding the young leader and to make these observations: first, if some self-directed youth were to decide today that he was called to change the world, what qualities and what facilities would he need?

Obviously, he would need energy and belief in himself.

Billy was born with energy, and his athletic, outdoor life undoubtedly renewed it. From his high school days until now, he has possessed phenomenal drive.

Second, he has believed in himself and in his ability to achieve the extraordinary, because he has experienced such achievement time and again. He is the proof of that truism which states that the most important element in teaching young people to lead is to provide opportunities for leadership. Napoleon said it better when he stated that "every soldier carries a marshal's baton in his knapsack."

Moreover, Billy had faith in God, absorbed through daily participation in the religious observances of his childhood and cultivated in his years of maturing. He understood that he was called by Christ, hence set apart, and that God answered prayer; and he knew that such a person, if filled by the Spirit, could not fail, because God was in command.

But there is more to becoming a national force and an international celebrity than personal qualities. One needs facilities for "the multiplication of the executive self," as a corporation consultant has put it. He needs a kind of supporting cast which, being like-minded, is moved to expand and extend the leader's instinctive program, to advise, to consult, but chiefly to carry out and carry on.

And ultimately he needs a structural organization with its intimate, internal lines of effort and discipline and communication, so that a few men become as a mighty army. To build such a group has been the design of every true leader since time began. General George C. Marshall, chief of our World War II forces, once told me, "One man is one man. Two men working in complete harmony are four times as effective as one. Three men are nine times as good. Four men are sixteen times as strong, five men are twenty-five times as powerful."

The Twelve who followed Jesus must have known that.

1945. Mark the year. During it Billy was to meet and work with many men who added to his vision and outreach, all of them concerned with young people and their spiritual destiny; and two of them, George Wilson and Cliff Barrows, were to become his closest friends and co-workers.

In many U.S. cities, young leaders were emerging spontaneously to put a new zing into religious activities for young people. The old-fashioned Young People's Unions, Epworth Leagues, Christian Endeavors, and Pilgrim Fellowships were appropriate to another day, not to VE-day minus three months. Modern YFC rallies were tagged and advertised by such names as "Youth-o-rama," "Quizzerama," "Spookerama" (for Hallowe'en), "Funspiration," and "Weirdstown." Many of them combined the features of a college pep session, amateur night at the Bijou, and a revivalist camp meeting. But their primary purpose was always to win a hearing by teenagers of God's Word.

Their first responsibility was to draw a crowd, their second, to deliver God's message. They used music, famous athletes, and stunts and promoted their sessions, as though they were Gene Autry rodeos, with advertising and publicity. They invariably outgrew the churches in which most of them began and moved to larger quarters in municipal auditoriums and ball parks.

One ingenious leader invented a "Spacerama" and pretended that he would take everyone to Mars. In the hall each boy and girl was fastened in his seat with a paper safety belt. Rockets decorated the platform. The toastmaster was the "Master of Spacemonies." Every song referred to the "Great Beyond." The Bible message was called "An Out of This World Talk on Eternity."

Many rallies involved a contest: for the best boy preacher, best boy song-leader, best vocal trio, best instrumental trio, best memory for Bible verses. Contestants invented uniforms that ranged from Comanche war paint to Hottentot headpieces.

It was corny, it was mad, it was fun, and it was much more, too. Youth for Christ was a ministry, not a shindig, as demonstrated by the creed they adopted in 1945. Some of its tenets were:

"We believe the Bible to be the inspired, the infallible, the authoritative word of God. . . .

"That there is one God, eternally existent in three persons, Father, Son, and Holy Spirit. . . .

"We believe in the deity of Our Lord Jesus Christ, in His Virgin Birth, in His sinless life, in His miracles, in His vicarious and atoning death through His shed Blood, in His bodily resurrection, in His ascension to the right hand of the Father, and in His personal return to glory and power."

Martin Luther could not have asked for more.

Finding the right speaker to deliver their message was often a problem, and Billy was swamped with urgent invitations. To assist ministers who took part in the programs, young leaders sometimes handed them this printed guidance:

"This is not a church service but a different kind of approach altogether. Dwell on the positive aspects of salvation, and leave doctrinal hobbies alone. We must preach the Gospel and let indoctrination be the job of the local churches. State clearly how to be saved. Don't poke fun at the local church and the pastor. We pray that we may aid and supplement pastoral work, not compete with it."

In the above, at least one of the columns upholding Graham's subsequent crusade program was erected. "We don't go anywhere unless we are invited by the local churches," he says. "We seek the united support of all denominations and pastors, and we refer all our inquirers to the church of their choice."

Speakers were also encouraged to talk man to man, even boy to boy, with slang and vernacular replacing sesquipedalian utterances. One youth evangelist began with this opening:

"Sitting there with your mortal hulk draped over that chair, or wherever you are, my friend, you are *lost*. You plan to be an upright, honest, ever-lovin' citizen. Great! But you could become the world's number one Who's Who and still be heading straight for hellfire and brimstone. Get what I mean? Being lost means you are separated from God. Salvation is what God has provided through the death and resurrection of His Son, the Lord Jesus Christ. How do you get salvation? Brother, the Bible lays it on the line so simply it takes only a 'yes' to make it yours.

"First, realize that you are lost, a sinner.

"Second, face the fact that God has provided salvation for you.

"'Third, receive by faith that salvation.

"'Will you do it?'"

Their program produced results. In the YFC archives that Billy Graham himself established are hundreds of case histories. One tells about a boy named Ted who looked his alcoholic father in the eye at the breakfast table and said, "Please wait a minute 'till I ask a blessing." And the father snapped back, "I'll do no such thing." So the boy prayed silently. It happened each morning for months. One day the young minister whose rallies had converted Ted got a phone call. "I'm Ted's father," the faltering voice said. "I want to tell you that I'm swearin' off drinking. I want to accept Christ. I've seen what He's done for my boy."

After one rally another leader was visited by a twelve-year-old girl who wanted to join his Bible club. She was a working prostitute, she said, and her weekend earnings were as high as a hundred dollars. The club treated her as they would any sinner, praying for her singly and as a group. Where others had avoided her, they offered friendship. During a later rally, she went forward to repent her sins and accept Christ.

In Texas a liquor store owner was shot dead by three youths. They got away, leaving no clues. Mel Larson tells the end of the story in *20th Century Crusade:*

"One day one of the three men walked into the Houston city hall. With him were two young ministers. He confessed the hold-up murder. Police doubted his story, but the facts fitted. The two other young men were picked up.

"Why had he confessed? What had brought him hundreds of miles back to Houston to make a clean breast of things?

"At a Youth for Christ rally in San Diego, California, twenty-year-old John Robertson had accepted Christ as his Savior. He knew he had to make things right, no matter what the cost."

Despite thousands of conversions, despite clear evidence

that young Graham's rallies were straightening out a host of confused young people, a good many pastors could not adjust to the new climate. George Wilson tells of a trip he took into the Southland with a male quartet from Northwestern Schools. Their purpose was to sing at arbor meetings and revivals. Rooming in private homes, they sang at night and spent idle afternoons in a private swimming pool at the edge of town.

One day a minister delivered a stern warning. "Your behavior is hurting your testimony," he told them.

"What behavior?" George asked.

"Why, because of that hell hole you go to every day."

"What hell hole, sir?"

"I mean that swimming pool at the edge of town with it's mixed bathing."

In 1944, the same year that Billy Graham was winning his spurs as a small-town pastor and regional broadcaster, a powerful youth movement was emerging in Minneapolis under Wilson's dynamic guidance. In his twenties, he had already established a booming book store and publishing business, become assistant to Dr. W. B. Riley, president of Northwestern Schools and also pastor of the city's influential First Baptist Church. His dedication to righteousness can be measured, possibly, by the fact that he also drove sixty miles each weekend for more than four years to serve as lay preacher for a small church in Clinton Falls, Minnesota.

The youth movement that he founded in the sanctuary of the First Baptist Church quickly outgrew its 2,500 seats, and Wilson and YFC had to move to the city's auditorium, which would hold ten thousand.

His initial invitation to Billy was accepted and then abruptly canceled. Billy had the mumps. His second invitation named a day in mid-winter. Billy accepted again, although he could not imagine that anybody would come to a rally in Minnesota's below-zero temperatures. He reckoned without young Wilson's promotional skill, a talent subsequently formalized in a helpful booklet entitled *Thirty-three Ways to Promote a YFC Rally*.

He called his rally a "Singspiration," and his drawing card was music and more music, musicians and more musicians. A newsman dubbed it, "the poor man's opera." An attractive feature that regularly pulled in large crowds was a night named for some sizeable town within a one-hundred-mile radius. Automatically, it guaranteed publicity and musicians. On the appointed evening, he bussed the town's high school band into the city to play an opening concert, and they invariably brought along a large cheering section plus a sprinkling of parents. Meeting them at the city limits with a police escort, he rushed them through traffic lights (to their pop-eyed amazement), gave them a tour of the Post Office Building, herded them through a downtown cafeteria, and escorted them to the civic auditorium where they were welcomed by a mayor named Hubert Horatio Humphrey. Their passage was usually sufficient to inform all within hearing that something remarkable was happening.

As a special annual attraction, Wilson thrice borrowed 102 pianos from every piano store in the twin cities, deployed them around his stage in a piano symphony orchestra, and gave standing-room-only concerts on Saturday and Sunday.

Striking a different promotional note, for three years he organized the world's largest smorgasbord, one particular year feeding 2,497 youngsters for $1.25 each—three less than his guarantee of 2,500—before marching them into a special section of reserved seats for the rally. Another time, with the thermometer registering ten degrees below zero, his auditorium was filled by over ten thousand young people, with almost half again as many turned away.

When Billy Graham arrived in Minneapolis to preach at Wilson's rally, he was still worried about the crowd. But not for long. Great floodlights slanted through the sky, and the auditorium was lit up as if for a Hollywood opening. That night he saw the largest audience of his lifetime when he faced eleven thousand teenagers. To that date it was the largest assembly in YFC history.

The consequences of that evening were to be incalculable. First, he met George Wilson and became intimately aware of his organizational wizardry and energy. "He's got more bounce to the ounce than any Christian I know," Billy said later.

Second, he became involved in the ambitions of a "gray-haired old Christian warrior"—these are Graham's words —Dr. W. B. Riley, George Wilson's boss, described as a man who, at eighty years of age, had succeeded at everything except turning back the clock. Riley was looking for a successor.

He invited Billy to return soon to Minneapolis to address the students of Northwestern Schools, which he had founded, and to preach from the pulpit of the First Baptist Church.

Billy was profoundly flattered by the saintly old man's interest, and he agreed to hurry back. He had no idea that the wily old gentleman was plotting, in his single-minded way, to redirect young Graham's career into education rather than soul-saving.

Next day Billy flew on to another rally, to another sleepless night—for insomnia was plaguing him now—and to tiresome but necessary committee meetings. Exhorting, raising money, counseling confused young people who hung on his words, he gave all he could and then tried to find within himself resources to give more.

The days were exhausting, but they were precious in

that they fortified his knack of inspiring and deputizing. Already, he had started carrying a briefcase full of books to occupy the many sleepless hours during which he continued the studies he had begun in college. This was a habit that would endure throughout his lifetime and cost him a pretty penny in airline overweight charges.

That July of 1945 he and some associates landed at an airport outside of Asheville, a few miles from Montreat and Ruth. In western North Carolina, July is Bible-assembly time. Ministers, missionaries, and religious workers assemble in those cool valleys to recharge their spiritual batteries, and now Billy was among them, invited to present a Youth for Christ service at a conference sponsored by the Columbia Bible College. He had accepted because it brought him back home—if Ruth's second-floor room in Dr. Nelson Bell's house could be called home—but he also wanted to get Ruth's opinion on several ideas he was polishing up for use around the country. Most important, perhaps, he wanted to show her off to his YFC associates and to prove his boast that "she's so pretty she gets wolf whistles even on Bible college campuses." Moreover, she was several months pregnant.

On the day set for his meeting, a large crowd gathered. For some reason Billy's YFC song-leader failed to arrive. Because music was an important feature of his service, he asked if an experienced leader might be found among the persons attending the assembly.

A friend said, "There's a honeymoon couple here from California. He's just out of Bob Jones College, but he's had some experience. She's a pianist, and he plays a trombone."

Billy said, "This is no job for an amateur."

But no one else was available. So young Cliff Barrows and his wife Billie were called from the audience and brought to Billy shortly before the meeting. One can imagine the two men sizing up each other. Graham, the lean football-end type; Cliff, the burly fullback; Graham, the blond; Barrows, the brunet; both possessing extraordinary vitality.

Then the service began under Barrows' warm guidance, and the sound of joyous voices led by a velvety trombone filled the Blue Ridge. As choir and audience responded to Cliff's breezy western manner, the old hymns never sounded better. Listening and watching closely, Billy must have recalled other evangelistic teams whose exploits fill the history of revivalism: John Wesley and his brother Charles; Moody and Sankey, whose evangelizing shook the British Isles and the United States; and Billy Sunday and Homer Rhodeheaver, the latter another trombonist.

"Barrows is good," he told himself. "We need his kind in Youth for Christ." Later they talked about that and formed a partnership of unsuspected significance.

A month later, a score or so of young YFC leaders from eight states and twenty-one cities met in their own first international convention at Winona Lake, Indiana. First, they asked each other pointed questions:

How can we help one another?

What new wrinkle in promotion builds crowds best?

What help are local churches giving? What opposition?

What is the best blend of hoopla and Scripture?

Point by point, they hammered out answers, defined their beliefs, and elected a slate of international officers. Full-time president was Torrey Johnson, the international vice-president was Billy Graham, the international secretary was George Wilson. Within two years, there would be a thousand YFC's meeting in a thousand cities.

British youth leaders sent them a message urging the dispatch of a task force to introduce Youth for Christ to Great Britain. Johnson accepted the invitation, and a team was designated, including Billy Graham.

216

They were to leave the next spring.

From Montreat, Ruth wrote that her time was near and asked Billy to come home a few days ahead of schedule. He promised. Then a friend asked him to preach in Mobile, Alabama, at a two-night stand. By his calculation, he could do it.

The inevitable Western Union wire reached him in Mobile. Ruth had been rushed to an Asheville hospital where she gave birth to a girl. Billy got home two days late and helped name the child Virginia, for Ruth's mother. The Chinese-speaking Bells gave her their own loving nickname, calling her Gi-gi, which is Chinese for Little Sister.

In his personal life, Billy had heard himself criticized as a "Christian gypsy." He had lost weight steadily and had been warned by worried physicians to slow down. His reply was invariably, "I cain't! The world's on fire, and I've only got a bucket of faith."

He only had a bucket of faith, but in those days he was also building his bucket brigade.

Beverly Shea, a rising singer, had been his first recruit.

Cliff Barrows, an emerging song-leader, had joined the movement.

In Minneapolis, George Wilson was back at his job at Northwestern Schools, but he was also waiting in the wings.

Meanwhile, Graham's day-by-day bouts with YFC organizational problems were multiplying his own capacities. Soon, in England, he would need talent of a different sort.

The team selected to visit Europe as representatives of Youth for Christ International consisted of Torrey Johnson, as leader, Billy, Charles Templeton, and Stratton Shufelt, the singer. William Randolph Hearst's International News Service ordered Wesley Hartzell, of its Chicago office, to go along and report the story.

On a Sunday night in March, 1946, over four thousand young persons jammed themselves into Chicago's Moody Memorial Church for a farewell service. Dr. Harry Ironside, pastor, gave a prayer of dedication. Earlier a going-away meeting for the team had been held in Detroit with eighteen thousand youths packing Olympia Stadium.

On the cold, rainy morning of March 18, 1946, Billy, Torrey, and their companions boarded a plane for England. Nobody in Chicago had ever seen a departure like it. A thousand teenagers gathered in the rain to sing hymns and say good-bye. Many knelt in prayer beside the plane. Radio mikes picked up Billy's farewell message and broadcast it throughout the West.

A mechanic asked, "What's this all about?"

"Some young preachers are going to England."

Billy's voice boomed through the rain. "Please pray for us," he begged. "We need your prayers. We need 'em real bad."

As the rain came down, a brass band gurgled through "Blessed Be the Tie that Binds."

Twenty-four hours later, he and his team were under military arrest in Stevensville, Newfoundland.

Perhaps "arrest" is not quite accurate, if one thinks only of bars and cells, but their confinement was real. What happened when their big C-54 landed in Newfoundland was inevitable, given a collision between a military mind and a quartet of zealous soul-winners. Future historians may decide that the event had no relevance to the evangelist's career, but I think it illustrates an initiative that the modern church has sometimes lost and which Graham has helped to revive.

The story, a tragi-comedy, begins when their storm-bound craft landed at an emergency base in Newfoundland. The boys went into a makeshift restaurant, hungry and full of enthusiasm. When they learned that they would be grounded for hours, somebody said, "Why not hold a service here for these soldiers?"

They telephoned the social director, who agreed to cooperate. However, she misunderstood the nature of their "show," swearing later that she thought they were members of a USO troupe. She rushed ahead with single-minded energy, sending out word of a sudden, special program. When the movie theater was jammed with eager servicemen, she stopped the regularly scheduled movie and waved her "entertainers" onto the stage.

All except Torrey were embarrassed. By now they knew the social director had misinterpreted their telephone conversation. Templeton spoke first, and the audience assumed he was a come-on for the girls. Shofelt sang "Short'nin' Bread," and a puzzled restlessness spread through the theater. Several men began to boo. Billy was next.

"I stood up and said I was going to tell them what had happened to me a few years ago when I was converted," he recalls. Now it was clearly evident to the audience that this "entertainment" was not from Broadway but from the Bible. The boos got louder.

Part of the audience clumped out. But as Billy talked, those who remained became quiet. When he finished, they departed in glum silence.

The commanding officer of the base was furious, claiming that he smelled a missionary effort to proselytize his men. Mincing no words, he ordered the evangelists grounded until he had completed an investigation. They were assigned quarters and told to remain there until called to testify.

Wesley Hartzell, Hearst newsman, stepped forward. He assured the colonel of the good faith of his traveling companions. He did not tell the colonel, though he could have, that his story, if published by the powerful Hearst press, could make that officer look very ridiculous indeed and cancel forever his hope of becoming a general. Instead he spoke of justice and mercy, and the military mind agreed to relent and forget.

When their airliner was ready to take off, the YFC team was escorted aboard.

Next day they met with youth leaders in London's Bonnington Hotel, prior to preaching engagements and youth conferences that would take them, in six weeks, through Scotland, Ireland, England, and Scandinavia.

Young Graham felt the strong pull of history as he walked through English streets. London was massive and bustling, but he got the feeling that it had become a spiritual cemetery. World War II had recently ended, and the city was still disfigured by heaps of rubble and bombed-out buildings.

Once, the now sickly capital had been the crossroads of the world, and its citizens had initiated great social movements. Here Henry VIII had divorced church and state, and himself from Catherine of Aragon. In Great Britain, George Fox had established the Society of Friends, John Knox had established Presbyterianism, and John Wesley had laid the foundation of Methodism. Here John Smyth had lived before he crossed the channel to establish the first Baptist church in Holland.

Billy saw in London the Baptist Church House once associated with John Bunyan, who had written *Pilgrim's Progress* as well as an engrossing description of his conversion.

"At some times I could feel my very body, as well as my mind, to shake and totter under the sense of the dreadful judgement of God," said Bunyan. "I felt also such clogging and heat at my stomach, by reason of this terror, that I was, especially at some times, as if my breast-bone would have split asunder. Thus did I wind, and twine and shrink . . . so that I could neither stand, nor go, nor lie, either at rest or quiet."

220

Conversion was the core of Graham's evangelism, but British pastors seemed to know little about it. One young prelate said, "If we had an old-fashioned Puritan conversion in one of our churches today, it would scare the vicar to death."

Always an eager listener to the strange accents he heard, Graham learned much that surprised him. England might be exhausted and poor, but her Christians possessed a Christian quality that Americans lacked. They could discuss their faith in specific terms, without fumbling, without embarrassment. If only their young people could be stirred, he felt, the harvest would be great.

"I determined to come back as soon as possible to conduct a series of evangelistic campaigns," he says.

He submitted his plan to Torrey Johnson, who agreed to help raise expense money. In America, Youth for Christ had succeeded best after moving from meetinghouses to auditoriums and ball parks. Young British leaders, men of energy and imagination, volunteered to form committees to help take the word of God out of half-empty churches to wherever the people were.

When Billy left for the U.S.A., plans were under way for a nonstop British crusade of twenty-seven revivals in twenty-seven cities in twenty-seven weeks. But where could he find the money?

Dashing about the United States, he infected everyone with excitement about the opportunity afforded by England, and he begged for help. It came in dribs, in drabs, in checks for a hundred dollars from a real estate man, in pledges for three thousand dollars from a group of Gideons. By autumn he had raised eight thousand dollars.

Cliff and Billie Barrows shared his vision and agreed to accompany him back to Britain. George Wilson cleared his busy schedule for six weeks and volunteered to go along to help get things started.

When they landed in England that October, they began

following a route that repeatedly crisscrossed the British Isles. Fortunately, they could not know at the outset to what depths or heights it would lead. Committees were already at work. Graham and the team focused on their objectives:

First, to win people to Christ.

Second, to encourage the churches of Great Britain.

Third, to help organize Youth for Christ rallies.

Fourth, to learn all they could from their British friends.

A town committee usually met first with George Wilson, the team's advance man, who was responsible for persuading local ministers that the meeting should be held in a public auditorium. Dipping into his own Minneapolis experience, he further advised them on advertising, on cooperation among the community's churches, and on the use of music and song to boost participation. A dozen advance campaigns were soon humming as silkily as any YFC "Singspiration."

"Britain in those days was dark and grimy," Graham recalls. "Food was still rationed. No cleaning fluids were available, so clothes were still dirty from the war. The blackouts and brownouts continued, so that at night everything was pitch black. Also, it was the coldest winter in a hundred years, and little fuel was available. However, the spirit of the people was not only remarkable, it was fantastic. Their smiles, their faith, and their courage were a lesson that I will never forget."

The maturing Graham's knowledge of people deepened almost daily, as he met one amazing character after another. One was an elderly Manchester man who had lost three sons in the war. His house had been destroyed by a bomb. His wife had died of a heart attack during a bombing raid. But when he met Billy, he said, with a smile on his face, "Rejoice, brother. The Lord is risen."

222

As always, Graham preached "for a decision." He had come to Great Britain to turn men around, to see them "born again," by the moving of the Holy Spirit. Years earlier, British evangelists had regularly given their altar call, crying out, "Fall down! Fall down!" Falling down, in that era, was the accepted symbol of human surrender. Now almost no pastors preached rebirth or asked for a public acknowledgment of Christ. Most sermons had become lectures. Billy persisted in demanding a decision, asking for the raising of a hand or for a brief walk to the altar.

The harvest surprised the Americans and astounded their English collaborators. Billy recalls, "From the beginning, the meetings proved to be far beyond anything we had ever imagined."

In Belfast a twelve-year-old dead-end type stopped him on the street. "You're that Yankee preacher, aintcha?"

"Yes, I am."

"I want to know, sir . . . can a feller like me be saved?"

"Anyone can be saved if he's sorry for what he's done and is willing to follow Christ."

A townsman said, "That lad's a bad one. Leads a regular band of sneaks. You'll not see him again."

But the young gangster came to a service and accepted Jesus, and then he helped convert sixteen other juvenile delinquents. Finally, he led a big man to the altar to pray with the others. The city had posted a police detective to watch the gang, and now he had surrendered, too.

The subsequent march of events was chronicled in *Christian Life* by Donald E. Hoke. "When the conservative Londoners got over the shock of the loud clothes and bow ties, they jammed heatless St. John's church . . . and four hundred persons professed conversion in a week.

"In Edinburgh, Graham was forced to don an ecclesiastical robe, and with red bow tie protruding from the surplice, he mounted the high pulpit one Sunday to preach a simple Gospel sermon. At the pastor's suggestion, an invitation was given, and eighty-two came forward, including several church officers.

" 'You're here to pray with some of the penitents?' the vicar asked one church elder. 'No,' he sobbed, 'I've never been converted.'

"In Newcastle-on-Tyne a tall, turbaned Negro came forward during the invitation. After confessing Christ as his Savior, he revealed he was a university student and the son of a Nigerian chief. 'Now I want to take the Gospel back to my own people,' he said, beaming."

What moved so many so greatly? Certainly, the American approach was vigorous and different. Meetings were organized ahead of time, many churches in a community were involved so that the revival became a joint effort, choirs were selected and rehearsed in advance and given intensive training by Cliff Barrows prior to the first service. Graham's informal style and simple message attracted many.

His willingness to face hardship won respect, too. He preached in one unheated Anglican church so full of fog that he could see only about two-thirds of his audience. In each city, in order to save expense money, they rented rooms in homes or accepted the hospitality of local laymen. In Wales they lived in a room so cold and furnished with bedclothes so flimsy that he and Wilson—or perhaps it was Barrows, he cannot remember which—slept together in a single bed for warmth. Their host, a miner, earned less than ten dollars a week. This was the best he could offer, and the young evangelists were grateful.

This British experience was surely a time of seasoning, of maturing. Like clay hardening in the fire of a baking kiln, his flesh and spirit were being "fired" in the give and

224

take of personal experience. Three incidents illustrate the process.

Without warning, arrangements for the use of a public hall in Birmingham, England, were canceled. Influential clergymen of that community had apparently agreed with newspaper accounts which referred to Graham and Barrows as "those Yankee upstarts." The blow sent Billy to his knees. When he rose, he asked his helpers to arrange a meeting with his principal critic.

A young evangelist is a bundle of emerging talents. He must be as logical as a lawyer, as tactful as a diplomat, as magnetic as a sales manager, as humble as a busboy, and also possess the knack of turning mountains into molehills. Arriving in Birmingham, he was met by a young worker and taken to meet the city's most powerful clergyman.

Billy came to the point at once. "I'm not here to argue the use of the Birmingham auditorium," he said. "My purpose is to lay our objectives before you, so you will know what we are trying to achieve."

The churchman inspected the slender, towering young man with the luminous blue eyes. His parchment face gave no sign as he put his fingertips together and said, "I'll be glad to listen, Mr. Graham. Please tell me all you think I should know."

Billy asked, "Could we pray together first, sir?"

Later, when Billy emerged from that encounter, he had won a supporter and an influential friend. Billy visited every other critical clergyman in turn and told the same simple story. As a result, the auditorium was made available to the revival committee again, and there were no dissidents among the clergy.

A youth leader asked an opposing minister, "Why did you change?"

"I was opposed because we already had plenty of soul-winners in Birmingham," the pastor said. "But when Billy called on me, I ended up wanting to hug that twenty-seven-year-old boy. I called my church officers, and we disrupted all our plans for the nine days of his wonderful visit."

On other occasions all the fates seemed to conspire against them. Once in Redding, near London, Billy's microphone balked in the midst of his sermon, so that many in the crowd could not hear. Minutes later, a platform chair collapsed with a crash like thunder, depositing its overweight occupant full-length on the floor. Next, as Billy was making his final point, a local minister stood up in the midst of the audience and shouted, "I don't believe a word of it. You're preaching the doctrine of Rome." His wife pulled him down. A lady several rows away answered him, and the ensuing argument, carried on at the tops of their voices, stopped the meeting cold. Billy asked the ushers to remove the protesting minister, but by now the audience was in no mood for an invitation, so he ended the service by asking those who wanted to accept Christ to go directly to the nearby prayer room. The harvest numbered 150 souls, including the son of a Baptist preacher, a prostitute, the scion of a noble family, an eighty-two-year-old man, a sailor, a soldier, and scores of others.

The third difficulty he encountered was more of the flesh, less of the spirit. In Dublin, where he and Cliff were holding a revival at the invitation of Irish Protestant ministers, he became seriously ill. His home in the rain-soaked city was a small hotel standing hard against a seawall over which waves splashed all night long. As the rains came down, his fever went up. The long campaign had already drained much of his strength and reduced his weight. This attack dropped him as if poleaxed.

Cliff Barrows, assisted in the music department by his wife Billie, assumed the burden of preaching. The meetings continued with mounting attendance, while Billy Graham huddled miserably in his damp bedclothes. If

226

ever he faced discouragement, this was such a time, for an additional burden suddenly dropped its weight on his shoulders:

He and Cliff were out of money.

A quick reckoning of the situation showed three more months of scheduled campaigning. Several bills were already overdue. They would need another seven thousand dollars to complete their mission.

They racked their brains, exploring sources on which they might draw. Seeking money for the Lord's work, laymen learn, is a holy task from which ministers of the Word cannot shrink. But to whom could they turn? The Youth for Christ office in America could not help. Praying hard, Billy became aware that a name had slipped into his consciousness, that of the American philanthropist-businessman, R. G. LeTourneau.

He quickly composed a letter describing their plight and dispatched it. When he was able to travel, they spent their last cash for tickets to London, the scene of their next meeting. En route, they prayed hour after hour. The old pattern of that memorable Florida Bible Institute prayer meeting was being repeated again, as their faith reached out to find God's will.

Arriving in London, they were handed a letter from Mr. LeTourneau. "We hardly dared open it," Billy says. "With our hearts in our mouths, we finally did, and inside was a check for seven thousand dollars."

They completed their itinerary, preaching four Protestant sermons in Catholic Paris during the Christmas season. Graham then recuperated in the sun of the Riviera (nursed by Ruth, who had decided that her husband needed her for the moment more than her daughter, whom she left with her mother). They were back soon enough, however, slogging their way through the remainder of a dismal English winter.

When, in March, he prepared to leave England for America, the "upstart" evangelist heard himself praised in extraordinary terms:

The Lord Mayor of York said, "Last night's meeting was one of the finest exhibitions of religious programming I have ever watched. It can lead Britain back to God."

The *Christian Magazine,* a Manchester periodical, said, "Not only is Billy Graham a great evangelist but also a mighty teacher of the Word. He holds a Bible reverently all the time he is speaking."

The Rev. R. M. McMillen said, "I expected platitudes, but my soul was stirred almost to bursting to be out and about to win young people to Christ. We have seen a revelation. . . . Billy Graham's challenge is the greatest I've ever heard in my life."

And the Bishop of Birmingham, the city in which Graham had met the greatest trouble, invited him to address a general meeting of his Church of England diocese on the subject of modern evangelism. Such a move was unprecedented, but it was also a measure of the religious growth of the twenty-seven-year-old Carolinian, and one day the implications of that precedent would be realized in the physical presence of the Church of England's highest prelate, the Archbishop of Canterbury, on Graham's platform.

In the spring of 1947 the YFC team returned to America, and every member of it knew that he was looking at his homeland through different eyes. "My spiritual life had deepened," Billy says. "I was beginning to understand what it means to lead a daily, victorious life in Christ. I had found a new cutting edge to my preaching."

Moreover he and Cliff Barrows had perfected their way of working together until it was an instinctive and harmonious whole, which it remains to this day. Both of them believed that the ten thousand converts whose confessions

228

they had witnessed in England were but the forerunner of a world revival. Both were confident that the methods they had used in England could be applied to city-wide revivals throughout the United States.

And, although no evangelist had dared undertake such a task for many years, they were itching to try it.

Chapter Eighteen

"To everything there is a season, and a time to every purpose under heaven . . . a time to plant, and a time to pluck that which is planted."—Ecclesiastes III

For twenty-eight years, the young evangelist had planted with all his energetic enthusiasm. And "everything came up roses." But in 1948 and 1949, clearly a time for plucking that which had been planted, he found himself beset by three separate dilemmas.

The first involved a great-hearted effort to turn his work from evangelism to Christian education.

The second was the consequence of several inadequate revivals that he and his team conducted, of outright failure (and the lack of God's blessing) in several key American cities.

The third was a spiritual weakness that gradually devastated his mind, growing from—in his words—"serious doubts concerning the authority and inspiration of the Scriptures."

This last perplexity reached its peak in 1949, driving him to intensive study of the Bible, to prayer, and to an ultimate surrender that surely accounts for much of the force he eventually acquired.

A contemporary historian cannot peer into any man's mind, but he can put two and two together. From the evidence, from observation, and from my unique interest in and collaboration with his work, I believe that Graham's escape from these refractory problems was one of the most exciting dramas in recent religious history.

Its first scene was laid in Minneapolis, the home of the Rev. William Bell Riley.

Dr. Riley was a scholar and a man of action. He saw Billy Graham once, he heard him preach once, and he decided immediately that this Southern youth with the flaming sincerity and great organizing ability should be his successor.

To succeed such a man as Riley was no small honor. William Jennings Bryan once called him "the greatest Christian statesman in the American pulpit." He had also been a battler for social improvements in his native Minneapolis. Yet, no matter how bitter the battle, he never held a grudge. He was a powerful preacher and a skilled administrator.

Mrs. Riley reported later, "In Billy Graham, I think he saw himself sixty years ago." His judgment was unerring with regard to the young evangelist's potential. Unfortunately for him, the fire that burned in Graham was nourished by a fuel the great old man could not understand.

He repeatedly made his hopes known to Billy, who refused to take them seriously. Then, finally cornered, Graham answered with a flat but polite "Thank you, no!" So the astute old preacher chose to bargain for half a loaf:

"Give three days a week to your evangelizing," he said. "Spend the remainder of your week at Northwestern."

"Sorry, sir, no!"

"Think it over. I'd like to have your decision so we can announce it at the 1947 commencement."

They corresponded fitfully, with Billy writing, "I've sought to discern the will of God. . . . May I have until July 21?"

231

Another letter was written in July, saying, "I have been waiting for Heaven's signal. I have not received it. . . ."

In midsummer, Billy opened a telegram summoning him to Minneapolis to Riley's bedside. The old crusader, near the end of his strength, was calling for him. As he hurried to the Riley residence, an August thunderstorm broke, pouring its torrents onto the darkling city.

Graham says, "I'll never forget the darkness of his room, broken only by flashes of lightning, and the bony finger he pointed at me as he said, 'You are the man to become my successor, and I will not be content until you give me your commitment.' "

Reportedly, the veteran minister then opened his Bible to First Samuel which told of the Prophet choosing a king for Israel among the sons of Jesse. Each was examined and rejected, until finally the youngest named David was summoned from a hillside. " 'He was ruddy and had beautiful eyes and was handsome,' " Riley read. " 'And the Lord said, "Arise, anoint him! For it is he." And the Spirit of the Lord came mightily upon David from that day forward.' "

No one will ever know what thoughts pounded through Graham's brain when the old Doctor added, "Beloved, as Samuel appointed David, I appoint you head of these schools. I'll meet you at the judgment throne of Christ and tell you how well you've done."

Such a prophetic injunction was beyond Graham's immediate power of resistance. So he compromised, agreeing to act as interim president in case of Riley's early death.

Billy says, "He dropped back on his couch with a sigh of relief. Then we had a prayer together, and I left him with trouble in my heart."

As always, he took his problem to Ruth, this time by telephone and by letter, and heard her dissect it with unfeminine logic. With all her persuasiveness, she counseled against it. Later she told me, "I felt it was a sort of trap. I just don't believe that any Christian has the right to point his finger in another Christian's face and say 'This is God's will for you.' Each person has to discover God's will for himself. We can advise, but we cannot state categorically that this is it."

Soon it was October, nothing had been decided, and a minister in Grand Rapids, Michigan, was on the telephone. Billy had decided to hold his first American revival in the furniture city.

Thus act two began. Few of his projects have been less likely to reach a happy ending.

He and Cliff were eager to conduct a revival, perhaps too eager, in a typical American city and to employ the organizational and doctrinal features they had utilized in England. Friends in Grand Rapids had invited them to "open" in the Michigan city.

Graham had formulated a kind of creed which, if British experience could be trusted, would bring success. It required:

1. Cooperation by a city's ministerial association.

2. Involvement in the campaign by many church congregations.

3. An unprecedented use of printing, publicity, and advertising.

4. The earnest use of consecrated music to prepare restless souls.

5. The supplications of countless Christians on their knees in prayer.

6. A simple Gospel message adorned with Gospel texts geared to the times.

In Grand Rapids committees had been appointed to obtain city-wide participation. They succeeded partially. Although some fundamentalist congregations gave their support, many churches abstained. Newspaper publicity was almost nonexistent. Advertising was inadequate. The period of prayer preparation was too brief.

The first meetings were poorly attended. Midweek crowds continued low. Only at the weekend was their attendance large enough to warrant moving the service to the civic auditorium. By the time word got around that a wonderful revival was being conducted, the campaign was over. Their converts numbered many less than expected.

What change in God's plan could this failure indicate? Graham studied his campaign like a defeated general. His errors discovered and spotlighted, he humbly asked God's pardon and promised not to make the same mistakes again. The next campaign would be more firmly managed, and the next would be in his own home town of Charlotte, North Carolina.

Older residents still remember his arrival. For weeks ahead of time, citizens had been urged to get out and greet the "home-town boy who had made good." Working the local angle, the appeal was distributed by the campaign committee through every conceivable medium. They broadcast radio spots, placed cards on restaurant tables, shoved leaflets under hotel room doors, and strung banners across the principal thoroughfares.

When Billy, Bev, and Cliff arrived, they were joined by Grady Wilson, now a successful pastor in Charleston, South Carolina. A reception committee of VIP's, plus a silver cornet band, met them. Next, they all marched through the crowded business district. Though local eyes blinked at the attention given this stripling of a preacher, only the ungracious were critical. This was Billy Graham's homecoming and a community's tribute to a boy who, not long ago, had delivered their morning milk.

A local headline read, "Boy Preacher of Charlotte Gets Welcome." A decade later a reporter attended a subsequent Charlotte crusade. Sixty churches had supported the first one in 1947. Nearly nine hundred supported the second. He wrote, "Then they watched a gaunt, twenty-nine-year-old stringbean; today they see a tanned, silky-smooth Graham who is breaking all records."

His homecoming revival made newspaper headlines almost every day, and Billy's sermons were reprinted word for word. Cliff Barrows' choir, as well as his neckties, became the talk of the town. A National Guard armory was their tabernacle, and its three thousand seats were occupied night after night. In three weeks, twelve hundred new converts confessed Christ, and two thousand church members renewed their dedication to the Lord.

In December Dr. Riley took to his bed for the last time. A phone call soon came for Billy, asking him to preach the old warrior's funeral.

In Minneapolis the board of Northwestern Schools expected him to redeem his pledge that he would act as interim president until a suitable replacement could be found. Facing the college's trustees, Graham said, "My role as an educator is not clear to me. If I'm certain about anything, it is that I'm called of God to win souls. I haven't the power to alter this. So I must tell you that Dr. Riley's proposal is full of danger for you and for me."

They asked him to take the presidency for a trial period of six months. This he accepted.

So at the age of twenty-nine he found himself filling three jobs. He was the administrative head of a group of three schools (a liberal arts college, a Bible school, and a seminary) with eight hundred students, he was the international secretary of Youth for Christ International, and he was a crusading evangelist.

His first task as the new administrator was clear. Northwestern's treasury was almost empty.

In a few hectic weeks he strengthened the staff with the full- and part-time help of several aggressive associates borrowed from the Youth for Christ organization. T. W. Wilson, his old chum of Fuller Brush days and Grady's brother, became his vice-president and principal assistant. George Wilson (no relation), recently Riley's assistant and the college's business manager, brought his administrative acumen to bear on finance and management.

Together with the old faculty and staff, they reviewed courses and gave extra emphasis to mission work and evangelism.

They opened the only radio station in America devoted full time to religion.

They raised money for better faculty salaries, more classrooms, and a larger endowment.

They moved from their musty quarters to a million-dollar structure begun by Dr. Riley.

They attracted important speakers to their campus, not only scholars and preachers but Christians who were also judges, senators, and businessmen. The formula that built his first men's club in Western Springs, Illinois, still worked.

One day he received an urgent call from the Mission Hospital in Asheville. Doctor Bell and Ruth were there awaiting the arrival of another child. He flew south and arrived at the hospital while Ruth was still in labor. Sinking wearily into a waiting-room chair, he fell asleep. Later someone shook him awake.

"You're the father of a girl baby," Doctor Bell told him, smiling. "And your wife is doing fine."

A remodeled cottage with a two-crib nursery awaited them. Ruth had bought a tumbledown structure across the street from her parents' home. Their resources were strained to raise the purchase price of four thousand dollars, but the Billy Graham family was becoming too large to impose further on the Bells.

"I'd been looking pretty hard for a place," she told me once, "because Bill was on the road, and I felt we needed

236

a place of our own. I don't know whether we found it together or not. It was a vacant summer house across from Mother and Daddy, on a corner lot with a little stream on it. We ran into some problems, but we finally got it. And then it cost so much more than we could afford. Fortunately, it turned out to be a good investment."

Ruth Graham is a great house-changer, with a passion for early mountaineering furniture. "We bought soon after the war when it was still hard to get materials," she continued. "We paneled some of the walls inside with wood and covered the house on the outside with stone. It was charming. I'm still crazy about it."

Graham's salary had been raised to one hundred dollars a week. They had two children and a mortgage. But at least Ruth's parents were across the street, potential baby-sitters.

When he took Ruth and tiny Anne to their new home, he gazed into the peaceful spaces beyond their windows and said, "It's beautiful. It's so good to be here."

"Will you ever come home to stay?" she wondered. Woman-like, she knew the answer before she asked.

Hurrying back to his post on the campus of Northwestern Schools, Graham experienced a strange depression. Suddenly, the burden he was trying to carry became so tangible that he had to examine it carefully.

He had commitments to Youth for Christ, to the Northwestern Schools, to God's call to evangelism, and to Ruth and his family.

Since this book is concerned with the making of a crusader, we shall omit most of the details of his eventual arrangements with Youth for Christ and Northwestern Schools. In fact, so many fine young leaders had emerged from the mushrooming youth movement that he was called upon to deliver sermons only at key rallies.

But it was four more years before the dilemma would be wholly resolved. His one solid conviction during that period appears to have been his belief in his call to mass evangelism. But evangelism can take different shapes and find various ways of expressing itself. While searching for the means to that "multiplication of self" which was mentioned earlier, Billy found Northwestern an attractive vehicle.

It gave him a magazine with a circulation of twenty thousand, and he was the editor-in-chief.

It gave him a radio station with a large audience.

It gave him a student body which had jumped to twelve hundred eager young people. "In my rationalization, I thought perhaps we could train men with a passion to present the Gospel, and perhaps through Christian education we could multiply my ministry," he recalls.

But Ruth disagreed with tender firmness. When the subject of moving the family to Minneapolis arose, time and again she postponed it, and each deferment was her signal that she was less willing than he to change horses in midstream. Having surrendered her own call to carry the Bible into Tibet, she felt a responsibility to his central career, evangelism, and she felt that God would soon lead him to this realization.

Thus, throughout a lifetime, she has been the loving critic. On one early occasion, Billy is supposed to have asked her to comment on a certain sermon.

"It was fine," she said, "except for the timing."

"Timing? What do you mean?"

She said, "You preached eleven minutes on a wife's duty to her husband and only seven minutes on a husband's duty to his wife."

In the eyes of Ruth Graham all Christian callings are of equal importance, whether it be homemaking or soul-saving. A motto that she borrowed from a Scotch Presby-

238

terian lady emphasized this point. It hung above the kitchen sink in which she washed her dishes, saying "Divine services are held here three times daily."

What should not be underestimated, however, was the concern that both Ruth and Billy felt for a revival of Christian faith in America.

He knew that God wanted him to preach to sinners and to turn them around, but this must be understood in the light of what many evangelical ministers were feeling in those days which followed World War II. They were united and prayerfully hopeful that a world revival might be in the making. Who would lead it, no one knew. It might be a priest like Wesley, a shoe salesman like Moody, a ballplayer like Sunday, an illiterate like Gipsy Smith. But of all God's children, one of the least likely candidates was a young Carolinian torn and pulled in a half-dozen directions . . . one Billy Graham.

Revivalism has been called Christian *revitalization*.

Quite unexpectedly, in those postwar years, for reasons beyond man's comprehension, masses of people became aware of God's sovereignty and gave their fealty to him. It occurs periodically; someone has estimated the intervals at about forty years. Its modern history began with a group of Oxford University students moving to London and preaching in the streets and parks and unoccupied buildings. Their leaders were John and Charles Wesley and George Whitefield.

About the same time in America's English colonies, there began an emotional stirring that is now called the "Great Awakening." Growing in New England under the lashing tongue of Jonathan Edwards, it rolled down the coast to Pennsylvania and into Virginia. Later the revival spirit moved like a gale along the new frontier of the United States in Kentucky and Tennessee, as has been mentioned in an earlier chapter, and it spawned 150 years of back-country camp meetings and brush arbor convocations.

Since then, many pastors and evangelists have impatiently awaited the return of the Holy Spirit. Most of them have lived their span and died, their dream unrealized. But the expectation was strong in the 1940's. Indeed, it is still there, and sometimes remarkable events feed their hope.

During his first visit to England in 1946–1947, Billy had visited the small room at Oxford's Lincoln College in which John Wesley and his fellow students had created the Holy Club, the germ of the Methodist Church. Its walls held pictures of the two Wesleys, Whitefield, and others. "This is holy ground," he said.

He had already become a student of revivals, and all that happened to him subsequently was filed away in his memory to be used when needed. So, as he turned over the crowded pages of his calendar in 1948, he was sustained by the hope that revival would come in his day and that he might contribute to it, thus speeding God's promise of salvation. And daily, as he moved across the earth, he was excited by the never-ending challenge of man's sin of separation from God.

He wrote a sermon naming sins of omission.

1. The sin of thanklessness, of not being grateful to God for all we have.

2. The sin of lack of *love* for God.

3. The sin of neglect of God's Word.

4. The sin of unbelief. "Do you know that every time you don't believe in God, you are really saying, 'God, you are a liar'?"

5. The sin of neglecting prayer.

6. The sin of failing to attend church services.

He named others: lack of passion to lead unbelievers to know Christ, neglect of family duty; and he enumerated sins of commission, too: worldliness, pride, envy, gossiping

240

and slander, lying, cheating, hypocrisy, temper, malice. . . .

In constant contact with college youths, and occasionally with their parents, he became aware of the American distemper called immorality. Several years later, this concern would be reiterated in a magazine article in which he named the enemies of morality.

"A generation ago we took God out of our educational system," he dictated to me.

"The Supreme Court ordered the Bible out of our schools.

"Our movies have featured sex, sin, crime, or alcohol for two decades.

"Some newspapers have played up crime so much that it is made to seem glamorous.

"When a Hollywood star marries for the fourth time, she is pictured on the front pages across the nation in spite of the fact that she is breaking the seventh commandment and living in adultery.

"We have taught that morals are relative and not absolute.

"Other enemies are the ease and luxury in which we live, the filthy literature on our stands, undue emphasis on sex, and the broken home."

And then he added the conviction which has nourished him for a decade: "No nation in history has ever improved morally apart from a revival. I want to repeat that. No nation has ever improved apart from a *revival*."

So, during the winter of 1948–1949, his thinking was less about revival in a single city and more about national revival in our nation, and his concern was for how he could contribute to it.

Considering invitations to hold campaigns in several cities, he accepted Des Moines, Augusta, Altoona, and Baltimore. But these evangelistic adventures alternately exalted him and depressed him . . . and for good reason. In Augusta, Georgia, his campaign was nondenominational and sponsored by the Augusta Ministerial Association. It represented a kind of Rubicon which he crossed at his own peril, for he thereby served notice that his work would not be bound by sectarian or denominational limits. Some fundamentalists have never forgiven him for this "crossing." For the time being, rivalries were forgotten.

In 1569, Martin Luther had written, "A preacher must be both a soldier and shepherd. He must nourish, defend, and teach. He must have teeth in his mouth and be able to bite and fight."

Young Billy became all of those things as he fought the devil in Augusta, and the seven-thousand-seat auditorium became too small. There he learned to deliver thumbnail sermons to the overflow crowd and to provide for extra halls equipped with loudspeakers and chairs for overflow crowds. As a wave of religious feeling rolled across the city, businessmen carried Bibles to lunch, movie theaters stood almost empty, and a total of fourteen hundred converts accepted Billy's call.

A stranger telephoned Billy's hotel room. "What shall I do to be saved?" he demanded.

"Come to our meeting tonight," Billy said.

"I can't wait," the man argued. "I'm convicted of my sins right this minute. I want to repent and accept Christ."

Step by step, Billy led him to a decision over the phone. It happened again and again. He wondered, *why not do the same thing on radio or television?* The idea was born, but just as quickly it was overwhelmed by more immediate duties.

Every sermon drained away part of his strength. He ate five meals a day and lost weight, but his weariness was of the body and not of the mind or heart. Knowing him so well, friends saw that this was different from the bone-tiredness of his Wheaton College years.

The phone rang constantly. "Minneapolis calling!" They

required Billy's opinion on an urgent matter. "Baltimore calling!" Would he speak to the Junior Chamber of Commerce? "Milwaukee!" Could he attend a Bible conference? "Los Angeles!" A committee wanted him to lead a city-wide, old-fashioned tent revival.

He told Ruth of this last invitation, his blue eyes lighting up as if someone had pressed a switch. "That's a real big city, Ruth. Next to New York and Chicago, it's about the most important place in the country. They say they'll put up the biggest tent in the history of evangelism." He thought of the sawdust trail in Mordecai Ham's tabernacle and then of the vastness of a great tent in which people would sit listening.

"It'll take all your time for months." Her level gaze challenged him. "Billy, can you be a good evangelist and a good college president at the same time?"

He flung his hands outward, releasing the tension born of a vision. The Apostle Paul had gone to key cities to talk of a risen Savior, and modern Los Angeles was such a key city.

Graham faced his wife, the urgency of his emotion flowing into words. "Wherever I go, I feel fear. Men thought that science would bring peace, but they were wrong. They thought that education would abolish greed, and they were wrong. Now they're trying to take the Bible out of our public schools. People are uprooted and lost. They need God, but they can't find him." He crossed the room, arms spread wide, and crossed back again. "Our time is short. If we're to escape God's judgment in America, millions must repent. Somehow, I must find a way to tell them."

That summer he had gone to the first international Youth for Christ convention in Beatenberg, Switzerland, and his spirit had been baptized afresh. "I rubbed shoulders with scores of men from all over the world, representing all races and many cultures." The country boy needed those contacts, and he thrilled to them. "My world vision was greatly enlarged," he says.

From Beatenberg he traveled to Nîmes, France, and preached to twenty thousand young people gathered in a coliseum in which Roman soldiers had once tossed Christians to hungry lions.

In Brussels he joined hundreds of religious leaders who were assembled for the first session of the World Council of Churches. Again he talked and dined and prayed with men of all colors and creeds. For the first time, he heard a speech by the legendary Dr. Karl Barth, a leading German theologian. "It was one of the most thrilling and exciting experiences of my life," he says.

At every turn he encountered leaders who were the pillars of great denominations. He felt humble and out of place, yet full of expectancy. One night, in his hotel room, he was awakened by the hum of muffled voices. Several bishops had taken the next room, and as he listened, he perceived that they were praying. "I'd already gone to bed and been asleep," he recalls. "I felt ashamed. I felt convicted of sin."

Back in America, as he dedicated himself to his coming Augusta campaign, he felt that America might be almost ready for a national revival. Postwar pressures had mounted to unprecedented heights, and everywhere people were asking, "Who am I?" "What am I doing here on earth?" "Where can I find peace?"

As millions turned to religion, best-seller books were *Peace of Soul* by Bishop Sheen, *The Greatest Story Ever Told* by Fulton Oursler, and *A Guide to Confident Living* by Norman Vincent Peale.

On Sundays churches began to fill their balconies for the first time in years, and congregations which had limped

244

along, pastorless, set up a plea for regular ministers. Here and there, communities, stirred by some evangelist, plunged into programs of good works.

Revival could be on its way, Graham reasoned, so he mapped his future courageously, but as yet with none of the dazzling certainty of later years. One difference, however, could be noted between him and contemporary evangelists. He was not alone.

Other talents were being mixed with his own. Indeed, in the light of future events, it might be said that they were learning how to multiply his own. Cliff Barrows, seasoned now in scores of Youth for Christ assemblies; Grady Wilson, loyal friend and now well-experienced in pastoral and evangelistic matters; George Beverly Shea, whose powerful ministry of song had turned auditoriums and air waves into sanctuaries. Young men, united, ardent, they moved confidently into a sequence of meetings that would take them from California to the East.

Two of their crusades were moderately succesful, one in Modesto, California, which was a city near Cliff's home town, and the other in Miami, Florida, where Billy felt relaxed and at home in his native Southland. But a dozen other revivalists could have reported about the same kind of harvest.

Then they campaigned in Altoona and Baltimore, either of which might be called the Valley Forge of Billy Graham's career.

Altoona's invitation had come from a group of conservative ministers and not from the ministerial association. Church support, in consequence, was spotty. Most of the citizenry would not budge from their comfortable homes. Though the evangelists stirred themselves to prodigious activity, the community remained indifferent. "If ever I conducted a flop, that was it," he says. "The people were

245

apathetic, the organization was poor, the crowds were small, and the results were insignificant. I left Altoona completely discouraged."

To one whose course is guided by that lodestone called God's will, this collapse demanded the closest scrutiny. That it had significance, some special meaning, he had no doubt. But did it mean that he had somehow failed, or that God intended him for other things—say, for the presidency of Northwestern Schools instead of evangelism?

He was now aware of deep personal tensions, of tiredness, of a loss of the physical buoyancy on which he had always been able to count in times of trouble. Ruth had her own theory: he needed to rest and then to reach a decision on which road to follow. She pressed her point with modest determination.

But he found a better explanation:

He was losing his faith.

Chapter Nineteen

In one of his sermons Billy Graham describes the record book that God keeps in Heaven, preparatory to judgment, which contains the names of all His children. I wonder what entries are written beside Graham's name for the first eight months of 1949.

He tells a story which illustrates his difficulty. "An acrobat was rolling a wheelbarrow back and forth on a tightrope over Niagara Falls, and thousands of people were shouting him on. He put a two-hundred-pound sack of dirt in the wheelbarrow and rolled it across, and then he rolled it back. Turning to the crowd he said, 'How many of you believe that I can roll a *man* across?'

"Everybody shouted approval, and one spectator became very excited in his belief. So the acrobat pointed his finger at him and said, 'All right, sir, you're next.'

"Well, you couldn't see that man for the dust. He actually didn't believe it. He said he believed it, he thought he believed it, but he was not willing to get in the wheelbarrow."

Graham's difficulty was that he, for a time, could not get into God's wheelbarrow.

Why not? What had happened? Well, he talks very little about it. Yet we can deduce certain pressures. A dilemma so intimate has two dimensions, the external and the internal. I shall try to avoid a misinterpretation of either.

He has revealed this much: "One of my closest and dearest friends began to experience a change of heart. He was a successful minister, about my own age, and taking special studies at a famous seminary. Now he came to doubt the divine authority of the Bible. Listening to him, my own mind became somewhat unsettled. I became bothered by doubt, not about the deity of Jesus Christ, not about the Gospel I was preaching, but concerning the authority and inspiration of the Scriptures. Suddenly I wondered if the Bible could be trusted completely."

His good friend told him, "Billy, your faith is too simple. You'll have to get a new jargon if you want to communicate to this generation."

Could that be right, he wondered? Were the biblical stories, the scriptural morals, the Christian beliefs of two thousand years now invalid? Rusted by this doubt, the sword in his mouth turned to a reed, and his preaching lost its power. He felt it first during his crusade in Baltimore. He saw it confirmed further in Altoona. Before the final service, he had gathered his committees and assistants into a room for a special prayer meeting, begging God to fill the house. His prayer was not answered until the last night.

One must imagine the state of his mind. He was the president of a Bible college with a student body grown to twelve hundred. He was speaking frequently to Youth for Christ groups and to church gatherings. Everywhere he was thought to be the fair-haired champion of stalwart orthodoxy.

"If you will not believe," the Prophet Isaiah said, "surely you shall not be established."

Billy's search for the full measure of faith took him back to his Bible studies and back to a few intimate friends. His need was urgent, because the most important crusade of his career lay ahead, requiring his total energy, intelligence, and righteousness:

248

A group of West Coast laymen known as "Christ for Greater Los Angeles, Inc." had invited him to conduct a revival there. Their backing consisted of two hundred churches, and their budget for promotional expenses was five thousand dollars. Billy, Cliff, Bev Shea, and Grady Wilson had accepted with two provisos. First, the committee would have to bring many more churches into the campaign. Second, they would have to increase the budget to twenty-five thousand dollars.

The temerity of this proposal seems much less when compared with the million-dollar budget subsequently raised by the Billy Graham committee sponsoring the 1956 crusade in New York City. But in those days, a tally of twenty-five to fifty persons coming forward during any evangelistic service was considered a success, and publicity was usually limited to a few inches of space on a newspaper's church page.

"I was almost sorry," Graham says, "when a letter came from the Los Angeles Committee agreeing to meet our condition. I felt I was not mentally, physically, or spiritually ready for such an undertaking."

Listening to his authoritative, incisive voice in the 1960's, one finds it difficult to imagine that it was ever otherwise. He alone knows how great is the difference. "I continued my preaching," he says, "but some of the effectiveness was gone."

His search among the writings of great thinkers did little to help his intellect to accept the Bible's authority. For the first time in his life, he craved proof of things unseen and demonstrations that would satisfy the rational mind. For six months, the uncertainty and pain continued.

Of course, the experience would benefit him ultimately, though this could not have been foretold at the time. Without the wrestling and testing, he probably would have continued to be a successful preacher, powerful, but limited to his college and his church. Yet the very stresses which he tried to resist were those that forced his growth.

A quick review of their source and nature reveals a part, but only part, of his ordeal.

Born and bred to the tradition of unswerving faith in the literal interpretation of the Bible, he was never assaulted in his youth by the least doubt of anything in the King James Version. His attendance at Bible school provided no significant challenge, nor did Wheaton College. When his success as a young pastor in Western Springs gave way to the intense activity of working for Youth for Christ, he became far too busy to be able to afford any long hard look at his world.

Of course, astonishing things were happening. First, the Protestant church had split into acrimonious segments fighting over, among other things, literalism. And beyond the Protestants were the disciples of Kant and Hegel and their intellectual descendants called "Humanists." The humanist credo was interesting:

"We regard the universe as self-existing and not created," they proclaimed. "We believe that man is a part of nature and that he has emerged as the result of a continuous process. We reject the traditional dualism of mind and body. We assert that modern sciences make unacceptable any supernatural or cosmic guarantee of human values. We are convinced that the time has passed for theism, deism, and modernism."

Humanists abolished, in short, the Holy Trinity, all miracles, absolute moral values, and divine inspiration. As their ideas flowed into American and European seminaries, Graham has said, "some of the greatest institutions in the land began to turn out men as preachers and teachers who were nothing more than humanists in clerical collars."

At the other extreme the fundamentalist Right had split among themselves and were battling with such violence

250

that many young preachers were driven away. Remarkably, young Graham found his personal credo in his Bible where he read, "By this shall men know that ye are my disciples, that ye have love for one another." And he resolved to fulfill that single commandment by not taking sides, even though he might fail with others. "I was determined that I was going to love Christians whether they called themselves Catholic or Protestant," he told me, "or whether they wore the label of 'liberal' or 'fundamentalist.'"

In 1946 the King James Version of the Bible, the rock on which fundamentalism rested, was abruptly shaken. The Revised Standard Version of the Bible, a translation based on more recent manuscripts and the result of impeccable modern scholarship, was published. It contained hundreds of changes, none important in terms of fundamental Christianity, but the old literalists screamed with distress, and the battle raged more violently than ever.

Graham was hurt and appalled by this warfare between brothers. His emotional upset even brought on a physical pain that hammered persistently at the base of his skull. For a while he thought of leaving Northwestern Schools, of going back to the University of Chicago to earn a Ph. D., or to Oxford in England, but the idea proved impractical.

Moreover, one of his close friends was becoming enamoured of the new critical theology. John Pollock mentions it in his recent biography *Billy Graham*. "The two friends met for hours of debate and prayer," he says. "Graham could see that his friend's 'doubts concerning the authority of the Scripture were intensified. I felt that we were now moving in opposite directions.'

"As he debated and read more, Graham grew confused. Could he continue to accept the authority of the Bible in the face of problems too hard to resolve? It was as if the Adversary, having failed to deflect him by a desk in North-

western, now sought to silence him by the primeval insinu-
ation: 'Hath God said?' "

Of all the minds to which Billy turned in those days, I
believe that the most comforting and supportive was Ruth's.
With her loving knowledge of the Bible, she was anchored
in her faith. Another pillar was Dr. Nelson Bell, her father,
who had become a giant among Presbyterians, and one of
the young evangelist's most stable backers.

Then, too soon for his peace of mind, it was time to drive
west to address one thousand university students at a college
briefing conference in the California mountains.

With Grady Wilson, Graham set out in the car to cross
the prairies, mountains, and desert. One day Billy suddenly
exclaimed, "Grady, I just don't think I can go any further.
I can't go out there feeling like I do and face that meeting."

Grady's faith accepted the challenge. Up ahead he saw
an old jeep track branching away from the highway. He
said, "Let's stop and talk to God about that."

They turned off the asphalt and followed the flinty desert trail until they were utterly alone. "We prayed for an
hour," Grady says. "And then we drove on to California."

A remarkable woman named Henrietta Mears was their
hostess. Many magazine articles and at least one inspiring
book have been written about her life. As religious education director for Hollywood's First Presbyterian Church,
she ran student conferences each summer. Graham has
called her "one of the most fabulous women that I ever
met . . . articulate in the faith . . . one of the best Bible
teachers in the country." She had established Forest Home
as a retreat for confused and harried college students.
When Billy presented himself that August day, she had no
idea that he was possibly the most confused and harried of
all.

That first day he climbed a forested mountain and tried

252

to arrange his thoughts. His nerves, never very relaxed, were as tight as bowstrings. As time passed, he sat with young leaders from England and the U.S.A., discussing man's purpose and the authority that guides his mission. Responding to the probing of Miss Mears, many hearts were bared. In day-long convocations and in private seminars in friendly cabins, Billy stumbled through the dialectics of rational thought and found no satisfaction. A rumor that cut deeply reached his ears. His old friend was telling others, "Poor Billy, he's fifty years out of date. People no longer accept the Bible as inspired. They won't listen. I'm sorry for him."

He remembers hurrying back to his room and shutting the door, facing the crisis in the only way he knew. Searching the pages of his Bible, he recalled an assertion that the biblical phrase most often used by the Prophets themselves was "The Lord said. . . ." Two thousand times, it was claimed.

In Revelations, that strange book which concludes the New Testament, the Almighty had once dictated a message to the fainthearted of the church at Laodicea. He declared, "I know your works; you are neither hot nor cold. Would that you were cold or hot. So, because you are lukewarm, and neither cold nor hot, I will spew you out of my mouth." It was ominously pertinent.

Since early times, man has known the power of belief. To acquire it he has taken what believers called "the leap of faith." By means of it he could bridge the unbridgeable, crossing a void to find firm footing in soil known only to believers. But where was such a land in the modern world? Was it possible that pure faith had become old-fashioned and that the Bible was on the intellectual level of magic?

A country woman once tried to explain her difficulty in

putting her faith into words. She said, "You can no more tell what you ain't seen than you can describe where you ain't been."

For many relationships science offers no explanation. It can define a mother, but it cannot formulate mother love. Dr. Karl Barth, the great contemporary theologian to whom Billy had listened in Brussels, wrote, "If you want to know the truth, go to Jesus and the men around him." In short, go to the New Testament to read what Christ and his followers said about the Scriptures.

Billy searched out hundreds of these passages, noting Jesus' respect for them, the loving detail with which they were repeated, and the crucial situations in which he used them. Obviously, Jesus himself believed in Scripture.

Now his dilemma pressed him to a decision.

"I took a walk that night in the moonlight," Billy says. He knew that unless his agony were healed, he could not continue his ministry. "My heart was heavy and burdened. The great issue burning in my soul was: Can I trust the Bible?"

He knew further that unless he could find faith again he was not competent to try to understand the Bible's teachings, for the fullness of that meaning becomes clear only with the inflowing of Holy Spirit which is born of faith. Spreading his Bible on a stump, he dropped to his knees.

A glorious moment of revelation rewards some persons in their search. Dr. Howard Atwood Kelly, a scientist at Johns Hopkins, once wrote in *A Scientific Man and His Bible* that such an illumination came to him as he recuperated from an illness. "There came as I sat propped up in my bed an overwhelming sense of a great light in the room and of the certainty of the near presence of God, lasting perhaps a few minutes and fading away, leaving a realization and conviction never afterwards to be questioned in all the vicissitudes of life, whatever they might be, a certainty above and beyond the processes of human reasoning."

In the Book of Mark, the father of an afflicted boy begged Jesus to heal his son. When Jesus said, "All things are possible to him who believes," the man cried, "Lord, I believe, but help thou my unbelief."

Faith, fidelity, fealty . . . the essence of these words is the only unguent for a Christian. Recently, Nils Ferrer, theologian, has asserted that if a man can believe only that which he sees, then he is lost, "for when authority becomes so clear to our sight that faith is no longer required, then that authority is no longer Christian."

Faith is of the essence.

And in that darkened moment on the mountain, Billy Graham bowed his head and his intellect in total surrender. With the moon silvering the pages of his Bible, he made the final leap.

"O God, there are many things I do not understand," he prayed. "But God, I am going to accept this Book as your Word by faith. I'm going to allow my faith to go beyond my intellect and believe that this is Thy inspired word."

He stood up, breathing deeply, feeling a startling resurgence. "Apparently I was still alone in the night," he remembers, "but I sensed the presence and the power of God as I had not felt him for months. And I knew that I had passed an important crisis in my ministry."

Once again he wore the whole armor of Ephesians 6:13, and was protected by "the shield of faith, with which you can quench the darts of the evil one." And in his hand was the "sword of the Spirit, which is the Word of God."

Chapter Twenty

In Baltimore Billy Graham had difficulty in filling a theater of twenty-eight hundred seats. In Los Angeles, his six-thousand-seat tent was enlarged to hold nine thousand persons.

The original engagement of three weeks was extended to eight weeks.

A total of 350,000 persons came to listen. Three thousand made decisions.

The Associated Press reported, "Old style religion is sweeping Los Angeles."

Time magazine reported, "No one since Billy Sunday has wielded the revival sickle with such success."

Billy was barely thirty-one years old.

A newsman asked the noted Bible scholar and theologian Dr. Wilbur Smith what he thought. The famous man replied, "This is the most important evangelistic meeting in America."

A Los Angeles pastor said, "This city with its one thousand ministers preaching every Sunday was going lazily along, with the man on the street unimpressed. Then came Billy Graham. In eight weeks, he had more people thinking and talking about the claims of Christ than had all the city's pulpiteers in a year's time. My church got a dozen new members, but it got more than members. It got new inspiration, zeal, and a spiritual uplift that can never be described."

256

What had happened?

Dr. Charles E. Fuller, known for his "Old Fashioned Revival Hour" broadcast, said, "Truly the hand of God is upon our Brother Graham, who has come to us in humility and with the true revival spirit."

Billy Graham says, "To this day, I do not understand the unprecedented series of events that took place. As I arrived to prepare for the crusade, I felt God's strength as never before."

He needed it.

He had brought sermons for two weeks only, plus enough unfinished outlines to fill out the third week. During the extra five weeks, he had to write a new sermon every day, give interviews, consult with ministers and laymen, and counsel literally hundreds of inquirers, including such headliners as Stuart Hamblin, Jim Vaus, Mickey Cohen, Louis Zamperini.

Stanley High has summarized the experience: "Until Los Angeles he had been another evangelist . . . not notably different from scores of others. By the end of the Los Angeles crusade . . . new authority had been added to his preaching; new significance had been added to its results; and a new prospect had been opened for his future."

On a more worldly level such astounding results were certainly more hoped for than anticipated. Billy, Grady, Cliff, and Bev were literally a self-taught evangelistic team without benefit of seminary education or big city pastoral experience. They had charm and verve and a flair for leadership developed during Youth for Christ rallies, but their other qualities were wholly unknown to their Los Angeles collaborators.

Within recent months they had campaigned in Baltimore and in Altoona with disappointing results. Then, as either a cause or a consequence—Billy did not know which—his belief in the authority of the Bible had wavered until that climactic night of decision in the California mountains.

As they approached Los Angeles, who knows what doubts may have stirred in their own hearts?

Certain of their preliminary steps are worthy of examination. Since their first city-wide campaign in Manchester, England, both Billy and Cliff agreed that a successful revival required the cooperation of all of a community's religious elements. All, or at least a large majority, of its churches should become involved. In Billy Sunday's day the practice was old; in 1949 it was suddenly new.

"We need a united campaign," Graham told the Christ for Greater Los Angeles committee.

"We'll do what we can," they replied, shaking their heads. They knew that denominational competition was fierce in southern California and that rivalry between churches and ministers was sometimes even fiercer.

"We need prayers," Billy added. "We need thousands of prayer groups meeting for months ahead of our campaign, asking God to bless our efforts."

They said, "We'll do our best."

What were prayer groups? Moody had used them, so had every other revivalist. Somebody has remarked that prayer is the gymnasium of the soul. Given the exercise of prayer, the weak and the backslid become Christian athletes.

"God must hear at least a hundred thousand prayers," Billy insisted.

To organize this work he once again summoned his boyhood chum Grady Wilson away from his pastorate in the South and installed him as an associate evangelist in Los Angeles. Grady's tireless rounds of lay and ministerial groups of the city soon brought results. Prayer chains were forged which divided the day into segments, with responsibility assigned to specific teams for certain hours, so that prayers were said around the clock. As the idea took hold, young ministers repeated the pattern on their own, and

258

scores of sanctuaries and private homes became the meeting place for praying Christians.

Another tool of evangelism is the so-called "personal worker," the person who, by training and custom, moves through tabernacle aisles to offer his urging and his arm to reluctant or timid prospects. Moody and Sunday had called them "personal workers," but the Graham team renamed them "counselors" and gives them intensive training for weeks prior to a crusade, in sessions that start as early as 6:30 A.M. But this development came later.

In Los Angeles they calculated that three hundred volunteers would be adequate. (Seventeen years later they had to train nineteen thousand for the London crusade.)

Up to now their efforts had succeeded without benefit of "small miracles." However, they now ran headlong into a quandary for which a miracle was the only solution. The local committee which had been expecting to pitch the revival tent on a gigantic parking lot at the intersection of Hill and Washington was abruptly informed that the space was not available; a circus had leased it.

Then the theological front erupted. An influential Los Angeles pastor submitted fifty questions to Billy, each of which posed an ecclesiastical conundrum. Before he could support Graham, he said, he would have to read Billy Graham's answers. Billy studied them in Minneapolis, where he was trying to dispose of pressing matters for Northwestern Schools. He did not reply.

"Instead, I wrote him a love letter," he recalls.

Among other things, he followed the Biblical injunction, "Let every man be quick to hear, slow to speak, and slow to anger, for the anger of man does not work to the righteousness of God."

And he invited the undecided pastor to sit on the platform in a place of honor on the opening night to hear for himself.

Other ministers demanded to know in advance what kind of revival Graham proposed to hold. Would it be loud, gaudy, or emotional? Persons accustomed to seventeen years of big-time evangelism as practiced by Billy Graham cannot appreciate the low opinion in which mass revivalism was held in 1949 when he began. Seminarians pronounced it as out of style as the surrey with the fringe on top. Others who recalled Billy Sunday's jaw-breaking tirades were afraid of the consequences of such uninhibited speech.

Sunday had called Presbyterians, "Those ossified, petrified, mildewed, dyed-in-the-wool, stamped-in-the-cork, blow-in-the-bottle, horizontal, perpendicular Presbyterians."

To him a saloon-keeper was "red-nosed, buttermilk-eyed, beetle-browed, peanut-brained, and stall-fed."

He described Pilate's wife as "a miserable, pliable, plastic, two-faced, two-by-four, lick-spittle, toot-my-own-horn sort of woman."

And he pledged his undying opposition to John Barleycorn in these words: "As long as I have a foot, I'll kick it. As long as I have a fist, I'll hit it. As long as I have a tooth, I'll bite it. As long as I have a head, I'll butt it. And when I'm old and gray and bootless and toothless, I'll gum it till I go to heaven and it goes to hell."

Billy, Grady, Cliff, and Bev, in their final planning session, resolved to keep all excesses to a minimum. They would try to avoid emotional outbursts. They would prohibit applause in the tent-sanctuary.

Billy, reminding his committeemen of Saint Paul's declaration in Asia Minor, said, "I shall preach nothing but Christ, and Him crucified."

Just in time, pieces of the crusade jigsaw began to fit together. One piece was the all-important downtown lot that had been preempted by a circus. Its owners called and said, "We've changed our minds. The lot is yours."

The problem of their need for an outsize tent was resolved by persuading a manufacturer to sew two tents together. When it was safely erected, Grady Wilson mopped his brow and reviewed the projects which made up this first fully planned, modern, religious mass meeting. Choir volunteers by the hundreds had been chosen and were waiting for Cliff's arrival. Personal workers, drilled in Scripture, were ready. Prayer groups were active in the mountains, in the valley, and along the coast, giving Billy his hundred thousand prayers.

All around the town, posters and window cards heralded the "Revival Campaign for Greater Los Angeles." Radio announcements generated excitement, and the newspaper ads went along these lines:

"Hear Billy Graham, America's Sensational Young Evangelist!"

"Visit the Mammoth Tent Cathedral!"

"Don't Miss the Glorious Music, the Dazzling Array of Gospel Talent!"

"Twenty-two Tremendous Nights!"

A billboard painting showed a preacher spreading butter on a slice of bread. The caption said, "It's a sin to spread it thin." Another line asked, "Brother, can you spare a prayer?"

A battery of searchlights was ordered to form "a steeple of light."

It all sounds a bit Hollywoodish, but a volunteer committee insisted that extraordinary efforts would be needed to make a dent in their calloused, careless town.

After the tent went up, its aisles were packed with sawdust, and thirty loudspeakers were placed where they could turn a whisper into a shout. And Grady Wilson paced nervously among the silent benches, remembering Baltimore and Altoona and wondering if perhaps their dream had been too big.

The crusade opened in the midst of one of the worst downpours in Los Angeles history. Rain fell by the bucketful and flooded the parking lot, seeped through the canvas roof, turning sawdust and dirt into a dismal swamp. But the faithful donned their galoshes and came by car and busload. They almost filled the tent.

"Wires and cables arrived from all parts of the world," Mel Larson says in his *Tasting Revival*. "Northwestern Schools took an entire day off from classes to remember their leader."

For two weeks the pattern of the Charlotte and Augusta campaigns was repeated with fair attendance and moderate success. When the weather turned warm and dry, the "tent cathedral" assumed the loveliness of a gigantic sanctuary. Above the fern-and-flower-burdened platform, gold letters spelled out "My Life for Christ." At one side an illuminated blue panel said, "Jesus Saves." At the other side its twin said, "Jesus Keeps." A massive oil painting twenty feet high represented an open Bible. Youth for Christ and Christian Endeavor flags stood at either side.

Larson says, "Skeptics who came to find fault with Graham's preaching went away with but one conclusion. They could not argue with Graham. Their argument was with the Word of God."

One day Billy said, "I want to speak on the subject, 'The choice that is before Los Angeles during these next three weeks.'" He told of his six trips to Europe since the war, of seeing cities that had been blasted into rubble, and he asserted his belief that America was spared because its people prayed, and because God might still use America to evangelize the world, which could be the reason God was now giving America a desperate choice of either revival or judgment.

"There is no other alternative," he declared, "and I particularly believe this applies to the city of Los Angeles,
262

this city of wickedness and sin, this city that is known around the world because of its sin and immorality. God is going to bring judgment upon this city unless people repent and believe—unless God sends an old-fashioned, heaven-sent, Holy Ghost revival."

He flung out figures. Ninety-five per cent of the citizens of Los Angeles said they believed in God, but only 27 per cent were members of a church. "And only 8 per cent go to church more than once a year."

He reminded listeners that history demonstrated the wages of wickedness. "The people of Sodom and Gomorrah heard Abraham and Lot ask them to repent. But they refused, and fire and brimstone from the hand of God rained down upon those cities.

"The antediluvian civilization heard Noah as he stood and preached repentance. For 120 years people scoffed and did not repent. You know what God said? 'My spirit shall not always strive with man.' And he said, 'It repented me that I ever made man.' Then judgment came upon that great civilization.

"One day the Apostle Paul passed by the city of Pompeii. The sin and immorality of Pompeii were known throughout the Roman Empire. Pompeii would not listen or repent; and God caused Vesuvius to erupt. The city was destroyed and every living thing in the city."

He named three conditions for revival. First, the people must desire it. Second, they must repent, which meant confession of sin and renouncing sin. Third, people must pray. All people of all sects.

"This means that we must love one another, and our hearts must be bound together. When we love one another, there won't be any pride . . . any jealousy . . . any envy . . . any gossip . . . any sins, because love binds us together and presents us to God in the purity of Christ."

In closing he told Christians, "If this is going to be just

263

another campaign, if we are going to take it half-heartedly, we might as well stop right now. But this may be God's last call to Los Angeles. I am going to ask you to make your business secondary, to make your family secondary, to make everything else secondary for three weeks. Try God, believe God, prove God, and come to these meetings. Pray and work as if your life and soul depended on it. Then watch God work during these days . . ."

Finally he turned to nonbelievers. "What can you do? Right now you can turn to Jesus. Let Christ come into your heart and cleanse you from sin, and He can give you the assurance that if you died tonight, you would go to Heaven. Will you accept Him?"

This was the old-but-new revival message in all its power, as Billy had preached it before and would preach it afterwards all over the world.

During the first two weeks small changes were made in the usual order of worship. They omitted a benediction but always sang the chorus of "Send a Great Revival in my Soul." It became a theme song that crowds hummed on their way home in streetcars and busses.

For the first time, Billy used a lapel microphone, and his preaching gained astonishingly in its effectiveness as he moved about the broad platform.

New Christians were given special attention following their acceptance of Christ. Counselors in the five-hundred-capacity "prayer tent" not only answered every question but also passed their names and addresses on to concerned ministers. This practice became a key policy in Graham's subsequent campaigns and eliminated one of the strongest and oldest arguments against mass evangelism, that evangelists were more interested in converting large numbers of people than in the subsequent nourishment of their souls.

I have questioned Walter Smythe, Graham's able Director of Crusades, on the difference between today's campaigns and those of Moody and Sunday. He replied: "The big difference is our concern about what happens to a new Christian." Since Los Angeles, various methods have been used to introduce "babes in Christ" into the Christian community. Every convert is card-filed, sent mailings of Christian literature and study courses, telephoned by local ministers, or called on by community committees. At least that is the intent of the follow-up program which must succeed or fail according to the degree of cooperation given it by local pastors and laymen who remain at their posts after the Graham team moves on.

By the third week in Los Angeles a modest advertising campaign plus word-of-mouth comment about Graham's preaching had stimulated enough interest to fill the tent. At a farewell minister's breakfast given that week, instead of the expected three hundred or so, almost double that number came. According to the original schedule, the following Sunday would be their last. As in every campaign, the question of continuing for another week arose.

Several important committee members, noting the average attendance of three thousand for week nights and four thousand for weekends, felt that the campaign had run its course. Others wanted to continue. Billy and Cliff persuaded them to carry on for one more week. In prayer, they asked God for a sign of blessing.

Succeeding events astonished all America and made Billy Graham famous. The first was the conversion of Stuart Hamblin, Hollywood radio star, ex-cowboy champion, racing stable owner, and two-fisted, hard-living he-man.

He and Billy had met a week before the crusade began at a session of a Hollywood Christian group in the home of Henrietta Mears. Hamblin's father was a Methodist minister, and his wife Suzy was a Christian. Though he believed that evangelists were in their racket for the money,

Billy seemed so different that he offered to plug his campaign on his radio show. Attending four revival meetings with Suzy, he began to feel the impact of Graham's appeal and to resent it. Once he got so angry, Billy recalls, "he actually shook his fist at me as he walked out of the tent."

In the third and supposedly final week Hamblin knew he had to surrender or else leave town. He took a hunting trip. On his return, Suzy said, "I've got a surprise. The meetings are going to continue for another week."

Hamblin has told his story in *Decision* magazine. "Next evening we were back in our seats . . . and that finger of Billy's began pointing again in my direction. 'There's a person here tonight,' Graham was saying, 'who is a phony.' I was furious. I got up and bolted out of that tent. I told my wife to go home. I went first to one bar and then another, but I couldn't stand the taste of the drinks they poured me. At last, I gave up and started home, and on the way Christ spoke to me.

"It was as though he said, 'Hamblin, for three weeks one of my best pitchers has been pitching to you. Now I'm stepping into the pitcher's box myself. Either you're going to play on my team or I'm going to strike you out.' "

At his home he told his wife what had happened. They prayed together, but nothing happened. Finally, he decided that his problem was Graham's fault. At two o'clock in the morning he called Billy on the phone. Billy said, "Stuart, I'm glad you called. Come on down."

Billy and Grady were waiting when Hamblin and Suzy arrived.

Hamblin said, "I want you to pray for me."

Graham's answer stunned him. "I'm not going to do it," he said. For a moment he-man Hamblin considered socking the minister.

"Come in and I'll tell you why," Billy added. "We've been friends, but tonight you come to me in a different ca-

266

pacity. I'm your friend, but I'm also an ambassador of Christ. You've never had Him fooled, Satan fooled, or us fooled. I want you to understand what it means to wear Christ's mark on your forehead."

After two hours of talk Hamblin was still arguing. Billy waved toward the door. "Go back home if you're not going all the way to let Jesus Christ be the Lord of every area of your life. Don't ask me to pray with you. And don't waste anybody else's time."

The hands of the clock indicated it was five in the morning when Hamblin suddenly blurted out, "Okay, Billy. I'll go for it."

At long last Graham said, "Now, let's pray."

Hamblin recalls that they got on their knees and Billy began, "Lord, you're hearing a new voice this morning . . ."

On Hamblin's next radio broadcast he told the world what had happened. That same night he went forward publicly in the tent cathedral to accept Christ as Lord.

He immediately renounced drinking and gambling; then he sold his string of race horses. Turning his talent to song writing, he composed "It's No Secret What God Can Do," "He Bought My Soul at Calvary," and "Teach Me, Lord, to Wait." Eventually he became a lay minister, and since that night he has visited almost every prison in America and talked to hundreds of youth groups.

The West Coast began to buzz with stories about the big tent. The team faced another weekend and another decision. Committee members asked, "What are we going to do?"

Billy replied, "I've asked the Lord. We'll make an announcement tonight."

Billy and Cliff had put out another fleece, asking for a sign. They went to the tent that night as usual, unaware of what was in store.

As soon as their cars reached the curb, newsmen and photographers came running from all directions, flash-bulbs popping.

A friend asked, "What you been up to, Billy?"

"Not a thing."

"Then why all this fuss?"

"I haven't the slightest idea." He turned to a reporter, asking, "What's happening?"

The man replied, "You've been kissed by William Randolph Hearst."

Graham knew that two powerful Los Angeles papers were owned by Hearst, but he couldn't understand being "kissed." When he began the service, photographers continued to snap pictures. Once he had to stop and ask a cameraman to remove himself and his stepladder, please, from before the pulpit.

He soon was able to find out what had happened. William Randolph Hearst, rusticating at his fabulous San Simeon castle, had sent his Los Angeles editor a telegram ordering, "Puff Graham." Cynics claim that the old newspaperman was interested only in the new readers a big religious story would bring, but others recall Hearst's previous support of the Youth for Christ movement. Whatever his reason, his action confronted Billy with a crucial decision for which nothing in his experience had prepared him. It involved the mixed blessing of unstinting newspaper publicity and its proper use in the Lord's cause. Fortunately, he understood its implications—or was divinely guided—and was soon able to include it, with hardly a bobble, in the arsenal of his evangelistic weapons.

To the young evangelist so timely a manifestation could not be an accident. It had to be as significant as Gideon's recovery of a dry fleece from soil that was soaking wet. Thus Billy was able to announce, "We are going to extend our

268

crusade for one more week. Tell your friends, tell your neighbors. . . ."

He could have saved his breath. Newspaper headlines were now heralding whatever he said and whatever he did. The young evangelist was front-page news.

At the end of that week Billy sought divine guidance for the third time. Bad weather was expected. The California winter was approaching. "Newspapers reported that a terrible storm was coming our way," he recalls. "We prayed that if it was God's will for us to continue, the storm might not reach Los Angeles. Next morning the papers reported that it had mysteriously disappeared at sea. So the crusade went into the sixth week."

By now he was exhausted and losing weight. He was writing a new sermon every day. The Associated Press distributed a story about the revival in Los Angeles that was front-paged across the nation. Yellowed headlines in 1949 newspapers tell part of the tale:

"Colonel Zack hits the sawdust trail." Zack was a famous show-business personality.

"Zamperini converted at Revival." Louis Zamperini had been an Olympic miler in 1936. During the war he had survived forty-seven days on a life raft, then thirty months in a Japanese prison camp. Back home he had lost his grip and taken to drink. Now he was a tarnished hero, but a headline maker.

"Jane Russell attends Revival." Few people knew that the movie star was already the leader of an important Hollywood Christian group.

Those racking days taught young Graham a most important lesson about his ministry. "Physically, I wanted the campaign to close, but I knew that God wanted it to continue," he told me. "There comes a time when the evangelist becomes physically exhausted and his entire dependence

269

has to be upon God for messages and for strength. It's at that very point that the greatest spiritual impact is made. I learned that a strange spiritual law operates. Truly, 'God's strength is made perfect in weakness.' The weaker I became, the more powerful became my preaching."

Ruth had come out for the final week, and the unexpected series of extensions trapped her in a whirlwind of activities. Billy wanted her, needing her logic and understanding as he tried to deal with the pressures of becoming an "instant celebrity." They had no time for thought or rest or planning.

"We felt we were just spectators," Ruth says. "God was doing something, and Billy and I were just watching."

Then came the most improbable event of all, the conversion of a preacher's renegade son, Jim Vaus, today an evangelist working in Harlem but then a private eye and wiretapper in the army of gang lord Mickey Cohen, California's Public Hoodlum No. 1. The Hearst press proclaimed the event in banner headlines, and rival newspers were forced to follow suit.

James Vaus was no ordinary sinner. He had attended Wheaton, Graham's old Alma Mater, but the authorities had requested him not to return. Enrolling in a Bible school, he accepted money for the publication of a yearbook and absconded with it. Forgiven, he came home to the parsonage of his minister-father, borrowed his car and gun one night, and held up an aged man. Clumsily, he dropped a card carrying his name and address. Police found it and arrested him. Newspapers named him the "calling card bandit." The judge sent him to jail for a year.

After Pearl Harbor he enlisted in the Air Force and rose to the rank of captain, specializing in electronics, but his love for electronic equipment soon overcame his conscience. He stole some government property and was caught. His

270

sentence of ten years was reduced to five and then, with the coming of victory, to only one year which he served at McNeil Island penitentiary. Incredibly enough, he was finally given an honorable discharge.

Next he opened a shop in Hollywood called Electronic Engineering Consultants. Needing equipment, he visited friends in supply houses and walked out with whatever he wanted. One day Mickey Cohen dropped in and asked for help.

"I think my place is bugged," he said. "Can you find it?"

Vaus found it, and he also found a dynamite bomb set to explode in a few moments. At his own risk he defused it, and Cohen became his patron. It wasn't long before he owned a big Cadillac, a fine home, and an endless supply of folding money.

This is the story he told me of his visit to the canvas cathedral:

"I knew I hadn't lived right, but I figured I could make a big killing and turn over a new leaf. At the tent Billy's voice was saying, 'There's a man here tonight who once again is saying no to God. He's hardening his heart, and he's going to leave this place without Christ.' Suddenly I felt the weight of all the wrongs I had done. I could hear Father's prayers and see every hurt I'd put in Mother's eyes. I couldn't bear it.

"A skinny man walked over to me and said, 'Brother, won't you give your heart . . . ?'

"I was looking for a place to throw him when I saw he was praying. I can't hit a man when he's praying. Then the choir sang, 'Almost Persuaded,' and Billy shouted, 'Man, wherever you are, just say "Lord, I receive thee."' All at once, I cried out, 'I'm coming Lord. I'm coming.'"

Next morning a million Californians gaped at the newest headline, "Wiretapper Vaus Hits the Sawdust Trail."

271

That night Graham's audience would have filled two tents. At long last the un-churched were coming and filling every empty bench.

If the conversion of an underworld princeling was news, Vaus's spectacular program for getting right with God set the town on its ear. He went to city officials and told them he had lied to an investigating jury. That was perjury, and he knew it, but he had to get it off his chest because he had helped frame an innocent policeman. He went to stores from which he had stolen a total of fifteen thousand dollars' worth of equipment and promised to pay up. He confessed how he had collaborated with movie stars to trap unfaithful wives, and with politicians to frame their rivals. A couple of times interested parties beat him up. But he continued to correct his sins, and the Los Angeles *Mirror* published his defiant statement:

"God has changed my life, and whereas I have lied and cheated men and women in the past, I purpose to live fearlessly for God and make amends for the wrongs I have done."

At the big tent he made himself invaluable checking the loudspeakers and giving public testimony. One day he told Billy, "Mickey Cohen would like for you to come and see him."

The papers smelled another sensation.

Billy says, "We arranged a secret meeting. Mickey came to the door, and I was surprised to see how short he was. He reminded me immediately of Zacchaeus in the Bible. He looked at me with his big, brown, curious eyes, and I doubt if he'd ever talked to a preacher before."

Cohen offered a drink, and Graham said, "I'll take a Coke." Cohen poured the drinks.

Jim Vaus told Mickey about his own conversion, and Billy followed with an explanation of the Gospel "from A to Z." Cohen said, "I'm of a different religion, but I respect what Jim Vaus has done. I hope he sticks to it."

After a prayer Billy and Jim departed.

Next day a reporter heard about the meeting and asked Cohen to confirm it. "When I need religion, I'll call a rabbi," he snarled.

The evangelist and the gangster met again, after wild cops-and-robbers chases through southern California, because newspaper editors had ordered their photographers to tail both parties and to get pictures. After that crusade closed, Cohen continued to seek Graham's company for years, and eventually he even asserted that the evangelist had loaned him a large sum of money. His claim was false, of course, and when he failed to explain his sizable income to Uncle Sam's revenuers, they haled him before a court that put him behind bars.

At a much later date Graham was musing about the encounter between him and the dapper gangster, an arms-length relationship which endured for almost ten years, I asked him, "After going through so many sessions, why did you keep seeing him?"

His forehead wrinkled wryly. "I wanted to lead him to Christ," he said. "He was a hero to thousands of young hooligans. If he had accepted Christ, his influence on delinquents would have been incalculable. I still think, if I could have found the right words, he might have become a tremendous force against evil in the underworld."

Eventually historians of religion will undoubtedly make a detailed study of the factors which made the "Christ for Greater Los Angeles" campaign so different from all other revivals of the past thirty years. In the meantime we can examine a significant assembly of facts.

Using a contemporary metaphor, I feel that Los Angeles

was the launching pad from which Billy Graham and his space age concept of revivalism took off. Like a rocket, he was lifted above the ruck of competing evangelists until he orbited the earth, a lonely and brilliant figure, and the California count-down deserves the closest scrutiny, because it became the basis of decisions which were to bear unsuspected fruit.

First, the significance of raising the advertising appropriation from a proposed five thousand to twenty-five thousand dollars can be seen. After the Los Angeles experience no lay committee, dedicated though it might be, would be able to hamstring Graham's effort to communicate his good news to the public. As an instance, the New York crusade, held only eight years later, spent more than one million dollars.

Second to be noted is the positive correlation between city-wide participation and success. At the beginning of the crusade two hundred Los Angeles churches were mobilized to support the revival, but at its end four times that number had enlisted. This unprecedented reinforcement was the expression of many influences, all of which emerged ultimately from the needs of thousands of individuals working in a unique place and time.

The third element in the Los Angeles success story is the weight of the prayers that were said by thousands of Christians for months prior to the crusade. Stanley High writes that this was Graham's first "well-organized" advance prayer campaign. Though other evangelists had made organized praying a part of their ministry, none since Billy Sunday had done so on such a grand scale. After Baltimore and Altoona, Graham felt that prayer power was crucial.

"Think how you would feel," he wrote later, "if you started preaching in a campaign which had had a regular prayer meeting in its behalf for a full nine months. How would you feel if every day at noon a prayer meeting was held by scores of people? How would you feel if several all-day prayer meetings had been conducted? And several all-night prayer meetings? And how would you feel if you were to receive letters, wires, and cablegrams saying the senders were praying for you?"

After the Los Angeles meeting many experts advanced their theories for its success. Accustomed to the art of building movie stars out of soda jerks and sweater girls, they believed that publicity made the big difference. They cited the prodigal support of the Hearst papers and the stories in international editions of *Time* and *Life,* which spread Graham's fame to the world's crossroads. Mentioning the spectacular conversions of Hamblin and Vaus, they licked their lips and moaned, "How lucky can you get? What news breaks!"

In a worldly sense they were right, but neither they nor the reporters who wrote the stories ever truly understood the six thousand inquirers who tramped up the sawdust aisles.

Graham's judgment after Los Angeles was, "The only difference between that crusade and all the others we had held to that time was more prayer. But that made all the difference."

After seventeen years a chronicler can record what has changed, what has endured. We can name several parameters of success. During the crusade in the canvas tabernacle a London editor phoned long distance and then wrote his story. He said, "Fixing the linen handkerchief protruding from his breast pocket and smoothing his startling Hollywood tie, Billy Graham said, 'We see the Word of God working here every night. Once, when I called for people who longed to be saved, a woman stood up at one end of the tent. A man rushed over and embraced her. They were husband and wife, just separated, planning a divorce, neither knowing the other was there. I tell you, the Devil is on the run when there's a revival in town.' "

Since that story appeared, the Hollywood tie has been replaced by unexceptionable habits of dress. As for the preaching, its components are essentially the same, and its consequence is that the Devil is still on the run.

Preliminary to a closer look, I think one should remember the time and the place. In 1949 the nation was disturbed by dislocations imposed by ten million demobilized servicemen, by Soviet efforts to drive us from Berlin, and by the croaking of prophets who remembered the economic collapse that followed World War I. Our nerves were on edge. World War III could start with any clash of U.S. and Soviet planes in the air corridor to Berlin. In Europe our handful of troops faced two hundred Communist divisions. Our atomic bomb was our only defense, and we knew that Moscow's spies had stolen our blueprints.

Given such conditions, members of that southern California audience were extraordinarily sensitive to their predicament. Beyond that, they were frequently strangers in a new land, too recently arrived to have put down roots, living in boomtowns and developments. Or they were retired, with much time on their hands to think of eternity; or physically ill, with much reason to fear the future. To be sure, builders and pioneers were among them, too, giving stability to their thrusting community. And so were mothers with children and fathers with dreams and teenagers full of rebellion and boredom.

These were the people who, in the context of their time, responded to Billy Graham's broadcast summons to worship in the tent cathedral.

What did they hear?

They heard music. They heard the old and glorious and almost forgotten hymns of evangelism, which some folk called the music of old-time religion.

By 1949 young Cliff Barrows, handsome as any Hollywood hero, had become one of the ablest choir directors in the land. Drawing his singers from scores of church choirs, he never failed to lead them to thrilling renditions or to turn the crowded tent into a titanic human organ.

George Beverly Shea, already a famous Gospel singer with a network program, commuted weekly between Chicago and Los Angeles. Then, as now, he sang two and sometimes three solos at every service.

But I think that both men conveyed much more than words and melody to their listeners; in his own way each communicated that love and spirit without which their lips would have turned to clay and that righteousness which is in their nature. Surely, in the words of another old hymn, when the roll is called up yonder, they'll be there.

And then, after the gathered thousands had sung, evoking who knows what memories, they heard the good news of the Gospel. After exhausting his two-week supply of sermons, Billy had been forced to dip constantly into the Bible, using from twenty-five to one hundred verses each night. His favorite phrase became "the Bible says . . . the Bible says. . . ." It obviously added power to his preaching.

Perhaps the most important innovation was the new tie-clip or lapel-type microphone that Graham was using, releasing him from a fixed position behind the pulpit. Harold Martin tells how it helps:

"As his message begins to stir in him," he writes, "his manner changes. His body tenses. His voice grows high and clear and takes on a note of desperate urgency. His eyes glow and flash, and his long arms slash the air or

277

thrust suddenly upward to hold the Bible aloft. With the open Bible in his hand, he moves like a boxer, weaving and crouching. Behind him, an associate, holding the thin microphone wire, plays him like a trout, reeling in as he comes closer, paying out as he moves away."

The message itself expresses the evangelist's concern, his solution for human problems, and his faith in God's redeeming love.

Then and now, he begins by saying, "Let us pray." His prayer is short and pointed. Recently he said, "Our father, we pray that thy Holy Spirit will exalt the Lord Jesus Christ until we shall see him and him alone. We pray that thou will speak in this audience and draw all men unto thyself whom thou has chosen in Christ. For we ask it in his name. Amen."

Since time began, friends have encouraged each other through words of mutual esteem. Graham does the same thing with his audiences. He praises their support, their attendance, their loyalty, their town, their friendliness, their generosity. Very often he seeks out some facet of the crusade that is the first, the biggest, the best.

"I think this is the largest opening night we've ever seen," he says. Or, "I have never felt God moving more powerfully in any place I've preached."

He invites the audience's partnership. On Youth Night (a feature of every crusade), he may ask every person under twenty-five years of age to stand up. "Wonderful," he'll drawl, "but I've never seen so many gray-haired, bald-headed people under twenty-five." And laughter surges through the crowd.

When he feels ready and in communication with his audience, he drops his bantering tone, opens his Bible, and says seriously, "Tonight I want you to turn with me to the fourth chapter of Romans. . . ." Then, holding his Bible

278

aloft, he orders, "Lift up your Bibles. Hold up your Bibles." If a celebrity is on the platform, he may say, "I want the governor (or the celebrity) to see how many Bibles we have here tonight."

Having read his text, he begins to expound. Words on a printed page cannot convey his impact. Long ago a publisher asked a famous evangelist for permission to reprint his sermons. "You may do so," the minister replied, "provided you include the thunder and lightning."

Listeners quickly learn Graham's basic doctrine. He holds that man is innately sinful but that all his sins were atoned for in the moment that Christ died on the cross. To find peace of mind and heart, therefore, man today needs only to repent his sins, to receive Christ in his heart, and to work thereafter in the body of his church.

Modernists criticize him for being old-fashioned. Far out fundamentalists criticize him for being too modern. He says that he "accepts the authority of the Scriptures, the virgin birth of Christ, the atoning death of Christ, his bodily resurrection, his second coming, and personal salvation by grace through faith."

But he is no literalist, as he explains by quoting a passage of scripture which tells of a person who died and "went up into Abraham's bosom." "Now this does not mean," he explains, "that he went and crawled into Abraham's body. It means that the man died and went to heaven."

He never makes Christianity easy. Some critics have said his outline of Christian living is too Utopian. I think they have not listened enough.

"It is hard to be a Christian," he warns. "Oh, it is easy to belong to a church. Some of our churches are like a social club. If the preacher talks beyond twelve o'clock, you are ready to look for a new preacher.

"Yes, you go to church, but it doesn't cost you anything. Oh, you throw a dollar in the collection plate . . . but there is no real following of Christ, no real surrender, no real dedication. You have not really met the Savior. . . ."

In another city he said: "I want you to see that the Bible teaches that Christian life is warfare. The Christian life is a battle, a fight, a struggle from beginning to end. Not one single Christian is ever exempt from fighting this battle."

Speaking in this vein to a youth group, he said, "There is always a penalty. Are you willing to take the scorn of high-school gangs? You might not be invited to a lot of things. . . . It will cost you some social standing and prestige if you give your life to Christ. If you're not willing to pay for it, forget the whole thing."

Christian life can be rough, but it has its rewards. "How I wish that every person could know how his life can be transformed through serving Christ," he says. "Believing in him, you have no fear. You become bold. You are joyful. You love and are beloved. In Christ you relax and are serene in the midst of the confusion and bewilderment and perplexities of this life."

Finally, the urgency with which the old prophets spoke creeps into his manner, but his words continue in today's vernacular. "You can't just come to Christ any old time you want," he says. "You can't just up and say, 'Well, here I am, Lord.' You can only come when the Holy Spirit is working and when He is preparing your heart and has already spoken to you. . . . Now the Bible says that if you harden your heart . . . you are in danger of being suddenly cut off and that without remedy. You had better not put it off. You had better not wait until tomorrow. There might not be a tomorrow."

To procrastinate is folly. He makes this abundantly clear, sometimes illustrating his point with a dramatic episode from local history. In Charlotte he concluded one powerful sermon with these words:

"Do you know what happened here about twenty-five years ago? There came a flash flood because of a rainstorm. A man drove up to a bridge, and it had washed away, but he did not see it in the rain, and he went over. He escaped from his car and went back to flag down other cars. That night eighteen cars plunged into that river. They refused to stop when they were flagged down.

"I am telling you that the bridge is washed out on the road you are on. The river is swirling ahead. It is going to claim your life here and the life to come unless you turn back. I am standing here tonight with a red flag saying, 'Stop, Look, and Listen!' So turn around! Change your way!"

In Los Angeles, in 1949, six thousand accepted his invitation, heeded his warning, and embarked on the difficult Christian life that he had outlined.

One convert even ran down the aisle midway through a sermon and asked to be converted then and there. He had been standing outside the tent, fighting off the impulse to surrender, when suddenly he found himself racing toward the pulpit.

Graham says, "That sermon was never completed, as God prompted me to give the invitation right then." Asking the audience to pray for the man and for others in the tent who might also wish to be saved, he concluded his invitation and waited. Hundreds of inquirers rose quickly and went into the prayer tent.

Some observers cried, "Fake," and tried to prove that those hurrying souls were sensation mongers and social misfits. Some psychologists charged that press agentry and drumbeating had produced a religious circus that mobilized the notoriously loose emotions of our tropical West. "It can never happen again," they chanted.

Others repeated the tired, seminary lament that "mass evangelism is dead." Neither the chilly North nor the sophisticated East, they asserted, would respond to such outdated methods and messages. The young evangelist would be a fool to crusade outside the Bible Belt.

As for Graham, he was as astonished as any. His bewilderment did not concern results; they were the consequence of God's will and his presence in the world. But why had he chosen Billy Graham? One night he called his mother in Charlotte. "You better come out here," he urged. "You won't believe what's happening."

God gave gifts to men, Paul writes in Ephesians. "And his gifts were that some should be apostles, some prophets, some evangelists . . ."

But why are some evangelists so favored and so effective?

What was the power that gave Billy Graham wings with which to circumnavigate the world? The turning point, admittedly, seems to have been the publicity support of William Randolph Hearst's newspaper chain, but the question next arises, "What urging in that time and hour moved Hearst?"

I once asked Graham, "Did you ever know Hearst? Did you talk to him?"

"I never met him," he said. "I never had any correspondence with him. Why he did what he did, I have no idea. I don't know what influence was brought to bear to make him do it. Only a few issues of his papers appeared before the others supported us, too, because when one paper picks up a crusade, the others come along. But it was Hearst who gave the first order. Why, I have no idea."

I said, "Some critics of Hearst have called him a very great sinner. Would you agree?"

He replied, "I couldn't make that judgment. I don't say anyone is a great sinner. I think we are all great sinners."

Is this perspicacity, this intuitive compassion for all men, perhaps his great secret? To be sure, he has reminded us great sinners are not only the Hitlers and Eichmanns. Great sinners are all of us who have not surrendered fully to the principles of Jesus Christ, though we rarely so think of ourselves. Moses handed down the law, which multiplied into countless volumes of interpretive "Don'ts." Jesus handed down principles that need no expanding.

In almost every sermon, Graham says:

God loves you.

God wants to forgive.

So repent of your rejection of him, of your separation from him.

Accept his son Jesus Christ as your Savior.

Believe.

And His Holy Spirit will fill your being and take care of all the rest.

That is his message. He has often explained that his role is that of a messenger boy. And it is clearly evident that the messenger boy of 1966 continues to be amazingly like the skinny youth who gave his first invitation in a converted butcher shop in Florida so many years ago. And of that audience of approximately one hundred persons it is recorded that about one-quarter of them came forward. In trailers camps and the Tampa mission and country churches they came forward, too. Even then the touchstone of evangelism had been revealed, whether he understood it or not. No "steeples of light," movie star testimonials, or gangster conversions accompanied his preaching then, yet the results were astonishing. Gaining stature, he has seen his audiences keep pace, until today his parish is global.

Some scientists believe that two sets of laws govern this earth; some laws are physical and can be quantified and understood; others are spiritual and remain a mystery.

Perhaps they will not always continue so, for already we perceive things about the spirit that were unknown to our ancestors. Among the first things we are coming to understand are the scientific principles on which Christian character can be founded. Among the things that *should* happen to children, science says, are these guidelines derived from the work of Dr. Ernest Ligon:

1. Teach the child that man is ruled by spiritual principles which, if discovered, can solve the problems of personality and society.

2. Seek to develop in him a powerful desire to discover those principles.

3. Teach him to believe that whatever happens is in accordance with those laws and that if he can discover them he can prevent evil and achieve great happiness for himself and for mankind.

4. Encourage him to make this vision the completely dominating purpose of his life.

5. Teach the child that the universe is fatherly and that the principle of fatherly love is the great spiritual power of the universe.

6. Let him, like a father for his child, become sensitive to the needs of the world.

7. Fill him with the desire to give every other person the opportunity to attain the happiest life of which he is capable.

8. Make him eager to solve the conflicts that tear men's minds with fears and angers, hates and suspicions; and to solve the conflicts that men have with one another and between social groups, classes, nations, and races.

9. Challenge him to be willing to sacrifice his very life, if necessary, for the attainment of these ends.

Two questions remain.

Are such selfless standards "practical" in our modern world?

Can one child so guided and motivated—or one thousand such children—grow up to change the shape of things to come?

If your answer is no, then you must ask one ultimate question: Is there any other, any better way?

If the answer is yes, then every parent must face squarely his unique Christian obligation and opportunity.

In Los Angeles, during the eighth incredible week of overflowing crowds, the air turned chilly and the fall rains gathered. Finally the great tent came down, and the corner of Hill and Washington Streets again became a parking lot. In the aftermath volunteers began to sort through the mountains of mail that had been delivered to Billy Graham's office.

It contained offers of stardom from two movie studios.

It contained over a thousand invitations to speak in clubs, churches, and at conventions.

It contained thousands of thank-you notes written by humble folk whose faith had been renewed.

Going to the railway station, Billy and Ruth were jostled by crowds of well-wishers and besieged by swarms of autograph seekers. At the depot, guards whisked them through gates, giving them the treatment reserved for celebrities.

"This was a new experience," Graham recalls. "We were happy and grateful, but we were also afraid that we did not have the capacity to live up to our new responsibilities."

As the train climbed the slope toward the Great Divide, they thought back to many things, to the dilemma posed by Northwestern Schools, to the weakness of spirit that had vanished so recently, and to the final service in Los Angeles with the tent packed two full hours ahead of time and throngs standing in the street.

Word came to their Pullman compartment from Kansas City, where the train would stop, that a huge crowd would be waiting at the station. In Minneapolis a "welcome home" reception was being planned. Whether he and Ruth liked it or not, the evangelist was now a celebrity, and their life would never again be quite the same.

The Apostle Paul had charted an itinerary for their special breed in a letter to the church at Corinth many hundreds of years ago. "Having this ministry by the mercy of God, we do not lose heart," he said. "We have renounced disgraceful, underhanded ways; we refuse to practice cunning or to tamper with God's word, but by the open statement of the truth, we would commend ourselves to every man's conscience in the sight of God. . . . For what we preach is not ourselves, but Jesus Christ as Lord, with ourselves as your servants, for Jesus' sake."

They had lost their claim to privacy. In the Los Angeles crusade they had forfeited their right to comfortable anonymity. But they had surely discovered Billy Graham's true mission.

The train sped them eastward toward a new world that was bright with the simplicity of a direction regained.

Go ye and tell. . . .

Ahead lay Boston, Columbus, Atlanta, London, Paris, New York, and the continents of Africa, South America and Australia. Ahead were the waiting millions of all creeds and colors, hungering and hoping and listening.

Clasping hands, he and Ruth sank to their knees.

CURTIS MITCHELL

Since his birth in 1902 in Montgomery City, Missouri, Curtis Mitchell has accumulated an impressive range of experience as writer, editor, administrator, and consultant to business and government.

His career as editor, which began in the print shop of a country weekly in Missouri, culminated in the 1930's with positions as vice-president and editorial director, first for Triangle Publications, then for the Dell Publishing Company.

Twice the government called upon Mr. Mitchell for special services. During World War II, he was awarded colonel's rank for his performance in the United States War Department's Bureau of Public Relations. Again in 1961, the Secretary of Labor and the Federal Aviation Agency obtained Mr. Mitchell's assistance.

Quite as diverse as his experience, Mr. Mitchell's intellectual interests encompass such subjects as religion, health, aviation, communism, science, and family life. His pen has kept pace with his mind. Mr. Mitchell's articles on health and science have appeared in a variety of magazines including *The Reader's Digest, The New York Times Sunday Magazine, Family Weekly,* and *Popular Science.*

Billy Graham, The Making of a Crusader is the latest of five books the author has written, the others being *God in the Garden, Isometrics. . . . First Step Toward Fitness, Fitness for the Whole Family,* a work he wrote in collaboration with Dr. Paul Dudley White, and *Those Who Came Forward,* the story of the people who have responded to the Graham crusades, which Chilton published in the spring of 1966.

Mr. Mitchell promises to extend this list. Currently living and writing in a country home in Westport, Connecticut, he means to keep his pen as active as it has ever been, perhaps more so.